NEGOTIATING THE CHRISTIAN PAST IN CHINA

WORLD CHRISTIANITY

Dale T. Irvin and Peter Phan, Series Editors

ADVISORY BOARD:
Akintunde E. Akinade
Adrian Hermann
Leo D. Lefebure
Elaine Padilla
Yolanda Pierce

Moving beyond descriptions of European-derived norms that have existed for hundreds of years, books in the World Christianity series reflect an understanding of global Christianity that embodies the wide diversity of its identity and expression. The series seeks to expand the scholarly field of world Christianity by interrogating boundary lines in church history, mission studies, ecumenical dialogue, and interreligious dialogue among Christians and non-Christians across geographic, geopolitical, and confessional divides. Beyond a mere history of missions to the world, books in the series examine local Christianity, how Christianity has been acculturated, and how its expression interacts with the world at large. Issues under investigation include how Christianity has been received and transformed in various countries; how migration has changed the nature and practice of Christianity and the new forms of the faith that result; and how seminary and theological education responds to the challenges of world Christianity.

OTHER BOOKS IN THE SERIES:
Krista E. Hughes, Dhawn Martin, and Elaine Padilla, eds., *Ecological Solidarities: Mobilizing Faith and Justice for an Entangled World*

Aminta Arrington, *Songs of the Lisu Hills: Practicing Christianity in Southwest China*

Arun W. Jones, ed., *Christian Interculture: Texts and Voices from Colonial and Postcolonial Worlds*

Edward Jarvis, *The Anglican Church in Burma: From Colonial Past to Global Future*

NEGOTIATING THE CHRISTIAN PAST IN CHINA

Memory and Missions in Contemporary Xiamen

Jifeng Liu

The Pennsylvania State University Press
University Park, Pennsylvania

Library of Congress Cataloging-in-Publication Data

Names: Liu, Jifeng, 1984– author.
Title: Negotiating the Christian past in China : memory and
    missions in contemporary Xiamen / Jifeng Liu.
Other titles: World Christianity (University Park, Pa.)
Description: University Park, Pennsylvania : The Pennsylvania State
    University Press, [2022] | Series: World Christianity | Includes
    bibliographical references and index.
Summary: "Focuses on the ways in which Christianity has become
    an integral part of Xiamen, a southeastern Chinese city
    profoundly influenced by western missionaries. Illustrates
    the complexities of memory and mission in shaping the
    city's cultural landscape, church-state dynamics, and global
    aspirations"—Provided by publisher.
Identifiers: LCCN 2022006300 | ISBN 9780271092874 (hardback) |
    ISBN 9780271092881 (paper)
Subjects: LCSH: Christianity—China—Xiamen (Xiamen Shi) |
    Christianity—Social aspects—China—Xiamen (Xiamen Shi) |
    Missions—China—Xiamen (Xiamen Shi) | Xiamen (Xiamen
    Shi, China)—Church history.
Classification: LCC BR1295.X53 L58 2022 | DDC 275.124/5—dc23/
    eng/20220302
LC record available at https://lccn.loc.gov/2022006300

Published by The Pennsylvania State University Press,
University Park, PA 16802–1003

The Pennsylvania State University Press is a member of the
Association of University Presses.

It is the policy of The Pennsylvania State University Press to use acid-
free paper. Publications on uncoated stock satisfy the minimum
requirements of American National Standard for Information

For my family

Contents

Illustrations

Acknowledgments

My heartfelt thanks go first to those in the Xiamen area who were willing to participate in this project. They are Simon Chen, Chen Miaozhen, Chen Yiping, Chen Yongpeng, Dai Zhaozhang, Fang Youyi (1931–2015), Hao Zhiqiang, He Bingzhong, Hong Buren (1928–2019), Huang You (1926–2015), Lan Yupei, Li Qixian, Lin Muli, Lin Shiyan (1928–2020), Peng Yiwan, Wang Shitai, Wu Zhifu, Ye Kehao, Zhan Zhaoxia, Zhang Xiaoliang, Zhu Libing, and those who are left anonymous for safety reasons under the uncertain political conditions.

I am also deeply indebted to Pastor Chen Shiyi, an octogenarian who served in Xiamen Trinity Church after retiring from the Nanjing Theological Seminary in the late 1980s and has been a citizen of the United States since the early 1990s. Since it was not convenient for Chen to access the internet, I e-mailed my questions to his daughter, who forwarded them to Chen, Chen then wrote down his answers on papers that were scanned and sent to me by his daughter. During my short stay in Wenzhou, Pastor Liang Pu accommodated me and opened his church to me. The ideas he shared helped me understand the situation of Christianity in Wenzhou in particular and in China in general.

I owe my greatest gratitude to Heleen Murre-van den Berg and Frank Pieke, my supervisors at Leiden who provided intellectual guidance and helpful encouragement throughout the project. Further debts are owed to Li Minghuan, who has greatly shaped my pursuit of an academic career and inspired me to take a broad vision in scholarship. I am grateful to Peter van der Veer, who accepted me as a research fellow at the Max Planck Institute for the Study of Religious and Ethnic Diversity and subsequently guided me to the field of religious transnationalism. His charm, humor, and encouragement has cheered many early career researchers specializing in Indian and Chinese religions.

This book has benefited from the helpful comments of Henrietta Harrison, Adam Chau, and Ernestine van der Wall on an earlier version of the full manuscript. As established scholars in modern Chinese history, the anthropology of Chinese religion, and the culture and history of Christianity respectively, these three preeminent scholars offered fair criticism and constructive suggestions from different perspectives. I wish to extend my gratitude to many people who have helped by reading draft chapters or discussing the themes found in this book with me, among them Bram Colijn, Markus Davidsen, and Barend ter Haar. My insights into Chinese religion have been sharpened from discussions with Nanlai Cao, Meiwen Chen, Tuz-lung Chiu, Alexander Chow, Khun Eng Kuah, Jie Kang, Yunfang Lyu, Zhen Ma, Mireille Mazard, Tam Ngo, Carsten Vala, Marina Wang, Xiaoxuan Wang, Fenggang Yang, Mayfair Yang, and many others.

I would like to give my special thanks to Chris White and Mark McLeister, who have been constant sources of inspiration and support for years. As specialists in Chinese Christianity, their benevolent presence is a warning to me not to muddle through anything. Thanks to their "inspection," many factual errors and misunderstandings have been avoided. Many thanks are due to Zhixi Wang whose introduction to a church in Xiamen sparked my interest in Chinese Christianity in 2011. I wish to express my gratitude to John de Velder (1944–2015) and his wife Linda Walvoord, as well as Huub de Jonge, for having helped me collect materials concerning the American medical missionary John Otte's experiences in the United States and the Netherlands.

Studying in Europe had been a long-cherished wish of mine that was made possible because of the financial support from the China Scholarship Council. Funding for field research for this project came from the Leiden University Fund, the Modern East Asia Research Centre at Leiden University, and the French Centre for Research on Contemporary China. I am also grateful to the Nordic Institute of Asian Studies at the University of Copenhagen for the SUPRA Nordic scholarship, which made my visit in September 2015 possible.

Some portions of this book appeared in earlier versions as "Reconstructing Missionary History in China Today: Cultural Heritage, Local Politics and Christianity in Xiamen," *Asia Pacific Journal of Anthropology* 18, no. 1 (2017): 54–72; "Old Pastor and Local Bureaucrats: Recasting Church-State Relations in Contemporary China," *Modern China* 45, no. 5 (2019): 564–90; and "The Passing of Glory: Urban Development, Local Politics and Christianity on Gulangyu," in *Protestantism in Xiamen: Then and Now*, ed. Chris White (Cham, Switzerland: Palgrave Macmillan, 2019), 77–101. I thank these journals and publishers for permission to use materials for this book.

Thanks are due to members of Pennsylvania State University Press for bringing this book to publication and two reviewers for their constructive comments and warm encouragement. I am grateful to Mireille Mazard,   xi
who invested a lot of time and creativity in editing the final manuscript. Needless to say, I am responsible for any remaining errors.

I am deeply indebted to my family for their years of emotional and financial support. This research is dedicated to the memory of my maternal grandfather, Zhang Dafu (1939–2010), who lived through the Second Sino-Japanese War and the Civil War between the Communists and the Nationalists. During the Land Reform Campaign in the early 1950s, his father was "wrongly" categorized as a landlord (even those "rightly" classified as landlords did not deserve persecution in many cases), and consequently he and his five older brothers were deprived of any chance to attend secondary education and therefore never had the opportunity to enter university. His identity was permanently restricted to that of a peasant and his dream of becoming a musician or an intellectual never came true. To my surprise, in his later years he appreciated Mao Zedong, the man primarily responsible for his unhappy experience of life, for creating an "equal" society; in contrast, he criticized Deng Xiaoping, who directed the national reform and opening-up policy in China, for the wide disparity between rich and poor. In the last three years of his life, I was reading for my master's degree. I was definitely an intellectual in his eyes. He implicitly expressed his wish that his life could be recorded. Having been bored with his repeated telling of his story since I was a teenager, I had no interest in his biography at that time. Not until I took up social memory and alternative history as themes in this research did I begin to understand his wish, that is, an ordinary person's history needs to be recorded. Although it is too late, I dedicate this book to my grandfather with a sense of guilt but in the hope that he knows about it.

Note on Romanization, Names, and Monetary Units

The pinyin system of romanization of Mandarin Chinese (Putonghua) is used for most Chinese expressions, except when the organization, individual, or author is better known under another spelling (for example, John Sung instead of Song Shangjie).

I have translated the Chinese names of churches and places into English, since these names are often descriptive. In some cases, it is important to note that urban changes have necessarily brought changes in names, or that some of these churches have inherited names from their predecessors. For example, the New District Gospel Church (Xinqu fuyin tang), located in Huli district, quite a new administrative district established only in 1987, was said to have been constructed to take the place of the abandoned Gulangyu Gospel Church. For most Chinese respondents referred to throughout the book, names are given in the Chinese order (surname followed by given name). However, when I refer to Chinese scholars whose publications are in English in the text, their full names follow the European order, in keeping with bibliographic standards (given name precedes surname).

All monetary units in this book refer to Chinese yuan (RMB) unless otherwise indicated. The official RMB-USD exchange rate was about RMB8.33 = USD1 in 1995. In 2013 it was around RMB6.15 = USD1.

Abbreviations

CAE	Chinese Academy of Engineering
CAS	Chinese Academy of Sciences
CCC	China Christian Council
CCP	Chinese Communist Party
CPPCC	Chinese People's Political Consultative Conference
GMC	Gulangyu Management Committee
HMC	Historical Materials Committee
HMRC	Historical Materials Research Committee
KMC	Kulangsu Municipal Council
LMS	London Missionary Society
NRAA	National Religious Affairs Administration
PCE	Presbyterian Church of England
PLA	People's Liberation Army
PRC	People's Republic of China
RAB	Religious Affairs Bureau
RCA	Reformed Church in America
SARA	State Administration for Religious Affairs
SEAC	State Ethnic Affairs Commission
TSPM	Three-Self Patriotic Movement
UFWD	United Front Work Department
WHS	World Heritage Site
XICF	Xiamen International Christian Fellowship
YMCA	Young Men's Christian Association
YWCA	Young Women's Christian Association

Characters

Districts of Xiamen City
Haicang 海沧
Huli 湖里
Jimei 集美
Siming 思明
Tong'an 同安
Xiang'an 翔安

Other Place Names
Anhui 安徽
Anping 安平
Anxi 安溪
Beijing 北京
Fujian 福建
Fuzhou 福州
Gaoyou 高邮
Guangdong 广东
Guangzhou 广州
Gulangyu 鼓浪屿
Gutian 古田
Henan 河南
Huian 惠安
Humen 虎门
Jiaheyu 嘉禾屿
Jiangsu 江苏
Jinggangshan 井冈山
Jinjiang 晋江
Jinmen (Kinmen) 金门
Longyan 龙岩
Lujiang dao 鹭江道
Min 闽
Minnan 闽南
Nanjing 南京
Nanyang 南洋
Ningbo 宁波

Penghu 澎湖
Pinghe 平和
Putian 莆田
Quanzhou 泉州
Qufu 曲阜
Rongcun 榕村
Ruijin 瑞金
Shandong 山东
Shanghai 上海
Shanxi 山西
Sichuan 四川
Taipei 台北
Taiwan 台湾
Tianjin 天津
Wei 潍
Weifang 潍坊
Wenzhou 温州
Xiamen 厦门
Xi'an 西安
Xiaoxi 小溪
Xinjiang 新疆
Yuegang 月港
Zengcuoan 曾厝垵
Zhangzhou 漳州
Zhejiang 浙江

Other Characters
aiguo aijiao 爱国爱教
aiguo zongjiao renshi 爱国宗教人士
ba shan yi shui yi fen tian 八山一水
    一分田
Bagua lou 八卦楼
Baihua qifang, baijia zhengming 百花
    齐放, 百家争鸣
Baosheng dadi 保生大帝

boluan fanzheng 拨乱反正

changzhu renkou 常住人口

chongyang meiwai 崇洋媚外

chuandao 传道

cunshi 存史

dang'an 档案

danwei 单位

Daonan 道南

daotai 道台

Dashengchan yundong 大生产运动

dazibao 大字报

difang wenshi zhuanjia 地方文史专家

difangzhi 地方志

diguozhuyi fenzi 帝国主义分子

diguozhuyi zougou 帝国主义走狗

douzheng dahui 斗争大会

fada de 发达的

fan 番

fandong fenzi 反动分子

fandong sixiang 反动思想

fangui 番鬼

fangzhi 方志

fanzai 番仔

Fanzai libaitang 番仔礼拜堂

Fanzai mu 番仔墓

fengjian de 封建的

fengjian mixin 封建迷信

fengjing liaoyangqu 风景疗养区

fengjing lüyouqu 风景旅游区

fu chuji 副处级

fu shengji 副省级

fu tingji 副厅级

Fuyin tang 福音堂

gaizheng 改正

Ganyu wei bei mohei de ren fanbai 敢
　于为被抹黑的人翻白

Gongbuju 工部局

Gongbuju lüli 工部局律例

gonggong zujie 公共租界

guanchang wenhua 官场文化

guanshu 官书

guanxi 关系

Guanyin 观音

Gulang yu 鼓浪语

guochi 国耻

Guoji libaitang 国际礼拜堂

guoji xingxiang 国际形象

Han 汉

heping jiefang 和平解放

heping yanbian 和平演变

hexin yicun dian 核心遗存点

Hong weibing 红卫兵

huji renkou 户籍人口

hukou 户口

Jiangdao tang 讲道堂

jianming 贱名

jiaoan 教案

jiaotang 教堂

jiating jiaohui 家庭教会

Jiayin 佳音

Jidujiao 基督教

jieji diren 阶级敌人

jihua dan lie shi 计划单列市

Jin 晋

jingji tequ 经济特区

jiu shehui 旧社会

Jiulong jiang 九龙江

Jiushi yiyuan 救世医院

jubaopen 聚宝盆

juhuidian 聚会点

kaihui 开会

Kongsu yundong 控诉运动

laishi de panwang 来世的盼望

laodong gaizao 劳动改造

laogai 劳改

Lianghui 两会

lianhe libai 联合礼拜

lingliang 灵粮

lishi xuwuzhuyi 历史虚无主义

Loushi ming 陋室铭

Lujiang bao 鹭江报

luohou de 落后的

Mazu 妈祖

mei wenhua 没文化

Ming 明

Minguo re 民国热

mingzhe baoshen 明哲保身

minjian shenyi 民间申遗

minjian youhao dashi 民间友好大使

Minnan dahui 闽南大会

Minnanhua 闽南话

mo zhe shitou guo he 摸着石头过河

mudaoyou 慕道友

niugui sheshen 牛鬼蛇神

nongmingong 农民工

ping'an xile 平安喜乐

pingfan 平反

pinyin 拼音

poxie 破鞋

Putao yuan 葡萄园

Putonghua 普通话

qiaoxiang 侨乡

Qing 清

Qingming 清明

qinjian 亲见

qinli 亲历

qinwen 亲闻

renmai 人脉

ruan shili 软实力

San gai yi chai 三改一拆

San gonghui 三公会

Sanjiang tang 三江堂

Sanyi fengyun 三一风云

Sanyi tang 三一堂

Sanzi aiguo yundong 三自爱国运动

Sanzi gexin yundong 三自革新运动

sanzuo dashan 三座大山

shehuizhuyi xin nongcun 社会主义
    新农村

shengmi zhu cheng shufan 生米煮成
    熟饭

Shengming shu 生命树

shengshi xiushi 盛世修史

shi 市 (city), 史 (history)

shili 失礼

Shuangjiang 霜降

shuling de 属灵的

shuling de shengming 属灵的生命

shuoli 说理

Song 宋

suku 诉苦

suzhi 素质

Tang 唐

tang zhuren 堂主任

Tanghua fanzi chuxue 唐话番字初学

Tianfeng 天风

tianguo de shiming 天国的使命

Tieguanyin 铁观音

tingji 厅级

tizhi nei 体制内

tongdi fan geming 通敌反革命

tuanjie 团结

Tudi gong 土地公

waidi de 外地的

waiguoren Jidujiao huodong linshi
    changsuo 外国人基督教活动临
    时场所

waijiao 外教

wairen 外人

Women yong bu renzhen de fangshi
    ban renzhen de shi 我们用不认
    真的方式办认真的事

Xia Ying da cidian 厦英大辞典

Xiagang tang 厦港堂

Xiamen ribao 厦门日报

Xiamen wanbao 厦门晚报

Xiamen wenshi ziliao 厦门文史资料

xiandai de 现代的

xianzhan houzou 先斩后奏

Xiaodao hui 小刀会

Xiaoxi libaitang 小溪礼拜堂

Xiehe libaitang 协和礼拜堂

xifang zichanjieji ziyouhua sichao 西
    方资产阶级自由化思潮

xin daomin 新岛民

Xinjiao 新教

Xinjie tang 新街堂

Xinqu fuyin tang 新区福音堂

xinxiang de Ma'na 馨香的吗哪

xueyuan pai 学院派

Xunyuan zhongxue 寻源中学

yangjiao 洋教

yifa yigui banjiao 依法依规办教

Yihequan 义和拳

yiku sitian 忆苦思甜

Ying Hua zhongxue 英华中学

Yingyu jiao 英语角

yinyuan 银元

yong bu xiaoshi de tiantang 永不消失
    的天堂

youpai 右派

Yuan 元

yuanze wenti 原则问题

Yude nüzhong 毓德女中

yuren 育人

zhanglao 长老

zhegai 遮盖

zheng chuji 正处级

zhengshu 政书

zhengzhi juewu 政治觉悟

zhi 志

zhishi 执事

Zhongguo tese shehuizhuyi 中国特色
    社会主义

Zhongguohua 中国化

Zhonghua diyi shengtang 中华第一
    圣堂

Zhonghua Jidu jiaohui 中华基督教会

zhongyuan 中原

zhuren mushi 主任牧师

Zhushu tang 竹树堂

zichuan 自传

ziyang 自养

zizheng 资政

zizhi 自治

zongjiao huodong changsuo 宗教活
    动场所

zuo de 左的

zuo guang zuo yan 做光做盐

INTRODUCTION

This study arises from a series of interrelated questions about Christianity in the region of Xiamen, in southeastern China.[1] Christianity in Xiamen dates back at least to 1842 and has become a prominent part of the city's social, political, and cultural life. The research explores how people in the Xiamen region engage with Christianity as a way of engaging with both history and modernity, particularly looking at Gulangyu (literally meaning Drum Wave Island, formerly known as Kulangsu or Koolangsu in the West), an islet off the main island of Xiamen, where Christianity has been present since the nineteenth century.

Though an important and prosperous part of China, situated in the economic powerhouse of Fujian Province, Xiamen is much less well known in the West than cities such as Beijing or Shanghai. One of the remarkable points I uncovered in my research is how Christianity in Xiamen has had a profound influence on the region's social and cultural development, as well as influencing society and religion in other parts of the globe, such as Southeast Asia, through the influence of transnational Chinese Christian networks.

Previous studies of Christianity in China have tended to view Christianity in opposition to the state. Yet recently, researchers have begun to attend to the complexities of the relationship between the two, which goes beyond simple antagonism. Christianity has been profoundly implicated in shaping modernity in the Xiamen region, even as the state offers competing visions of what modernization means. The past is important to the people of Xiamen, who view it with an interest and nostalgia that reveals more profound preoccupations with the changes brought about by modernization, and this preoccupation with both history and modernity, and their connections to Christianity, is the central theme of this book.

Some studies have focused on analyzing the growth in the numbers of Christians in China, or the evangelization tactics employed by churches. This research takes a different approach, addressing the relevance of Christianity to ideological negotiations with officially established authority. I explore this topic by asking how history enthusiasts negotiate Christianity-related ideology, reconstructing the Christian past, and reproducing religious histories that redefine local power structures in contemporary China. By taking this tack, I hope to move away from viewing Christianity simply as a religious system and focus on how it has become deeply embedded in and relevant to society as a whole. I employ detailed analyses of different events to unpack the dynamic interactions between different stakeholders and assess what Christianity means to Chinese people. In this sense, it moves beyond a Eurocentric approach to reflect on the acculturation of Christianity in the Chinese context and the place of Chinese Christianity on the global stage.

Understanding World Christianity in the Context of East Asia

For a long time, the predominant theory in the sociology of religion was Peter Berger's idea of secularization, predicting that the significance of religion would continue to decline in modern society.[2] Time has proved his prognosis untenable. It seems religion is not doomed to disappear; on the contrary, religious revivals are underway around the world. Even Berger himself has frankly admitted the failure of his theory.[3] In their more recent research, Berger and his colleagues now point out the importance of attending to regional variations. They note that Europe is a relatively secular part of the world in global terms, in contrast to "religious America."[4]

Elsewhere, as well, religion is shaping the meaning of modernity. Scholars of world religion can no longer elide the differences in religions and religiosities worldwide, and as Brian Stanley reminds us, "No single global narrative of secularization is evident across the century as a whole.... Radically divergent patterns of believing and belonging [are] discernible, even within Europe itself."[5] In this light, the thriving Christian communities in

East Asia are prime examples of how Christianity (or Christianities) can not only thrive in the presence of modernization but become more diverse through complex interactions with their historical, social, and political contexts.

3

One of the most important changes in global Christianity in the past century has been its rapid rise in the non-Western world. A few distinguished scholars of Christianity, such as Philip Jenkins and Lamin Sanneh, have pointed out the steady southward advance of Christianity into countries in the "Global South" (particularly in Africa, Latin America, and Asia), and the concomitant shift in the balance of religious power between these newly established centers and the old heartland of Christianity in Europe. This trend, described as Christianity's "southern expansion," seems set to continue in the foreseeable future. Conversely, this dynamic growth in the Global South has coincided with the twilight of the Western phase of Christianity. In other words, though the Western world dominated Christianity for most of the second millennium, it is now primarily a non-European religion.[6]

The theory of Christianity's southern shift encompasses a kind of macroview of world Christianity, often looking at demographic growth as a significant factor in this broader shift. Yet the rising importance of the Global South in Christianity worldwide should not be perceived as merely a numbers game. It is crucial to attend to differences in how Christianity is developing in different social contexts. When it comes to Christianity in Asia, in particular, Julius Bautista argues that "there are some specificities about the Asian experience of secularism, nationalism, ethnicity, and statehood that we should take into consideration" to understand its rise and cultural manifestations.[7]

Advocates of the southern shift theory have pointed out that statistically speaking, Africa and Latin America, rather than Asia, will be the new Christian centers. Yet they still tend to be amazed by the booming Christian population and indigenous churches in East Asia, especially South Korea and China. South Korea today is probably one of the most Christianized countries in the non-Western world, where the faithful constitute more than a quarter of the population as a whole.[8] And since the 1980s, Christianity has been a prominent part of the general resurgence of religion in China.

For part of China's history, Christianity—along with other religions— was sharply repressed, particularly after the founding of the People's Republic of China (PRC). In spite of the state's atheistic ideology and restrictive regulations, Christianity survived the harshly repressive political movements of the Maoist era (1949–76), going on to see remarkable development in the past few decades.[9] At present, there are enormous numbers of Christians across the country: while no reliable figures can be found, a well-informed estimate would put their numbers in the tens of millions. As Daniel Bays writes, "Today, on any given Sunday there are almost certainly more Protestants in church in China than in all of Europe."[10] A number of studies indicate that Christianity has evolved in step with changing local historical and political conditions in China. The most important outcome of this development is that indigenous denominations in modern China unquestionably have their roots in Chinese cultural, social, and political contexts.[11]

The context of East Asia affords us a good starting point from which to discuss the study of Christianity in the Global South. Many studies of the southern trend tend to overemphasize the diminishing influence of the nation-state. Indeed, the state might be losing influence in some regions where political loyalties are secondary to religious beliefs, as Jenkins has pointed out,[12] but in East Asia, national politics remain a crucial factor in how Christianity is developing and has developed in the past.[13]

This study of East Asian Christianity will not be confined to frameworks such as (de)secularization theory and trends in the Global South but will demonstrate that it is essential to engage in detailed, in-depth study of the cultural context in order to understand the place of Christianity in East Asia and the role of Chinese Christianity worldwide. Furthermore, regional variations are such that even within China, the religion cannot be considered homogeneous or monolithic.

Indeed, although researchers have paid little attention to the phenomenon so far, South-South and even South-North evangelism represent one of the most impressive phenomena in contemporary Christianity.[14] South Korea, a former recipient of Western missionaries, has been a prominent missionary-sending country in the past few decades. In 2018, according to a source from the Seoul-based Korea Research Institute for Mission, there were as many as 21,378 South Korean missionaries working through 154 mission agencies in 146 countries.[15] The United States, whose Protestant missionaries first entered Korea in 1885, has been continuously ranked as one of the top destinations for South Korean missionaries. Since the late 1970s, South Korean missionaries have been dedicated to evangelizing (mostly white) Americans and have achieved considerable success in cross-cultural evangelism, exporting missionaries back to the places from whence they once received them.[16]

Although it is prohibited by the socialist state, Chinese Christians now take a more active role in the global missions as well. One example is the "Back to Jerusalem" movement, a mission-oriented project to evangelize all of the nations between China and the Middle East. This movement is generally associated with unregistered churches rather than state-sanctioned churches in China.[17] Many Chinese missionaries are recruited and trained by South Korean mission agencies and then sent to Muslim-majority countries.[18]

Mark Mullins's book *Christianity Made in Japan* focuses on the "native" response rather than Western missionary efforts and intentions. In it, Mullins gives a clear illustration of how world Christianity has become localized in Japan, as it had previously been localized in Europe and America, where it developed into what is now recognized as "Western Christianity."[19] In a similar vein, inspired by Mullins's research, Peter Tze Ming Ng argues that in China "what we should be looking for is not 'what Western missionaries have done in China,' nor is it simply taking 'Christianity in China as an unfinished Western project,' it is rather the 'Christianity Made in China,' and indeed, it would turn out to be a new kind of Christianity found in China with Chinese Christians as the proper subject of our study."[20] A point of note, shown in empirical studies of contemporary Chinese Christianity, is that it is mainly Chinese believers rather than foreign missionaries who have revived the faith, and it is people from upwardly mobile social strata (for example, entrepreneurs, migrant workers, and educated youth) who are changing the makeup of today's Christian population.[21]

For societies that were the recipients of evangelism in the missionary era, the rise of Western discourses of modernity inevitably transformed their religious perceptions of the self, the community, and the state.[22] In modern East Asia, rather than being merely a system of belief and practice, Christianity has been an important source of ideas and knowledge for ordinary people, intellectuals, and politicians, helping them negotiate modernity, and giving them meaning when confronted with changing realities, such as when the sovereignty of their countries was under threat from imperialism and colonialism.

The negative discourse about Christianity in relation to Western imperialism emerged through nation-building projects in modern Asia. Kiri Paramore's book *Ideology and Christianity in Japan* sheds light on the historical development of anti-Christian ideas and their role in the construction of the modern Japanese state in the late nineteenth century.[23] Under Meiji rule, the discursive identification of State Shinto with an essentialized Japanese identity forced Japanese Christians into a struggle about being both Japanese and Christian at the same time.[24] Since the latter half of the twentieth century, finding their feet after their humiliation in the aftermath of the Second World War, extreme right-wing nationalist politicians in Japan have been making the case for the rehabilitation of disgraced State Shinto and for its installation as a civil religion.[25] As a minority religion in Japanese society, Christianity has always been forced to negotiate its place.

By sharp contrast, South Korea's differing historical experience of colonialism provides a good illustration of how Christianity can play a pivotal positive rather than negative role in national politics. In the early twentieth century, when Korea was under Japanese rule, Korean Christians were at the forefront of resistance against the colonizers' efforts to introduce Shinto. As a result, Christianity was naturally associated with emerging nationalism. In addition to the prestige it had acquired from its role in resistance to Japanese colonialism, postwar Christianity benefited from being the religion of the American liberators, at that time an overwhelming power compared to their Asian neighbors. The place of Christianity in South Korea was further boosted when the nation's postwar leadership was assumed by the Christian elite. These factors have granted Christianity plenty of social space for its development.[26] Even today, Christianity in South Korea retains its modernizing image—for example, it is invoked in the state's promotion of cremation, which the state and church see as a way of modernizing death practices.[27]

In China as well, Christianity has a complex relationship to nationalism and modernization. In some coastal cities, such as Fuzhou and Xiamen, Chinese Christians played a major role in the 1911 Revolution, which overthrew both the Manchu-ruled Qing Dynasty (1644–1911) and the system of imperial governance. After the 1911 Revolution, Chinese Christians also played a prominent role in building China's modern Republican state (1912–49 in the mainland) in Fuzhou and Xiamen. Christian individuals and organizations were deeply involved in the social and political life of these two cities during mainland China's late Qing and early Republican eras, playing leading roles in the movements against opium smoking and the abuse of slave girls, as well as being prominent in volunteer associations advocating social reform.[28] However, Christianity's contribution to state building was soon overshadowed by anti-Christian movements. As China entered its modern era, Christianity found itself caught in a dilemma. As Sanneh remarks, "Two central issues have defined China's encounter with the Western Christian movement: one was the demand for indigenous control against missionary domination, and the other was China's role in recent global Marxist movements. Christianity was a target on both fronts: one time as an obstacle to local empowerment, and another as an antagonistic ideology. On both issues Christianity yielded ground; first with respect to China's national interests, and next with respect to China's place in global revolutionary movements."[29] This point will be elaborated below.

Thus, although Christianity in China has at times been attacked as a tool of imperialism, it is clear that its success was at least partly due to what we might call its "indigenization" and how it was "mediated and understood" through local cultural and social values, as Albert Park and David Yoo have argued. In East Asia, "Protestant Christianity inspired new forms of subjectivity, visions of society, and conceptions of national identity."[30] What is needed is a more nuanced understanding of the state of East Asian Christianity and its role in the overall Christian world, coupled with insights into how Christianity has influenced the political, cultural, and social landscape of the region.

Christianity and the Making of History in China

Beyond the Church-State Dichotomy

The early People's Republic saw several turbulent decades when Christianity was widely attacked under successive political campaigns. Churches and all public activities were shut down under Maoism and did not resume until the late 1970s. All churches are now asked to register with the state-sanctioned Three-Self Patriotic Movement of Protestant Churches (TSPM, Sanzi aiguo yundong). Still, numerous congregations refuse to register and remain in a gray zone without an explicitly legal status. These are widely known in English as "house churches" (*jiating jiaohui*).[31]

Largely because of ongoing friction, scholars of Christianity in China have tended to understand it as being in opposition to the state. Many scholars tend to overemphasize the state's dominance in China, and the ways that churches, through avoidance or defiance, engage in resistance.[32] The Three-Self church structure that officially heads Christianity in China tends to be regarded in the literature as a governing tool of an overly restrictive regime.[33] Similarly, the religious revival in reform-era China is often regarded as a response to the repressive measures of the Maoist state.[34]

8

The prevalence of this model of state versus church owes much to Western theories of civil society. The idea that a civil society was emerging in China aroused widespread debate in the 1990s. Scholars reached a consensus that the concept of "civil society" as it has been applied to the Chinese context presupposed a (false) dichotomy between society and the state,[35] yet the theoretical framework of church versus state continued to inform studies of Chinese Christianity.[36] Furthermore, the concept of church-state separation in democratic societies has engendered assumptions about individuals needing full religious freedom to be autonomous and religious organizations needing to be independent from the state.

However, the separation of church and state is, in fact, a notion that is culturally situated in the liberal West. It cannot be taken for granted in the context of Chinese society, where, since ancient times, religion has never been independent from the state.[37] This has implications for the way we view the actions of religious leaders like Pastor Wen, described in chapter 3, and how they engage with religious affairs authorities. Rather than seeking independence, many Christians in China instead look for ways to maneuver alongside the state, employing networks of contacts as well as a range of licit and illicit means to pursue and expand their religious practice.

Recently, a growing number of scholars have realized that an approach viewing the church and state as fundamentally separate fails to capture the social complexity of religious dynamics in China, oversimplifying the interactions between multiple actors, especially at the local levels. The prevailing paradigm overlooks the fact that religious groups and government enjoy many areas of common interest.[38] They are not simply entrenched on opposite sides of religious issues. There is a rising awareness that religion in reform-era China cannot be properly understood unless the dichotomous approach is buttressed with greater local-level analysis. In particular, it is crucial to acknowledge that dominance and resistance are not the only possible positionalities in church-state relations, and while state repression plays an important role, it is only one aspect of the complex dynamics between a range of actors on the local, national, and international levels.[39]

A few years ago, a watershed moment occurred in church-state relations in contemporary China. In March 2013, the Zhejiang provincial government launched the three-year campaign known as "Three Rectifications, One Demolition" (San gai yi chai). Its goal was to renovate or "rectify" old residential neighborhoods, old factory grounds, and villages enclosed in newly urbanized areas, as well as to demolish illegal constructions. In the course of its implementation, buildings identified as "illegal" would be immediately torn down.

One of the targets of the campaign turned out to be Christian structures deemed to be illegal, leading to conflict with local Christian groups.[40] The situation escalated after the forced demolition of a church complex that began in March 2014. The Three Rivers Church (Sanjiang tang), a magnificent landmark building, became the focus of attention at home and abroad. Hundreds of Christians gathered spontaneously and organized themselves into human barricades, but the government refused to compromise. As the base of the church was blasted, the 180-foot-high spire collapsed, and it did not take long for the whole Gothic structure to be razed to the ground.[41]

What happened to the Wenzhou church in 2014 poses a serious challenge to scholars who privilege the negotiating capability of resourceful Chinese Christians, overlooking state rule and intrachurch politics.[42] Unexpectedly, the official demolition program did not cease after the Three Rivers event; instead, it has evolved into a widespread movement with a mission to remove crosses across Zhejiang. Although the government received extensive criticism from abroad, it has never compromised; indeed, repressive measures have even intensified. Disobedient pastors and Christian human rights lawyers who opposed the campaign have been arrested.[43]

It is believed that the Zhejiang movement has damaged church-state relations and forced members to detach themselves from the officially recognized Christian organizations that serve as the liaison with the state apparatus.[44] The campaign, a potential catalyst for millenarian beliefs within popular Christianity, may have had negative consequences for millions of Christians in Zhejiang and beyond, who interpret these events as "indicating that the 'Last Days' are imminent."[45]

This is by no means the end of the story. Soon afterward, the "rectifications" initiatives spread beyond Zhejiang, extending to Henan Province and elsewhere as well as to other religious institutions. Numerous religious buildings have been demolished; many unregistered churches have been raided and shut down. Some local authorities have exceeded the central government's expectations in order to demonstrate their loyalty to "socialist civilization." An extreme case is Gaoyou, a county-level city of Jiangsu Province whose government demolished as many as 5,911 Earth God (Tudi gong) shrines within a single month (March 2019) in the name of constructing "ecological space."[46]

The Zhejiang campaign has led scholars to look at how local clergy and congregants think of the mistreatment of their churches and, furthermore, to examine the current church-state relations from the perspective of theology.[47] Even in this context of high tension, researchers have continued to reflect on the limitations of the church-state binary and explore the negotiations between religion and state agencies at the grassroots.

This research is inspired by Karrie Koesel's recent enlightening research on religious groups under authoritarian governments in Russia and China, which shows how the religion-state nexus can be reconceptualized from an overemphasis on suppression and resistance to a more nuanced understanding that acknowledges a mutual alliance. Koesel's "interest-based theory" of religion-state interaction employs rational choice theory not in analyzing conversion or personal religious beliefs but rather as a framework for understanding the interplay between authorities and religious leaders.[48]

Taking all these points into consideration, this research departs from the notion of a church-state dichotomy, drawing on in-depth ethnography and previous studies of Christianity in China to show the complex dynamics of religion and government at the local level. More importantly, this project opens up a new field of research, exploring grassroots negotiations around Christianity's political history in contemporary China.

Christianity's Political History in China

Christianity has long been at the center of official narratives of "national humiliation" (*guochi*) in China. The discourse is closely related to the building of the modern nation-state and later to affirming the legitimacy of the Communist regime. Before China became a Communist-ruled country, previous political regimes already associated Christianity with imperialist invasion. The most violent attack against foreigners, one explicitly associated with Christian missionary activity, occurred around 1900. With the backing of the Qing government, motivated by protonationalist antiforeign sentiments, members of the Society of the Righteous and Harmonious Fists (Yihequan), generally known in the West as the "Boxers," killed perhaps 30,000 Chinese Catholics and Protestants and 250 foreigners, most of whom were missionaries.[49]

During the Republican period after the 1911 Revolution, large-scale, anti-Christian campaigns were already occurring.[50] In the twentieth century, patriotic Chinese people made endless references to the "century of humiliation" China had suffered at the hands of foreign imperialism, beginning with the Opium War (1839–42).[51] The British establishment viewed this war as a battle for free trade in general and open access to the Chinese domestic

market in particular. However, the Chinese saw it as a life-and-death struggle to retain their national sovereignty and maintain control over foreign
trade in order to remain free of manipulation by Western forces, especially
regarding the pernicious import of opium.

The Opium War led to the de facto guarantee that British ships could
continue transporting opium to China, "present[ing] the China coast
missionaries with something of a moral quandary," as Daniel Bays notes.[52]
The subsequent series of treaties gave missionaries increasing scope for their
activities in China, allowing their influence to grow. Shielded by the guarantee of "missionary freedom," they were not subject to management or
supervision by the Chinese government and enjoyed the protection of their
respective governments. As John Fairbank has commented, "The missionary . . . had the chance to preach and innovate in China only because he
was part of the Western invasion. Gunfire and the unequal treaties initially
gave him his privileged status and opportunity."[53] Irrevocably, the Western
missionary endeavor was linked to imperialism and colonialism, height-
ened by the fact that some missionaries actually participated in negotiating
and drafting the treaties.[54] The first foreign Protestant missionary in Xiamen
brought the gospel on a British warship during the Opium War, contributing to the political stigmatization of Christianity in the area.[55]

If the pre-1949 history of Christianity was overshadowed by the specter of imperialism, post-1949 narratives of missionary work were defined
by the political authority of Communist leader Mao Zedong (1893–1976). In
his 1939 essay "The Chinese Revolution and the Chinese Communist Party,"
Mao wrote, "The imperialist powers have never slackened in their efforts
to warp the minds of the Chinese people. It is embodied in their policy of
cultural aggression. It is implemented through missionary work, through
establishing hospitals and schools, publishing newspapers, and inducing
Chinese students to study abroad. Their aim is to train intellectuals who will
serve their interests and to deceive the people."[56] In another well-known article from 1949, "Friendship or Aggression?," Mao specifically targets "United
States imperialism" in detail and ridicules the role of American missionary
enterprise as "spiritual aggression" in the name of "friendship."[57]

Shortly before victory in the Communist revolution, Mao published
"Farewell, John Leighton Stuart," one of his most widely read articles. In
it, Mao fiercely criticizes and satirizes John Leighton Stuart (1876–1962), a
former American Presbyterian missionary, the first president of Yenching
University in Beijing, and later US ambassador to Republican China. In
Mao's eyes, he is a typical example of Western imperialists working hand

in glove with the Christian mission, education, and politics.[58] To ordinary people in the early People's Republic, Chairman Mao's works were like the word of God to devout Christians. Almost every citizen with basic literacy skills had one or more copies of the *Quotations of Chairman Mao* (commonly known in the West as the *Little Red Book*), and even the illiterate could recite large paragraphs from Mao's works. His judgment set the tone for decades of political discourses on the history of Christianity in modern China.

In the early days of the PRC, the top leaders on multiple occasions expressed their concern about "imperialism under the guise of Christianity" and the Western missionary enterprise that was linked to imperialism and colonialism.[59] At the outbreak of the Korean War in 1950, US imperialism was the greatest target of their ire. The top-down Three-Self Reform Movement (Sanzi gexin yundong) in the early 1950s confronted Western missionaries and the Christian enterprise with unprecedented challenges. Subsequently, a nationwide Accusation Movement (Kongsu yundong) against "American imperialists under the cloak of religion" was launched in Christian communities.[60]

Christianity's role in the "national humiliation," as a significant theme running through modern Chinese history, has redefined and thrown into even sharper relief the Chinese Communist Party's (CCP) historical role as a liberator of the people, cast in terms of the shared Chinese struggle against foreign imperialism. The conviction that Christianity is associated with imperialism has prevailed in the writing of history in modern China, led by the CCP. Gu Changsheng's book *Missionaries and Modern China* is the fruit of an official project to record Christian history and represents the mainstream view that Catholic and Protestant missionaries acted as tools of imperialist aggression.[61] This book went through four editions, the latest in 2013, even though Gu himself changed his position, particularly after becoming a citizen of the United States.[62]

At the turn of the century, government-sanctioned national Christian organizations were still publishing volumes criticizing the disgraceful role of Christianity in the imperialist invasion of China.[63] On the other hand, dozens of books have been published recounting the missionaries' contributions to China's modern science, medicine, education, and the like. More recently, a greater number of both translated and original books have become available in China that portray particular missionary figures (for example, John Dudgeon, Samuel Pollard, James Legge, Calvin Wilson Mateer, Peter Park, and William Edward Soothill) instead of missionaries in the abstract.[64] Publishing is still subject to strict censorship by the authorities, so without official approval, none of these works could possibly have appeared in China. How could these two situations exist simultaneously? What is the current role of Christian history in maintaining the CCP's political legitimacy?

Since the relevant officials seldom give interviews, the government's intentions can only be inferred, but from the perspective of its citizens, the state restriction on Christian history writing is not set in stone. The cases discussed in this research reveal that the government has begun to concede a broad space for rewriting the history of Chinese Christianity prior to 1949, meaning that the Christian past or particular historical missionaries can now be painted in a positive light. By contrast, the ruling Party is still unwilling to acknowledge its early mistakes, and the suffering of churches, foreign missionaries, and individual Christians at the hands of the Communist regime after 1949 remain a forbidden topic.[65]

The end of the Maoist era saw a turn to "socialism with Chinese characteristics" (*Zhongguo tese shehuizhuyi*) through the "reform and opening-up" policy. In the subsequent decline in Communist ideals, the reform-era state has had to confront a crisis of legitimacy. The events in Tiananmen Square in June 1989 triggered tighter ideological control to combat the influence of the so-called "Western bourgeois liberation trend" (*xifang zichanjieji ziyouhua sichao*). There was a revival in patriotism and nationalism as the ruling Party made China's "national humiliation" a central theme in the official production and propagation of history. Patriotic educators "entreat[ed the young] to 'not forget.'"[66] As Zheng Wang has described, "The legitimacy-challenged Chinese Communist Party has used history education as an instrument for the glorification of the party, for the consolidation of national identity, and for the justification of the political system of the CCP's one-party rule in the post-Tiananmen and post-Cold War eras."[67]

The Party has perceived religions, particularly Christianity, as competitors for the minds of the next generation. For example, in April 1990 Chen Yun (1905–1995), one of the top Party leaders, told then incumbent President Jiang Zemin that counterrevolutionary activities were being carried out in the name of religion, particularly stressing that they were competing for the youth.[68] As long as this state of affairs prevails, alternative versions of the Christian past cannot be easily produced.

The shift in the legitimacy of the Chinese state has been a factor not only in the rise of Christianity but also in the revival of Confucianism, Buddhism, Daoism, and popular religions. As Richard Madsen has argued,

Communist rule was legitimized by a Sinicized version of Marxism-Lenin-ism; as Marxism in China lost its former ideological authority, the CCP embarked on a new course, adopting the role of heir and protector of five thousand years of Chinese cultural heritage.[69] Cultural traditions that the state denounced as "feudalistic" (*fengjian de*) and "backward" (*luohou de*) only a few decades ago have become a new source of legitimacy for Commu-nist rule. In this rediscovery (and reinvention) of China's roots, Christianity has never been regarded as part of national culture. Instead, it is still seen by some government officials as an "alien species" causing an imbalance in the "religious ecology." Some even claim to be establishing resistance to Christianity by reviving Chinese popular religions and traditional cultural features, nominally contributing to national security.[70]

Precisely at this same critical juncture, Xi Jinping, the general secretary of the CCP and president of the PRC, and his administration have launched a series of political movements devised to strengthen ideological control and deliberately make the CCP a sacred object of worship as an integral part of a new "communist civil religion," which features an absolute "dedi-cation to the Party that is specifically religious, yet does not require belief, conviction, or faith in a doctrine."[71] To a certain extent, the party-state still perceives Christianity as a powerful competitor for ideological author-ity. Thus, the study of Christianity in China must take into account these broader ideological battles, which are implicated in events like the wide-spread resistance of government officials and Chinese nationalists to the construction of a magnificent Gothic church in Qufu City, Shandong Prov-ince, the birthplace of Confucius,[72] and in increasingly common bans on celebrating Christmas, a typical "foreign festival," initiated by local govern-ments and universities.[73]

The analysis of these events should not be limited to what is happen-ing on the surface. The current political situation has led the public to suppose that the Zhejiang campaign, which so explicitly targets Chris-tianity, actually reflects the intentions of the high leadership. Seeing the central government's acquiescence in the provincial government's harsh-ness toward Christianity, some attribute this to the notion that top leaders realized there had been a certain inefficiency in implementing its policies and consequently suspected the grassroots officials' political loyalty. Thus, the political loyalty of local government officials may be the central govern-ment's underlying concern.[74]

Painful memories of the state repression of Christianity under Maoism have profoundly affected believers' current religious practices and interactions with authorities, as shown in numerous studies of both Protestantism and Catholicism in China.[75] In contemporary Xiamen, some older people are still aware of what happened to foreign missionaries and local Christians during the rule of Mao Zedong. They have a strong sense of historical and cultural purpose to record the as-yet untold past in the hopes that they can pass on their collective memories to a younger generation.

However, younger Christians did not live through Maoism and may evince different ways of interacting with society and the state. In his study of Wenzhou Christianity, Nanlai Cao argues that the older generation of Christians who suffered during Maoist political campaigns are more likely to retain antistate emotions but are now taking a step back from public life. On the other hand, a younger generation of Christians who have not experienced the state's harsh religious repression are actively seeking to play a fuller role in economic and financial affairs.[76]

As I have observed, many Xiamen citizens who are versed in the city's history tend to negotiate alternative narratives around the discourse on modern, advanced societies. Many students of Chinese religion have attempted to discover the affinities between religion, modernity, and the nation-state.[77] A palpable tension exists between the modernist imagination of the Chinese nation-state, which emphasizes essentialism, territoriality, and fixity, and that of entrepreneurial capitalism, celebrating hybridity, deterritorialization, and fluidity.[78] People interpret modernity, especially its relationship with Christianity, in their own way. Inspired by Max Weber's notion of the relationship between the Protestant ethic and the spirit of capitalism, Wenzhou's private entrepreneurs attribute the region's economic success to their Christian belief (although only a rare few have actually read Weber's book).[79] For many Chinese, saying that one is a Christian is the equivalent of stating that one is Western, modern, and economically successful. Discussing this view, Fenggang Yang writes that many Chinese believe the most advanced societies are "Christian countries" with Christian traditions, and some Chinese converts in the United States express the conviction that "there is a causal connection between Christianity, on the one hand, and modern market economies and political democracy, on the other."[80] Western modernity is an important ingredient in the attraction Christianity holds for urban believers.

Christians and the post-Mao state actually share many important concepts, values, and aspirations for modernity, even concerns about Chinese society's perceived moral crisis.[81] As Nanlai Cao has argued, "Chinese Christians are not simply victims of the state modernizing project; nor is the post-Mao Christian revival a process of faithful believers resisting state ideology."[82] The revival of Christianity in China today is better understood as a dynamic process in which emerging socioeconomic groups, embedded in specific historical and cultural contexts, are trying to claim their own space in which to practice a long-established faith under changing economic and political conditions. As Yoshiko Ashiwa has pointed out, "Modernity is not a one-sided project of the state to discipline people's thoughts but is a reciprocal project of religions and states reshaping themselves and each other."[83]

As Bays points out, the Christian church in China is now regarded as a major nongovernmental entity, considering its size, resources, and nationwide activities.[84] Researchers are fascinated by the consequences Chinese Christianity could have for the future of civil society. Ryan Dunch insists that, despite the ongoing struggle to claim an autonomous space for religious activity in everyday experience, there is no direct correlation between Christian demands for autonomy and political opposition to the government.[85] Richard Madsen argues that the Catholic Church might prove to be more of a hindrance than a strength in attempts to form a civil society, since the Chinese Catholic Church, historically shaped by its Counter-Reformation theology, tends to be more authoritarian and less tolerant of moral pluralism. Consequently, present-day Catholics have inherited and sustained a way of life—particularism, dependence on vertical hierarchy, and factionalism—that was effective in building a strong communal identity in a preindustrial Chinese society but is not conducive to building a civil society in today's modernizing China.[86]

Wenzhou Christianity, as Nanlai Cao has argued, is unlikely to become any kind of national civil association contributing to China's political transformation. The privileged Christian entrepreneurs of Wenzhou are striving to carve out a position as members of the emerging local elite by embracing a rather motley assemblage of evangelical Christianity, rational masculinity, state connections, a freewheeling market, and a Western lifestyle, all at once. In this process of self-creation, having a Christian identity sets someone apart as a person with a claim to higher social status, who can also assert that he or she also holds the moral high ground, thereby honing the distinction between those who are successful and those who are less so.[87]

While I was in the field, I heard the popular term *civil society* employed only once, by an educated young person. In this research, it is not my plan to take up the correlations between cultural reinvention and the development of civil society in detail. The concept of civil society does not seem

16

to contribute to the understanding of collective motivations in the context of this research.

In Xiamen, the Christian past has become the raw material for the imagining of a modern society. Instead of the theoretically laden concept of "modernity," my respondents use more colloquial phrases such as "modern" (*xiandai de*) and "advanced" (*fada de*) to refer to their understanding of the past. From their point of view, pre-1949 Xiamen used to be much more modern and advanced than other regions of China as a direct result of the introduction of Christianity and Western civilization in a broad sense.

History enthusiasts in Xiamen are constructing a shared past of belonging simultaneously to the state-led modernization project and the construction of local pride. In the reproduction of discourses about what is modern and advanced, an inevitable tension arises between national narratives on Christianity's inglorious role in modern Chinese history and alternative, more positive versions of Christianity's image in local society. Negotiating mechanisms inevitably form around these contradictory visions.

Rediscovering and Rewriting the Christian Past in Xiamen

People from Xiamen display a particular enthusiasm for the history of Gulangyu, and many are now interested in rediscovering and celebrating the islet's Christian past. I found this striking because links with the past are so often overlooked in studies of Chinese Christianity. This research shows that without knowing the past of Christianity in a particular context, we cannot fully understand how Christianity became indigenized in Chinese society and how it shaped the social fabric, as well as how Chinese people perceive the role of Christianity in their social life.

Studies of China understandably emphasize official manipulations of social memory, yet they have generally neglected the way people respond to and engage with these manipulated narratives of the past, particularly when it comes to Christianity. While a few scholars have examined the influence of history in Chinese Catholicism,[88] when it comes to Chinese Protestantism, the uses and values of history remain an understudied topic.[89]

What is fascinating is that people in present-day Xiamen society are precisely now engaged in rediscovering the past. Since Christianity entered the region over 180 years ago, the faith has grown and become rooted in local sociocultural structures. Recently there has been a burgeoning movement in Xiamen to rewrite the Christian past and reconstruct its historical

18

narratives, as I describe in the following chapters. History enthusiasts, both Christian and non-Christian, are devoting themselves to reinterpreting the legacy of the church and publicly celebrating their connections to the past. This is a civil movement on a local level that questions, even challenges, official historical narratives. The citizens who are involved in this movement are local history experts (*difang wenshi zhuanjia*)—elderly people who, while not possessing any professional training in history, are interested in collecting documents and preserving or publicizing the city's history. Even the local government acknowledges and makes use of church heritage for pragmatic purposes.

The enthusiasm that people from Xiamen now have for reconstructing a glorious Christian past is, to some extent, an expression of present grievances. They lament recent social changes in Gulangyu and the subsequent decline of Christianity on the island. To them, Christianity in Gulangyu is inextricably intertwined with a certain vision of modernity. In the aftermath of China's defeat in the Opium War with Great Britain, Xiamen was forcibly opened up to the outside world as one of the five treaty ports ceded to the British, and Gulangyu was thrust into a Western-led modernization process. As I examine in the following chapters, Christianity, in conjunction with imperialism, played a major role in reshaping the sociocultural context of the island.

Trinity Church (Sanyi tang), built in 1934, bore witness to the heyday of Christianity on this small island. Remarkably, Trinity Church survived the repressive and violent political campaigns against religion during the Maoist era, and it was reopened and revived as a site of worship in 1979. However, the church is now doomed to a decline in numbers and influence because of government-led efforts to commercialize the island in a push to make it more tourist-friendly. When I was invited to the church's eightieth anniversary celebration in October 2014, I witnessed firsthand how church people responded to the state modernization project by reminiscing about its glorious past and grieving over its irreversible fate.

As an essential ingredient of the social fabric in Xiamen, the Christian past has drawn extensive attention from both within and beyond the Xiamen Christian community. When I went to Xiamen at the end of 2013, my respondents repeatedly mentioned a memorial service for an American missionary, John Otte, that had been organized by a non-Christian group several years earlier. Under Maoism, Otte had been denounced as an "imperialist rogue," yet the commemoration countered the charges that had been laid against him and highly commended him for the contributions he had made to Gulangyu. The ceremony reversed the grassroots discourse on missionaries in a broader sense.

The memorial for Otte to some extent inspired and encouraged local history experts to embark on a study of the Christian history of Xiamen. This was a bold step because the Chinese Communist regime has had a monopoly on the writing of history as a national project since it took power in 1949. Today, all publications on religion in mainland China continue to be published under strict censorship; some are banned from being printed, whereas some have to be revised, in particular those parts referring to religious repression after 1949.

The official Christian history of Xiamen, as yet unpublished and incomplete, is a prime example of how contentious this history can be. In the late 1980s, the Xiamen Religious Affairs Bureau (RAB), a branch of a local government that is in charge of regulating religious organizations, assigned the City's Christian community with the task of writing the history of Christianity in Xiamen. A manuscript was eventually completed in 1993 but failed to satisfy either the government or the church community. The assignment was passed on to several other writers, but so far no acceptable manuscript has been completed. The project apparently cannot reach a satisfactory conclusion. Meanwhile, local history experts have taken matters into their own hands and have translated English-language history books or written their own. Some have succeeded in having their work published through "unofficial" (to some extent "illegal") channels; others have failed. A growing number of people are beginning to narrate the past of their Christian families, including compiling genealogies that trace their families back to the first convert or circulating memoirs of their Christian ancestors.[90]

This phenomenon immediately raises the question: Why does the past of Christianity matter so much to the people of Xiamen? The answers to this are many and varied, but one major reason is that the version of the official narratives endorsed by the state conflicts so deeply with their own understanding of their shared past. Importantly, these unofficial, rather than the official, versions are providing people with an alternative historical knowledge of Christianity.

These negotiations of the Christian past are not only embodied in issues of memory or history; they are also seen in church practices. Trinity Church has sought the involvement of international Christian agencies in its efforts to revive the once thriving Christian movement on Gulangyu. One of the matters investigated in this book is a fellowship established by Chinese American missionaries under the aegis of an officially registered church. Contrary to the popular perception that Christianity is becoming indigenized in China, this American ministry is aware of the fascination the outside world holds for young Chinese people and does its best to display its "foreign" (especially American) features to attract young believers. This present-day transnational ministry diverges considerably from the perennially assumed connection to imperialism in the official discourse of the Chinese state. Its presentation of Christianity in a package with the modern image of the United States has deeply influenced young people, not only in their beliefs but also in their understanding of modern society and Christianity. Indeed, the cooperation between local churches and the American Christian agency has not been all plain sailing but has turned out to be troublesome for both sides.

To understand the collective passion for reinventing the past in Xiamen, it is important to understand the local sense of nostalgia, the way in which individuals or social groups seek to re-create the past to satisfy their present needs. As Peter Nosco describes, nostalgia can be a response to dissatisfaction with one's immediate situation, engendering a desire to idealize past events. By looking backward to an idealized past, one can momentarily disengage oneself from the unsatisfactory present.[91]

My respondents, consciously or unconsciously, often mentioned the glorious past of Gulangyu. Then they would shake their heads and heave a sigh about how the island had deteriorated culturally in the wake of the local government's efforts to expand tourist revenue. While the government unilaterally tried to discredit historical missionary activity, the people I spoke with invariably overembellish the city's past by intentionally dissociating Christianity from colonialism, and exaggerating the church's role in the modernization of Xiamen. What they are doing is in some ways similar to what the state does, rewriting historical narratives to fit with a specific version of the present; only they are operating from a diametrically opposite perspective. This fixation on an imagined past might explain why local people have no interest in the present-day American evangelists, even though they cherish missionary history and see the erstwhile missionaries as having made a valuable contribution to the region's prosperous past.

Success in cultural reinvention can only be achieved when the timing is right and when there is a certain degree of liberty to do so. The historical and sociopolitical contexts are too important to be overlooked. The previous decade saw a nationwide movement for recording oral history that at times challenged official narratives. One salient movement is the current "Republican fever" (Minguo re)—namely, the upsurge in public support in

China for the legacy of the Republican era. The roots of this great yearning for Republican freedom and democracy can be traced precisely to dissatisfaction with China's present situation.[92]

What is happening in Xiamen is occurring at a significant historical juncture. It is important to note that some locals share a collective need for this sort of reinvention and believe that writing their own history is essential to the survival of their social collectivity. A conviction about such a need pushes people to group together and join in the process. If the group enjoys a relaxed and liberal political climate, it could engage in cultural reinvention without fear of reprisals for its members and without its cultural practices being repressed. Nevertheless, the political climate in which this reinvention is taking place is far from liberal. We should bear in mind that, as a national project, social memory or history writing in modern China has been dominated by social engineers who invariably try to dictate citizens' remembrance and forgetting.[93] Even today, Chinese authorities seek to keep a tight rein on society's memories. Jun Jing puts it on three levels: "At the archival level, such control takes the form of restricting access to historical documents. At the level of mass media and public education, control is exercised through censorship, political propaganda, and the careful writing and rewriting of history textbooks. At a more personal level, control relies on intimidation and, sometimes, physical punishment of those who offer a radically different and unwelcome version of the past, particularly when it touches on the history of the Communist Party."[94]

Social Memory: Theoretical Considerations

Traditional historiography saw memory as being essentially different from history because memory was considered an unreliable source. However, more recently, scholars have reconsidered the distinction between memory and history, and memory has now become a newly valued source of evidence in historical research. Yet conversely, as a consequence of postmodernism, the way we understand "objective" truth and whether there is indeed a "truth" has changed, blurring the boundaries between history and memory.[95]

In this research, I have moved away from trying to distinguish memory and history, leaving this question to more eminent specialists. Terminologies like "social memory" and "history" will be used alternately without being strictly defined, but with the proviso that "history" is most often used to describe representations of the past that appear in written form, while "social memory" refers to living information about social events that members of a particular society conserve in their minds. Throughout the book, unless noted, these two terms always refer to the past.

Memory, Power, and the Invention of Tradition

French sociologist Maurice Halbwachs pioneered the study of what he termed "collective memory," which, as he established, is connected to particular social groups. He argued that there are as many collective memories as there are groups and institutions in a society, and all memories are structured by group identities. Therefore, the study of memory must be placed within a social framework, taking into account the impact of such social institutions as family, community, religious group, tradition, and social class.[96]

Following the Durkheimian understanding of social continuity, Halbwachs asserted that the past is a social construction mainly shaped by present concerns and developed the notion that present concerns determine what we remember. This influential idea has since been developed further by other scholars. George H. Mead, for example, claims that the past is construed from the standpoint of today's new problems.[97] Ian M. L. Hunter states that the primary function of memory "is not to conserve the past but to make possible adjustment to the requirements of the present."[98]

The invention of tradition approach argues that the past is shaped to suit the interests of dominant groups in the present. According to this perspective, the most prominent members of society tend to dominate its way of thinking and seize every means available to exploit public ideas about the past: public commemorations, school syllabuses, and the mass media, as well as sources such as official records and chronologies. As Paul Connerton writes, people's image of the past commonly legitimates the present social order.[99] Thus, power relations have become a central theme in memory studies. Michel Foucault's work has been influential in this regard, arguing that memory "is actually a very important factor in struggle . . . if one controls the memory of the people, one controls their dynamism. . . . It is vital to have possession of this memory, to control it, administer it, tell it what it must contain."[100]

In this approach, researchers have illustrated how new traditions and histories are invented to legitimize political structures, solidify social orders, and sustain national communities. Yet in defining social memories as inventions of the past, scholars tend to focus on the officially led institutionalization of remembrance or the creation of a master narrative of a common history to the exclusion of experiences outside of official narratives.

Eric Hobsbawm and Terence Ranger's *The Invention of Tradition* (1983) represents this perspective. "Traditions which appear or claim to be old," as Hobsbawm points out, "are often quite recent in origin and sometimes invented." Invented tradition, he postulates, is taken to mean "a set of practices, normally governed by overtly or tacitly accepted rules and of a ritual or symbolic nature, which seek to inculcate certain values and norms of behavior by repetition, which automatically implies continuity with the past."[101]

While the Durkheimian tradition argues that people remember collectively and selectively, the invention of tradition approach suggests more directly who is responsible for this selective remembering; that is, who controls or imposes the content of social memories. The official manipulation of these narratives of the past, resulting in the production of official memory, is embodied in both socially organized forgetting and socially organized remembering, legitimizing and stabilizing the political orders and interests of ruling groups.

This state-centered approach emphasizes the mechanism of state rituals as an effective means to produce official narrative. In the course of the last century, communist revolutions eliminated the rituals and symbols of the ancien régimes from which they took over and invented new ones to replace them. Paving the way for new social memories, communist regimes designed new flags, rewrote school textbooks, and thought up new national events to be commemorated.[102]

Undeniably, there is a long-standing tradition of ruling groups controlling the writing of history in China. Each of China's dynasties sought to legitimize its power through new interpretations of history. One of a dynasty's first acts to consolidate its rule was invariably to write the history of the preceding dynasty.[103] Since 1949, the People's Republic has continued this tradition, making Marxist historiography an important sphere of ideological control.[104] Under the rule of the CCP, the careful crafting of history has been a monopoly of the state, shaping social memory. In some areas, freedom of discussion is either absent or strictly limited; any conflict with official narratives invites persecution.[105]

The ruling groups in China are well aware that the only dependable way of making people effectively forget one thing without the aid of natural amnesia is to make them remember another with greater effect. The art of official amnesia, therefore, "always goes hand in hand with the art of political remembrance."[106] The political elites indicate which part of past experience should be remembered or forgotten according to the current political line.[107] Certain past episodes have been thoroughly erased from both official history and personal memory, leaving those who are ruled with a seemingly plausible representation of the past that elides a great deal of politically laden experiences. The colonization of public and private space, as Rubie Watson has declared, constitutes one of the hallmarks of state socialism.[108]

Numerous ethnographies of China since 1949 have shown that technologies of memory were deployed and embodied in various political movements, such as "speaking bitterness" (*suku*) and the Large-Scale Production Campaign (Dashengchan yundong).[109] "Speaking bitterness," in which people were pushed to mold their personal memories around Communist tropes of suffering and liberation, served as an important psychological mechanism to mobilize rural people against the politically constructed landlord class. Modern Chinese history has been written so as to maximize the gratitude due to the Communist Party. Therefore, written history serves as a record of debts that the ruled owed the rulers. Alongside this kind of history there has developed another practice known as *yiku sitian*—recalling the bitterness of the past so as to appreciate the sweetness of the present, establishing a debtor-creditor relationship with the state.[110]

When attention is paid to who controls or imposes invented memories, social memory appears as an ideology serving the interests of the powerful, an instrument of elite manipulation used to control lower classes. Because the social and cultural aspects of memory are underplayed, as Alon Confino points out, it "becomes a prisoner of political reductionism and functionalism."[111] Nevertheless, it is also misleading to equate memory with ideology. One of the chief purposes of ideology is to act as a sort of cement that will guarantee national cohesion; hence it is monolithic. On the other hand, although social memory can strengthen, it can also cause discord. It is crucial to remember that the memory of a social group cannot always be reduced to the political aim of sustaining relations of power as it is not necessarily solely imposed from above.

Popular Memory: Contesting Dominant Ideology

The official manipulation of social memory is not always effective. Individuals and subgroups have their own, often quite strong opinions, and therefore they will readily repudiate any depiction of the past that conflicts with what they personally can recollect and what they perceive to be the truth. As Michael Schudson has pointed out, "The past is not only the stories people tell of it; it is the claim of events that set the conditions about which people feel compelled to tell stories."[112] In other words, collective memory is not so easy to undermine or distort. A dominant power that ignores the authenticity and experience of memories held by any group under its sway risks being challenged or accused of unethical behavior. Moreover, the negative memories produced by a ruling group might challenge its legitimacy, and a regime could fall if it creates too many bad memories and fails to eradicate them.[113] It is not always possible to impose totally invented or fabricated traditions on people regardless of the political system, democratic or undemocratic. As Jun Jing writes, "The transmission of memory involves a large armamentarium of symbolic resources and moral evaluation, in which the worth of political control itself can be questioned and even challenged."[114] In this sense, this state-centered memory approach tends to presume the ruled to be passive recipients of assigned narratives and simplifies the multidimensional relations between the people and the state.

In discussions of the popular memory approach, scholars are particularly interested in the issue of unofficial narratives shared by members of certain social segments who do not necessarily adhere to the dominant, public, or official representations of the past. This approach, inspired by Foucault's notion of countermemory, observes that memories can be socially constituted from below as well as from above. The articulation of countermemories has been taken as evidence of resistance to various forms of domination.[115] Unlike the official memory approach, which assumes that memories are socially constituted from above, popular memory theory emphasizes that cogent memory can also be constructed from the grassroots.[116]

These forms of political control over society's memory have been extensively researched in terms of the relationship between the Chinese party-state and intellectuals.[117] But more research needs to be done, especially grassroots studies that focus on local reactions to official manipulations of social memory.

Memory as a Domain of Dynamic Negotiation

What this analysis of popular and official memory shows is that there are limitations to the construction of overarching official historical narratives. The past is often resistant to efforts to make it over; permanent and changing versions of history are always mutually imbricated. Taking this into consideration, we need to develop a more complex perspective, which acknowledges that dominant constructions of memory can be challenged

NEGOTIATING THE CHRISTIAN PAST IN CHINA

or even rejected by ordinary citizens, and that various elements are often simultaneously in play. Thus, memory is a domain of dynamic negotiation. This approach shifts our focus toward a more complex view of how past and present interact with each other in the formation of collective memory, positing that it is an operative process of sense-making over time.[118]

As Barbara Misztal argues, this perspective allows us to understand "commemoration as a struggle or negotiation between competing narratives and stresses that the dynamics of commemorative rituals involves a constant tension between creating, preserving, and destroying memories."[119] In this context, commemoration is seen as a socially constructed and contested process that is shaped by, and shapes, the present as well as the past. Social memory is viewed as a continuous exercise in dialogue and consequently, when examined, it reveals the restrictions placed on the ability of actors to refashion history in general or what might have happened to them personally to suit what they want to achieve now.[120] Hence, the dynamic negotiation perspective argues that memory is not constrained solely by the official narrative but recognizes that commemoration can also be constructed and contested by ordinary citizens. It sees memory as inhabiting the space left over between what is imposed by ideology and the possibility that there might be other ways of understanding and interpreting experience.

Generally speaking, the virtue of this approach is that it avoids political reductionism and functionalism. As Misztal notes, it "runs a lower risk of reifying collective memory as it is aware of the flexibility and ambiguities of memory and because it incorporates conflict, contest, and controversy as the hallmarks of memory."[121]

This research adopts the dynamic negotiation perspective, starting from the assumption that the history of Chinese Christianity is not a free field that can be repeatedly contrived to suit particular purposes. As I show in the following chapters, efforts to stamp out any alternative version of Christian history in Xiamen, or indeed to browbeat people into submission, have not been nor will be effective enough to guarantee that imposed interpretations of past events will find general acceptance.

Doing Fieldwork in Xiamen

This research is based on materials collected during fieldwork in Xiamen between 2011 and 2015. My field study was undertaken in three parts. The first began in May 2011 and continued up to the spring of 2012. At that time, I focused on transnational Christian networks, in particular a group of Chinese Americans who have devoted themselves to bridging the gap between Chinese society and American Christianity. The second part was conducted from December 2013 to May 2014, as well as in October 2014. The final trip came in November 2015. During my fieldwork, the School of Public Affairs of Xiamen University where I pursued my master's degree offered me letters of introduction bearing official seals to assist my visits to the Xiamen Archives and the Xiamen RAB. In China, a letter of introduction from an official or quasi-official agency is necessary to access government and other sorts of work units (*danwei*).

When interviewing people within or outside of the church community, I referred to my status as an affiliate of Leiden University. It turned out that my research benefited from the foreign associations conferred by a Western university. I would have been less welcome if I had come as a local student. My background prompted my respondents to discuss the decline in Christian beliefs in Europe (in particular the Netherlands, where they noted that prostitution, homosexual marriage, and personal use of marijuana are all legal) and also led to a request from local history experts who were looking for help locating foreign historical materials related to the Xiamen church.

Whenever I gained access to archives and interviewed officials in religious affairs, I showed letters of introduction from Xiamen University. Even so, most officials were hesitant to share their ideas about Christianity with me.

One afternoon in April 2014, I made a visit to the Xiamen Archives. Before I had even entered the door to the reception room, I heard the sounds of an emotional debate. A man who had requested access to his father's personnel file (*dang'an*) had been refused. A staff member explained the policy to him, stating that only his father himself was qualified to see it. "But my father is bedridden. Do I need to carry him over here?" He was filled with rage at the way he was being prevented from seeing his own father's file.

I was carrying an official letter of introduction in the hopes that it would give me access to church archives. After showing the letter, I was asked to fill in a form and to check the boxes associated with the subjects listed. I was surprised to see a short list indicating very limited information. Contrary to the list I had been given, when I had been to the archives I already knew that a local church member had copied hundreds of pages of historical documents relating to the city's Young Men's Christian Association (YMCA) just

28

two years earlier. Even worse, when the junior staff member submitted my request to her superior in charge, the latter rejected more than half of items on the list. What I was allowed to access were merely policy documents that had been made public and could be found online. They explained that a notice had been issued not long before stating that archives relating to sensitive religious questions were not open to the public; an official letter of introduction from religious affairs authorities would be required to grant me greater access. However, shortly afterward my request for such a letter was rejected by an RAB official. This experience depressed me, but it also helped me understand the difficulty in accessing church histories during the Maoist era. Historical archives concerning post-1949 Christianity are now under even stricter control than they were before.

Just one month after initiating the second phase of my field study, I was left feeling extremely frustrated. I was quite aware of the difficulties in investigating foreigners' transnational Christian activities because I had a thorough knowledge of the state policies and appreciated the complexities. Nevertheless, I still underestimated how challenging it would be. These Chinese American missionaries were alert to any potential risk when I explained my purpose. The problem, I later realized, was that I had assumed a fairly "open" landscape in the Xiamen church and that I would encounter no problems in doing research on such fashionable themes as modernity and transnationalism. My intention was to identify the characteristics of Christianity in Xiamen and compare it with other areas such as Wenzhou.

In his study of a Chinese Catholic community, Wu Fei has said, "Like a stonemason, I attempt to carve a regularly shaped artifact, to be named 'academic research,' out of a single piece of stone. However, is it really my work to dress or cut the stone according to my own likes and dislikes?"[122] When I realized the problem, I decided to depart from my intended focus and reacquaint myself with the Xiamen church community from another, hopefully more objective, angle. Then as I worked, I became conscious that my fieldwork was taking place at a historical juncture at which local people had just begun to be concerned about their Christian legacy. This prompted me to shift my focus to locals' efforts to reconstruct the Christian past.

The fact that I am not a Christian rarely proved to be a significant hindrance to my research but it did sometimes affect how people perceived and responded to me in the field. On one occasion an unregistered church leader refused my request for a conversation, even though I had been intro-duced by his fellow preacher. He gave a straightforward justification from a typically Christian perspective: "Such a non-Christian from a secular university could not understand our faith in Christ." I supposed that his reaction was prompted largely by safety reasons in the current political context, and I fully understood the fragility of his position as an unrecognized church leader. On many other occasions, Christians told me that I could not understand their faith and experience unless I accepted Jesus as my savior.

When I was in Wenzhou, a pastor who gave me accommodation reiterated this view over and over again. In one conversation, he mentioned a scholar from Beijing who once visited his church and authored an article on it. "I read her article. With all due respect, from the Christian view, these articles written by non-Christians are ridiculous." His contempt for nonbelievers' research turned up again and again in our everyday conversations and made me quite uncomfortable. I then responded, "With all due respect, from the non-Christian view, articles written by Christians are sometimes ridiculous too." He forced a slight, reluctant smile but did not say anything. My sudden impulsive response embarrassed him. Since then I have often pondered why many Christians insist that their beliefs could not be comprehended. Is it simply because of my lack of religious experience? The only thing I can assume is that these believers must have already generated their own interpretive systems that run contrary to the aims and assumptions of non-Christians.

In the past the composition of China's Christian population has frequently been described in Chinese as "three-many"—that is, many female, many old, and many illiterate believers.[123] Recently, however, an increasing number of young, educated people are attending urban churches in economically advanced regions, a trend that is gradually changing the composition of today's Christian population. Xiamen Christians invariably profess the city's long-standing Christian tradition and wish to demonstrate their cultural superiority. "Even the finest dignitaries," a local intellectual proudly said to me, "bow their noble heads when they set foot on Gulangyu."

Rather than identify myself as a "cultural Christian," a term popular in Chinese society to refer to someone who appreciates the Christian doctrine and the faith but has no personal commitment to the church,[124] when asked I replied that I regarded myself as a "seeker" (mudaoyou). This term is used in Chinese, both among Christians and more generally, to refer to someone who is keen to learn about a religion but has not yet converted to it.

My respondents often tried to convert me. Apparently, I disappointed all of them. They felt sorry to have to tell me that I would not be saved without Jesus as my savior. I often gave them an excuse, claiming that it was necessary to distance myself from the faith in order to maintain a certain degree of objectivity. I appreciated that many of them understood the requirements of scientific research. I attended various church services just as an ordinary Christian would do and became familiar with their faith by reading the Bible, listening to sermons, and singing hymns. As often as possible, I made my presence visible on various occasions. But I neither prayed in public nor participated in Communion, a rite reserved for church members only.

In October 2011, I attended a closed men's retreat held by a Chinese American fellowship. When sharing testimonies, my emotions spun out of control and I burst into tears. Since that time, I have become more aware of the dangers of becoming profoundly involved in religious experiences and reminded myself from time to time of my role as a researcher rather than a believer. However, precisely because of this unexpected episode, I caught the attention of the leader who believed that I would accept Jesus soon. Even though I did not convert, I did become more popular and credible among members of that fellowship, a step that greatly facilitated my investigation.

Although local history experts are keen to explore the Christian past, their efforts are often restricted because of limited sources and lack of foreign language skills. Ma Zhenyu, a retired engineer who was in charge of writing the history of Trinity Church, came to seek my assistance. The biggest difficulty in the construction of Trinity Church in 1936 had been constructing the roof. Thanks to a Dutch engineer from the Netherlands Harbor Works Company, who was living in Xiamen, a roof for the new structure was finally designed and the church building was completed one month before it hosted the second National Bible Assembly in July 1936. As the engineer had solved the most difficult part in the construction process, Ma believed that his name should be committed to memory. Ma did his utmost but still could not identify the engineer. When he heard that I was doing my doctoral research in the Netherlands, he invited me to lunch and requested my help. As soon as I returned to Leiden, I devoted myself to the matter. However, because of the multiple restructurings of the company, I was unable to locate the engineer's name. Ma then asked me to bring a picture of the current company building with me to the church. To my surprise, my picture was projected on a big screen during his testimony at the church's eightieth anniversary celebration. On behalf of the church, he spoke of his appreciation of my help and even listed my name among his most important sources. An American guest joked with me, saying, "Now you're famous."

Given my active involvement and assistance, Ma said to me, "You are no longer an outsider (*wairen*)." Every time he presented me to other church people, he introduced me with the words: "He is the young man from the Netherlands who tried to help us identify the Dutch engineer." Although my name was far from familiar among those Christians, after this the distance between me and these church members had indeed narrowed. My research benefited from becoming not just part of the church community but also part of the cause to which local people were so committed.

I collected historical materials for those who appreciate the past of the Xiamen region in general and the role of Christianity in particular. In so doing, I became far better acquainted with two key pastors and several local history experts, who were delighted to be of assistance. Quite apart from research purposes, I gladly contributed to the local cultural or church activities because I appreciate these people's growing cultural awareness and enthusiasm to narrate alternative histories. I have to say that the refocused theme of my research is more welcome among the local history experts who consider me as their companion in history issues, even though I have repeatedly explained my research subject. In a sense, they appreciate my research as they rightly think that their commitment and efforts are being recorded.

Being Chinese helped me avoid the official restrictions that often hinder foreign researchers from participating in Christians' everyday lives in China. I was well aware that the theme of my research could be quite sensitive and might cause my informants unwanted trouble. The first priority in my research was to avoid putting them into any kind of difficulty, even though Christians are no longer under pressure to renounce their religion (but still cannot join the CCP without doing so). Those who are still alive will remain anonymous throughout this research, despite prior public disclosure of persons and/or events existing in published forms (including newspaper and internet articles). However, I cannot keep the geographical site of my research anonymous, as many sociological or anthropological studies have traditionally done, because this research needs to be located in the historical, political, and social contexts of modern and contemporary Xiamen to make sense of the collective enthusiasm for connecting the past to the present and how this is undertaken. Moreover, the locality is referred to in detail, and some of the historical and geographical information would easily lead readers to Xiamen; any efforts to keep the place unidentified would be in vain.

When collecting my data, I conducted interviews and occasionally used participant observation. Sixty-one people acted as my respondents (some of them on a number of occasions; eighty-one interviews in total were carried out), including those with twelve pastors and eight local history experts. In most cases, informal conversations, rather than (semi)structured interviews, were preferable. I did design major questions but, in many cases, let them tell their stories freely. They were all aware of my identity as a researcher and what the purpose of our conversations was. Careful consideration was given to information derived from discussions that they specifically asked me not to publish. In the case of some quotations that are essential to the analysis, I have carefully changed the informants' personal details to preserve their anonymity.

I studied at Xiamen University from 2007 to 2012, giving me a sense of familiarity with the region. The Southern Fujian dialect (Minnanhua), which is significantly different from Mandarin (Putonghua), the official language, is used by many local people. Xiamen is a city of domestic migration in which a large proportion of the population are not native speakers of the local dialect. As a result, in my fieldwork all conversations were conducted in Mandarin. Even so, I was aware that the use of Mandarin could potentially color the research. To reduce any negative impact, each time I sensed something in interviews might be inaccurate or contradictory, I posed the same question to other respondents and compared their answers.

Throughout the research, I identified myself as a narrator who retells the stories of those who are recounting the Christian past. Locals may not always agree with my perspective, and unfortunately I expect that many will never have access to my research. However, I often think of Wu Fei's image of the stonemason as a metaphor for how we shape the raw material of our research, and I have tried to be as accurate and respectful as possible in presenting the narratives and thoughts they were generous enough to share with me.

Organization of the Book

In addition to the introduction, this book has five major chapters and conclusion. In chapter 1, I give a complete picture of the region of Xiamen, covering the geographical, administrative, historical, social, and cultural contexts of the broader region as well as Gulangyu Island, the focal point of my research. The social change that has affected Gulangyu and its Christian community are described in detail, showing the complex connections between Christianity, nationalism, imperialism, and Communist movements that serve as the backdrop for the present production of Christian history. Chapter 2 examines a memorial service held in Xiamen in 2010 for an American missionary who died and was buried there in 1910, and how local history enthusiasts, as well as government authorities, are reclaiming and rewriting ideas about the region's foreign missionaries. Chapter 3 recounts the eightieth anniversary celebration of Trinity Church in October 2014 and the life story of "Old Pastor" Wen, who was instrumental in the church's survival and revival through successive political movements. The chapter reflects on the fate of Christianity on the changing island and how the church has responded to state modernization projects, reinterpreting its glorious past, and grieving over its irreversible fate. In chapter 4, I depict tensions and connections in the creation and publication of Christian history texts between the state, churches, and enthusiastic amateur historians.

Chapter 5 explores the role of a foreign missionary organization in reviving the lagging Trinity Church, revealing the complex mechanisms at work in the interactions between churches, "new era" evangelists, and local authorities. Though it has been immensely successful and long-lasting by local standards, the international Christian agency has continued to experience tensions with the Chinese Christian community because of its political sensitivity, as well as its absence from the historical tradition and present-day social fabric. Finally, in the conclusion, I revisit the central themes of my research and point to some of its broader implications.

Chapter 1

XIAMEN HISTORY, SOCIETY, AND CHRISTIANITY

Understanding the lived history of Christianity in modernizing China is impossible without a fuller understanding of the rise of Xiamen, a city that occupies a special position in the Christian history of China and the opening of the nation to the outside world. This chapter begins with a concise introduction to Xiamen as a geographical and an administrative entity, followed by a historical and contemporary overview of Xiamen and the island of Gulangyu.

An Introduction to Xiamen

China is often referred to as the land of yellow earth, reflecting the hue of the thick soil covering the Yellow River Valley, where the earliest Chinese civilization is said to have emerged. But looking out from the islands of Xiamen or Gulangyu, the color that floods the mind is blue, the sparkling hue of the South China Sea that surrounds them.

Xiamen, formerly known to the West as Amoy, is an island city of over four million people nestled in the estuary of the Nine Dragons River (Jiulong jiang). Administratively and culturally, it belongs to Fujian Province, also known by its ancient appellation Min, which makes up a significant part of the southeastern coast of China. Three quarters of Xiamen are encircled by the prefectures of Zhangzhou in the west, and Quanzhou in the north

Map 1 China. Jun Kawaguchi / Shutterstock.com (http://www.Shutterstock.com). Graphic additions by author.

and east, which together make up the prosperous region of Southern Fujian (Minnan). Sailing east from Xiamen, one finds the island of Jinmen (also known as Kinmen), then, facing Xiamen across the Taiwan Strait, Taiwan and its dependencies, the Penghu or Pescadores Archipelago.

The Fujian mainland is known for its rugged terrain, described in a popular saying as "eight-tenths mountains, one-tenth water and one-tenth fields" (*ba shan yi shui yi fen tian*). The entire province is dotted with hillsides, with few plains; arable land per capita falls far short of the national average. In the northwest, it is bordered by mountain ranges; in the east, its long coastline hugs the South China Sea. Although these natural barriers have to some extent confined the people of Fujian within a narrow cultural universe, they did not prevent them from exploring the world beyond. Partly because of the limited availability of arable land, which led to increasing population pressure, the people of Southern Fujian turned to the sea and established elaborate maritime networks for overseas trade and migration.

The main everyday language spoken in the Xiamen region is a variant of the mutually unintelligible dialects spoken throughout Fujian and wherever Fujianese migrants have settled, such as Taiwan and parts of Southeast

Map 2 The administrative region of Xiamen. Wikimedia Commons / Chk2011 (CC BY-SA 3.0). Graphic additions by author.

Asia. These dialects vary so considerably that people cannot understand nonnative dialects without actually learning them, the difference being comparable to the differences between spoken German and Swiss German or Dutch. The principal dialects are the Southern Fujian dialect, the Fuzhou dialect, and the Hakka dialect. The Xiamen vernacular is dominant in most of Southern Fujian, a fact that is usually attributed to the city's prosperity and trade dominance since the late imperial period.[1]

The name "Xiamen" carries two distinct meanings. In the first instance, it refers to the municipality of Xiamen, including the city of Xiamen (Xiamen shi) and the suburbs in its immediate vicinity. The city is made up of six districts that straddle the island and the mainland: Siming and Huli on the island, Jimei, Haicang, Tong'an, and Xiang'an on the mainland of Fujian. Gulangyu Island, administered by the Gulangyu Management

Committee (GMC), has been affiliated with Siming district since the government administrative restructuring of 2003.

In the second instance, Xiamen is used to refer to the islands of Xiamen and Gulangyu, often by citizens of those places, who imbue the name of Xiamen with a sense of cosmopolitan superiority. Their attitude derives from the fact that these two islands make up the main part of Xiamen and have long been urbanized, but the other districts have only recently been merged into the administrative entity of Xiamen City. Even today, a boorish person can be ridiculed as a "Xiang'an farmer."

Xiamen has a land area of more than 1,573 sq km, of which the islands of Xiamen and Gulangyu make up 141 sq km, and a sea area of 390 sq km. By 2020, the city had a resident population (*changzhu renkou*) of 5.16 million. Of these, 2.73 million were registered household residents (*huji renkou*), and almost half (1.25 million, 46 percent) were living on Xiamen and Gulangyu Islands.[2] Residents of Xiamen have long enjoyed one of the highest standards of living in China and they are noted for their personal and economic links with the outside world.

By virtue of its location, Xiamen has long been one of the best deep-water harbors in China. Its history is entwined with the sea and with that of neighboring territories across the waters. Geographically and politically favorable conditions have recently allowed it to become an international seaport city. Its municipal infrastructure, neat cityscape, and higher standard of living make it one of the most popular Chinese cities to live in today and it enjoys the sobriquet of being a "garden of the sea." Legend has it that countless egrets once made it their home, hence its alternate name of Egret Island. In recent years, Xiamen has been officially designated a tourist city and attracts millions of visitors annually.

Within China, Xiamen is considered a second-tier city, with a smaller population and a lesser commercial importance than cities such as Beijing and Shanghai. It can be considered less global than the first-tier cities, which cater to mass movements of people from across the globe and function as hubs for global financial flows. Nevertheless, as Angela Lehmann shows, as a globalizing city Xiamen has recently hosted a growing number of international expatriates;[3] and historically, its links to the world beyond the island played an instrumental role in the geopolitics of the region, giving rise to pirate merchants, Taiwanese settlers, and the development of a native Chinese Protestant movement that was influential far beyond its borders.

The ethnographic research for this study was conducted on the main island of Xiamen and the smaller island of Gulangyu, while the historical research includes references to the broader region of Xiamen. Consequently, "Xiamen" in the text generally refers to the geographical and cultural region that covers the islands of Xiamen and Gulangyu, while Xiamen City refers to the municipality that straddles the mainland. The specific names of Xiamen Island and Gulangyu Island are used where necessary to distinguish these two areas throughout the book.

A Brief History of Xiamen

A thousand years ago, Xiamen was an isolated island remote from the civilization of the Central Plains of China known as *zhongyuan*, usually meaning the central state and dominant culture of China's Han ethnic majority. There are virtually no records of Xiamen before the Song Dynasty (960–1279).[4] According to a county gazetteer, in AD 282 the Jin court (266–420) established Tong'an County, which included the Xiamen area.[5] The next substantial change in Xiamen's administrative structure was recorded over a thousand years later. During the Yuan Dynasty (1271–1368), troops were stationed on Xiamen Island, giving an indication of the island's military importance.[6] It was then known as Jiaheyu, meaning "island of paddy fields." Government-sanctioned overseas trade flourished in Southern Fujian. More people moved to Xiamen Island in greater numbers and contributed to its economic development and population expansion. Gen. Zhou Dexing (?–1392) had a city wall built in the early years of the Ming Dynasty (1368–1644).[7] After this landmark event, the city was officially renamed "Xiamen," meaning "gate of the mansion."

During the sixteenth and seventeenth centuries, the official overseas trade in Southern Fujian began to decline. Thereafter, stimulated by the expansion of the commodity economy, a new type of private overseas trade rapidly emerged, centering on the ports of Yuegang (in Zhangzhou) and Anping (in Jinjiang), and these dislodged the leading position of the port of Quanzhou. After these two ports declined in their turn, Xiamen became one of southeast China's most important port cities.[8]

The Qing court pursued a policy of seeking greater control over outlying areas and centralizing bureaucratic management of the vast empire. As a long isolated and underdeveloped island, Xiamen had never really been tightly controlled by the successive central states. Although the dynasty seated itself firmly in the saddle, its authorities were not able to establish all-encompassing governance on the coast. Consequently, the cultural landscape of Xiamen was continually (re)shaped by factors that were not directly in the control of the imperial government, like trade or war sweeping in from the sea. In an effort to diminish, if not banish, the threat from the sea, on two separate occasions Ming and Qing emperors prohibited maritime trade. Only a few countries approved by the central government were exempted from this ban. In the years when the bans were at their strictest, coastal residents were forced to move inland; even touching seawater could lead to the death penalty. Yet in spite of severe penalties, even when the banning policy was at its most severe, coastal residents were still not deterred from trying their hand at smuggling or piracy, though they knew they ran the risk of being beheaded. In fact, the problem worsened as numerous bankrupt maritime businessmen and fishermen joined pirate bands.[9]

Meanwhile, private (illicit) sea trade thrived and rapidly expanded, especially under the rule of rebel leader Zheng Chenggong (also known as Koxinga, 1624–1662) who claimed loyalty to the Ming court after it had been defeated by Manchu invaders. Zheng led an uprising against the newly established Qing Dynasty in 1647 and captured the islands of Xiamen and Jinmen, where he set up an administrative body under the nominal governance of the usurped Ming imperial family. In 1661, he defeated Dutch colonists to take Taiwan under the jurisdiction of the Zheng family.[10] In response, the Qing state banned maritime trade in an attempt to cut off the rebels' connections and keep them isolated. By contrast, the Zheng group promoted foreign trade, which maintained military procurement and increased the commercial prosperity of Xiamen.[11]

The flourishing maritime trade was an enormous fillip to the shipbuilding, commerce, and handicraft industries in Xiamen and the surrounding areas. When the Qing government took over Xiamen, the court attached great importance to its military significance and moved the Fujian naval headquarters there from the provincial capital of Fuzhou. They established the Fujian Customs in Xiamen in 1684 to oversee merchant ships and centralize tax collection. The fact that its headquarters were located there, rather than in Fuzhou, is further proof of the prominence achieved by the port.[12]

In this era Xiamen gradually established itself as a leading port for both domestic and international trade. Liao Feipeng, a noted scholar-official of the Qianlong era (r. 1735–95), wrote, "There are tens of thousands of ships mooring in the port,"[13] an evocative image that bespeaks its prosperity at the time. In 1757, Emperor Qianlong shut down Xiamen Port along with all the other ports in the region except that in Guangzhou, ushering in nearly a century of seclusion. Despite this measure, trade between Xiamen and Southeast Asia (commonly referred to Nanyang in Chinese) was not completely severed.[14]

The Socioeconomic Rise of Xiamen

Under the Qing Dynasty, Xiamen emerged as the economic and military center of Southern Fujian, though the administrative centers of the region were situated in the neighboring prefectures of Quanzhou and Zhangzhou. The expansion in maritime trade during the Qing era stimulated the development of a complex coastal network radiating outward from Xiamen.[15]

Another factor that was to complicate the center-periphery relationship between the Qing court and Xiamen was the intervention of Western forces. Only one and a half centuries after Xiamen was absorbed into the Qing Empire, the court once more lost full control over the area. The city's fate changed completely in the 1840s. Defeated by the British in the Opium War, the Qing government was forced to sign the Treaty of Nanjing on August 29, 1842. Its terms opened up Xiamen as one of five treaty ports (along with Guangzhou, Fuzhou, Ningbo, and Shanghai) giving preferential and asymmetrical rights to foreign powers. It is at this point that our study of Protestant Christianity in Xiamen begins.[16]

In 1853, two centuries after Zheng Chenggong's rebellion, yet another event forced the Qing government to cede temporary control over Xiamen when the Small Sword secret society (Xiaodao hui) revolted against Manchu rule and occupied the island for six months.[17] As Ching May Bo has argued, although in the Ming and Qing periods the power of the state gradually expanded into South China, it was still possible for people to evade the arm of the state.[18] Xiamen had long remained a place with a reputation for "not being governed," where the state had to struggle to exercise efficient and consistent control.[19] In the following century, Xiamen was to be controlled by the late Qing government, the Chinese Nationalist government, and invading Japanese forces, before reverting to Nationalist rule in 1945.

On October 17, 1949, the People's Liberation Army (PLA) took over the islands of Xiamen and Gulangyu. The People's Government, led by the CCP, was established shortly thereafter. As one of the final battlefields of China's civil war between the Nationalist Party and the CCP, Xiamen was "liberated" by the Communist army, but at a high cost of life. During the civil war, defeated Nationalist troops had fled to Taiwan, where a Nationalist government had been established. Local officials on the islands of Xiamen and Gulangyu, many of whom had overseas ties, especially with Nationalist-ruled Taiwan, were considered potentially disloyal to China's new Communist regime. Therefore, upon the capture of the city, a large number of key positions were filled by demobilized military officials of the PLA. Later, in the 1950s, "politically loyal" young students recruited from Shanghai and Zhejiang were sent to Xiamen to strengthen the Party's leadership.[20]

In the aftermath of the Communist victory, a series of political events took place that unleashed a continuous transformation in the social structure of Xiamen as well as that of the whole country. Chronologically, these encompassed land reform, a campaign to suppress counterrevolutionaries, cooperation, the introduction of collectivization, the deprivatization of commerce and industry, the Hundred Flowers Campaign, the Anti-Rightist Movement, the Great Leap Forward, the Four Cleanups (or Socialist Education Campaign), the Cultural Revolution, and finally decollectivization and reprivatization of commerce and industry. Just as in other parts of the country, Xiamen's overseas connections were largely cut off under the rule of Chairman Mao.

In the light of the openly hostile political confrontation between the CCP and the Nationalist Party during most of the period between 1949 and 1978, Fujian was assigned the military and political mission of confronting Taiwan, a task it was to accomplish by building significant military fortifications. Fighting across the Taiwan Strait broke out around the offshore islands of Fujian throughout the 1950s. Xiamen in particular, the nearest place to Nationalist-ruled Jinmen Island, had to bear the brunt of heavy bombardment. Peaceable cross-strait exchanges were not resumed until 1987, when the Nationalist government in Taipei announced the lifting of martial law and permitted war veterans to visit their hometowns in mainland China.

In 1979, top-level reformers departed radically from the path marked out by their predecessors by proposing the use of foreign investment to promote exports and stimulate the domestic economy, and this goal required setting about raising managerial and technological levels. In the framework of the state's reform and opening-up policies, in 1980 Xiamen was designated one of five special economic zones (*jingji tequ*), which it was hoped would attract investment and new technology from overseas. In 1984, the boundary of the Special Economic Zone was extended from the original area of 2.5 sq km in the present-day Huli district to cover the whole of Xiamen Island (including the islet of Gulangyu). This meant lower enterprise tax rates, and thus much greater scope to encourage foreign investment.

In 1988, Xiamen gained the status of "a city with a separate listing in the plan" (*jihua dan lie shi*). This placed the mayor of Xiamen on an equal footing with the deputy-provincial governor, granting more room to maneuver with both the central and the provincial governments. The highest-ranking officials in Xiamen City are the Party secretary (who functions as the local deputy of the CCP, an extremely important role) and the city mayor, who reports to the Party secretary and governor of Fujian Province, respectively.[21] They enjoy a deputy provincial-level rank (*fu shengji*); a status even higher than their counterparts in Fuzhou, the provincial capital. On the level immediately below are the chief and deputy district Party secretaries and district administrators who head the six districts of Xiamen City, who rank at the chief and deputy department level (*tingji* and *fu tingji*).

In the past three decades, Xiamen City has witnessed a rapid rise in prosperity and industrialization. The most salient factor in the trajectory of Xiamen's development has been the special policy privileges granted by the central state.[22]

Several bridges over the channel and the Xiang'an Tunnel have been built. Nowadays, it takes only a few minutes to drive from Xiamen Island to the mainland. An international airport was inaugurated in 1983, giving easy access from Xiamen to other cities at home and abroad. Nowadays Xiamen Island is just a topographical concept, and the channel is no longer the barrier to top-down state control that it once was in the imperial era.

Xiamen as a Qiaoxiang

Xiamen is an important *qiaoxiang*, an area that traditionally produced numerous emigrants. In Southeast Asia and elsewhere, there are substantial communities of overseas Chinese with ancestors from Xiamen and who still speak Xiamen dialect. From the 1840s to the 1890s, 390,000 emigrants departed from the port of Xiamen. Emigration reached a peak of nearly 1.36 million (including contract laborers) from 1890 to 1930.[23] Not only did this enormous number of emigrants send home a large amount of money in the form of remittances, they also established strong overseas ties in their new places of residence, which they then drew on to promote regional development, trade relations, modern education, and transnational religious networks in Xiamen itself.

Although Xiamen never developed into a major industrial base, overseas Chinese capital nevertheless played a significant part in regional development there in the early decades of the twentieth century.[24] Wealthy and influential overseas Chinese involved themselves in the fields of business, finance, transportation, and real estate. Apart from these commercial activities, they also promoted the construction of modern infrastructure, as well as establishing education, medical services, and charitable facilities for the common people. A good example is Tan Kah Kee (1874–1961), who established Xiamen University as well as the Jimei primary/middle school and college campuses.

43

More importantly perhaps, overseas Chinese brought their vision of modernity back to Xiamen.[25] Since 1979, the region's extensive ties with overseas Chinese have been an enormous boost to local economic development. These overseas Chinese have been an important source of capital for Xiamen in particular and Fujian in general. Very much aware of this important resource, local governments have offered incentives to the families of overseas Chinese to encourage them to use their overseas relatives' knowledge and capital resources to open factories and develop businesses.

In the era of reform, as well as economic growth, the Southern Fujian region has also witnessed a revival of local traditions.[26] Overseas Chinese, in particular those from Southeast Asia, have played a vital role in the recovery of religious activities.[27] Kuah-Pearce's study in Anxi County reveals that, far from just contributing to economic development of the *qiaoxiang*, the "moral economy" that binds the overseas Chinese to their ancestral lands has also led to a religious revival.[28] For centuries, the cultural landscape in *qiaoxiang* has been heavily shaped by overseas Chinese. Although many of these emigrants have roots in the broader region rather than in Xiamen proper, they have tended to make investments in or contributions to Xiamen rather than their true ancestral lands, likely because of Xiamen's prosperity and prominent reputation at home and abroad.

Nostalgia and Social Change in Gulangyu

Gulangyu in the Late Qing and Republican Periods

Gulangyu, a smaller islet off the coast of Xiamen Island, is known within the region for its beauty and old-fashioned charm. Today, the people of Xiamen tend to glorify the past of Gulangyu with a kind of rose-tinted nostalgia, waxing poetic about its history and architecture. But neither Xiamen Island nor Gulangyu Island was considered much of a "paradise" when foreigners first took up residence there in the early 1840s. Rev. Philip

Wilson Pitcher (1856–1915), a missionary of the Reformed Church in America (RCA), known as the Reformed Protestant Dutch Church (of America) until 1867, paints a picture of Xiamen and Gulangyu in the early twentieth century that contrasts starkly with the romantic vision evoked in my interviews with local people.

> A city! But not the kind of city you have in mind. There are no wide avenues, beautiful private residences, magnificent public and mercantile buildings. All is directly opposite to this condition of things. The streets are narrow and crooked,—with the sewer underneath and plainly in sight thro[ugh] the chinks of the uneven flagstones,—ever winding and twisting, descending and ascending, and finally ending in the great nowhere. . . . There is no street either straight, or one even called "Straight" in Amoy. Then in addition to the crookedness, they must add another aggravation by making some of them very narrow. . . .
>
> There are streets in Amoy so narrow that you cannot carry an open umbrella. . . . The streets are alive with a teeming throng, and the unwary pedestrian is liable to be hustled about and shouted at unceremoniously. Here every aspect of Chinese life passes before you, presenting grotesque pictures. Here goes the motley crowd, from the wretched beggar clothed in filthy rags to the stately mandarin adorned in gorgeous array. On beholding such sights we stop and question ourselves if this is all real or whether it is not the working of our imagination. Men almost nude, hatless and bootless, go hurrying by, giving a grunt of warning for people to clear the road as they go struggling under the weight of some ponderous burden, while still others are bearing on their shoulders the sedan chair. What does it all mean? Have men turned themselves into "beasts of burden?" Indeed they present a sad phase of human life. But perhaps the beggars show a more wretched state of existence than these "heavily laden" ones.[29]

Pitcher was extremely depressed by his experiences in Xiamen and complained at length of the indignities he witnessed. Other foreigners' accounts paint a similar picture. Cecil A. V. Bowra (1869–1947), then commissioner of customs, wrote that "Amoy City is a hotbed of every form of disease, among which plague and cholera are prominent. The causes are the filthy state of the town, and the fact that the civilization of the people has not advanced to the point at which the advantages of hygiene is realized."[30]

Gulangyu, in particular, was singled out for criticism. Conditions there were so bad that it was considered even unhealthier than Xiamen City on account of its squalor and filth. When British troops were stationed on the island in 1841, hundreds of them were stricken with fever. Therefore, the island initially held no attraction for either missionaries or merchants. However, from the 1860s, they began to take up residence here very comfortably in well-built houses offering sea views on all sides, most situated at vantage points on higher elevations. Gulangyu slowly evolved into an ideal residential area, a reputation that has persisted until recent times.

In the wake of China's defeat in the First Sino-Japanese War in 1894, the Qing court ceded Taiwan to the rising state of Meiji Japan. Concerned about the threat of more territorial concessions, the Qing government decided to seek "international protection" for Xiamen to prevent it also being seized by Japan. In 1903, the island was officially declared an international settlement (*gonggong zujie*) on which thirteen countries, including Great Britain, the United States, the Netherlands, France, Japan, Germany, Spain, and Portugal, could enjoy extraterritorial privileges and set up their consulates. Along with Shanghai, it was one of only two international settlements in all of China. Gulangyu at that time was under the control of an international board of managers known as the Kulangsu Municipal Council (KMC, Gongbuju). The KMC, founded in 1903, was independent of the Qing government. Its board (elected annually) took care of the day-to-day running of the settlement.

The first Municipal Council was elected in January 1903 and began to exercise its authority on May 1 of the same year. The first KMC Board was composed of six non-Chinese members, plus one Chinese representative appointed by the Xiamen governor (*daotai*).[31] A set of resolutions similar to those that prevailed in the Shanghai International Settlement was adopted by the residents of the island and subsequently ratified by the Qing court. These in effect formed the KMC Regulations and Bylaws (Gongbuju lüli) by which the international settlement was governed. After the adoption of these regulations, Gulangyu was transformed into a sort of "paradise" for foreigners, as Reverend Pitcher would describe it. All the major business buildings and banks were located on the Xiamen side of the harbor. Besides the foreign residences on the island, Gulangyu was the preferred location for the schools and higher educational institutions of the three

45

major missions, the RCA-affiliated Hope Hospital, and the Union Church
in which services in English were held every Sunday. It also housed foreign
consulates, several post and telegraph offices, two clubhouses with reading
rooms and libraries, two hotels, and several pharmacies. Gulangyu boasted
one of the finest recreation grounds along the coast. Here foreigners could
pursue their sporting activities and indulge in healthy exercise, playing
tennis, cricket, and field hockey.

As Gulangyu was managed peacefully as an international community,
growing numbers of upper-class Chinese or returned overseas Chinese
from Southeast Asia, and those fleeing from Japanese-occupied Taiwan
(1895–1945), settled down on the island. In the mid-1870s, the incumbent
Xiamen governor conducted a census that revealed 2,835 Chinese inhabitants and 252 foreign nationals on Gulangyu.[32] According to a report of the
Xiamen Customs, in 1911 the total population on the island was approximately 12,000, including 300 foreign nationals.[33] Only twenty years later,
the number of residents had almost doubled. A Republican dossier reveals
that around 1930 it was home to over 567 foreigners and 20,465 Chinese
residents.[34]

For decades, China had been torn apart by successive wars. As a peaceful island under the governance of the KMC, Gulangyu attracted people
seeking stability and security, many of them prosperous. A large number of
laborers also settled on the island and made a living serving the wealthy. A
new social structure gradually emerged. Although the population soared,
the island remained a haven of law and order, except when it was occupied
by the Japanese.

Japan launched a full invasion of China in July 1937 and shortly afterward occupied Jinmen Island. Subsequently Xiamen found itself under
attack by Japanese fighter planes and warships. When Xiamen Island fell to
the Japanese on May 10, 1938, approximately forty-three thousand refugees
fled to Gulangyu in search of shelter. Gulangyu's status as an international
settlement offered it a temporary reprieve from the ravages of war. However,
after the outbreak of the Pacific War, Japanese troops swiftly occupied the
island from December 8, 1941, until the end of the war in 1945.

By and large, Gulangyu had enjoyed a century of comparative peace,
during which the Western-style modern education system from primary
school through college produced a number of educated people, many of
whom earned nationwide fame in medicine, education, science, and the
arts. The foreign nationals and overseas Chinese originating from Southern
Fujian initiated the Western modernization of Gulangyu and introduced

a Western lifestyle to the island. Gulangyu earned the moniker of Piano Island for having the highest per capita number of pianos in the world. Hundreds of Western buildings in a colonial Southeast Asian style were built or renovated, and even today the island is still noted for its cosmopolitan architecture.

Gulangyu in Post-1949 State Projects

Since October 1949, when the Communists assumed power in Xiamen, Gulangyu has never been detached from state control. The island was designated a "scenic wellness area" (*fengjing liaoyangqu*) in the 1950s and a couple of sanitariums were established there for Communist cadres and army and navy officers affiliated with the Fuzhou Military Region of the PLA. The municipal government's overall plan for Xiamen City clearly stated that the population size of the small island had to be strictly controlled by a household registration system based on the principle of "moving out allowed, moving in forbidden." Moreover, citizens were prohibited from building or importing factories or industrial activities, except those connected to tourist enterprises. In 1982 Gulangyu was redesignated a "scenic tourist area" (*fengjing lüyouqu*) and the number of permanent residents dropped to fewer than twenty thousand. In 1988, Gulangyu was recognized as a national-level scenic area (it was later selected as a 5A-class Scenic Area in 2008),[35] and in 1995 it was announced that all factories had to move out and the number of permanent residents was to be limited to no more than fifteen thousand.[36] People who wanted to obtain permanent residence on the island were subjected to a thorough investigation and faced exhausting and cumbersome approval procedures.

All this had a detrimental effect on the social life of the island. Gulangyu used to be a fully functional residential community with a population of over twenty thousand, run by various administrative organs and well supplied with hospitals, schools, and factories. When it was designated a specific tourist area, its function as a residential community became secondary. Factories were forced to move out, taking job opportunities with them. Hence people from Gulangyu have increasingly had to look for work on Xiamen Island and commute between the two islands on weekdays.

As the population shrank, the Second Hospital of Xiamen (the successor of the Hope Hospital, founded by the RCA missionary organization) also moved out. This caused the residents considerable inconvenience and led to several disturbing cases: two pregnant women were said to have given birth at the ferry terminal when they could not reach Xiamen Island in time, and renowned calligrapher Gao Huai (1914–2007) died due to a delay in treatment. Residents now bitterly complain, "There is no maternity ward in which to give birth; there is no mortuary in which to die." Schools, including the noted Gulangyu Piano School and the high school division of the Number Two Middle School of Xiamen (formerly known as the church-run Anglo-Chinese College, established in 1898), have likewise been moved to Xiamen Island because of the decreasing number of students. The exodus of schools and hospitals and the general overall inconvenience of life on the island eventually forced many residents to leave.

Coasting on its architecture, sandy beach, and reputation for being "Piano Island," Gulangyu enjoys a romantic image, attracting millions of domestic and international visitors every year. In 2018 alone, city statistics reveal that over ten million tourists landed on the tiny island.[37] However, growing numbers of Gulangyu locals have now moved to Xiamen, and many are seeking to transfer their *hukou* (household registration) there. Authorities did not become truly cognizant of the problem caused by the shrinking number of permanent residents until the launch of the island's bid to be listed as a UNESCO World Heritage Site in 2009 (discussed in the following chapter), which it gained in 2017.

Gulangyu is now stuck in a vicious circle. According to 2019 official data, 12,851 residents had their *hukou* registered on the island, of which thousands had retained their *hukou* but were living elsewhere. That same year, the number of births was 108, less than the number of deaths (125).[38] Another challenge for authorities is that while Gulangyu has been losing its young, educated, and wealthy residents, the ones who are most likely to stay put are the older, poorer, and less educated members of the native population, who are less able to find well-paying work on the main island and other parts of the Xiamen area, where the cost of living is going up.

Keeping pace with the rapid rise of tourism, thousands of businesspeople and laborers have come in as what the locals call "new islanders" (*xin daomin*). These "new islanders," particularly migrant workers from rural areas (known in Chinese as *nongmingong*, literally "peasant workers"), do not have Xiamen *hukou*. As the household registration system in China regulates access to social security, virtually none of them benefited from the city's social security systems in the past, including medical insurance and public schooling for their children, although the government is now implementing measures to remediate this problem (allowing them to join the local social security system in Xiamen without giving them the same rights as full residents). They usually leave their families in their native villages and strike out to make a living alone in Gulangyu, which also means they do not contribute to the birth rate on the island.

In locals' eyes, these "outside" (*waidi de*) workers from poor inland provinces are not as "civilized" as they are and will never become sophisticated "islanders." Gulangyu locals feel that migrant workers lack "high quality" (*suzhi*), a key term in contemporary Chinese society referring to a wide range of sociopolitical practices for population "improvement."[39] The notion of *suzhi* is often used pejoratively by the state and educational elites to refer to rural people and migrant workers. As the islanders quip, "When the people wearing leather shoes left, those with slippers arrived; when the piano players moved out, the laborers came in."[40] Thus, the government's strict population control measures have drastically altered the population and class structure of Gulangyu.

As tourists walk through the alleys under the dense shade of trees, enjoying the kinds of gorgeous views that are rare in modern cities, they have a chance to imagine the island's glorious past and perhaps envy the people lucky enough to live there in the present. However, the locals' sentiments are far more complex. In the new century, as some of my respondents have said, Gulangyu has quickly "deteriorated into a resort island full of seafood restaurants, barbecue stalls and souvenir shops." People from Xiamen frequently lament that "Gulangyu is dead." As far as they are concerned, Gulangyu is no longer the beautiful, clean, civilized, and romantic island they feel it once was. Meanwhile, a kind of nostalgic yearning has emerged among locals who view Gulangyu as the "heaven that never disappears" (*yong bu xiaoshi de tiantang*). Dwelling on Gulangyu's idealized past, for a moment residents can detach themselves from the unsatisfactory present, "imagin[ing] and construct[ing] a more pleasing idealized environment," as Peter Nosco writes in *Remembering Paradise*.[41]

In a critique of this wave of nostalgia, a respected senior scholar who grew up in Gulangyu once wrote in an online article, "Those who are longing for and have an attachment to Gulangyu do not have memories that reflect a true image of the island's glorious past. The only thing it allows some of them is to give full vent to the emotions aroused by these dilapidated buildings and the 1,200 existing historical houses. . . . Nevertheless, faced with reality, no praise or repair can return the past and all the sadness or outpouring of feelings are nothing but a sense of loss."[42]

NEGOTIATING THE CHRISTIAN PAST IN CHINA

Christianity in Modern Xiamen

50

The Arrival of Christianity in China and Xiamen

The question of when Christianity first entered China remains a matter of some debate. The earliest-known record is a nine-foot-high limestone stele erected in 781 and inscribed in both Chinese and Syriac that was unearthed in the Xi'an region in the 1620s, attesting to an early Nestorian Christian presence during the Tang Dynasty (618–907). In later centuries, Christianity gained a foothold in parts of the empire, but it almost disappeared from public view among the Han Chinese ethnic majority, pushed out by imperial efforts to control religious life.[43]

During the sixteenth century, in the late Ming Dynasty, European Jesuit missionaries came to China, including renowned Jesuit scholar Matteo Ricci (1552–1610). Ricci insisted on policies of accommodation and adaptation to Chinese culture and in many ways "exemplifies the best of the Jesuit approach to missions and attitude toward Chinese culture."[44] Roman Catholicism took root and gained some converts in China, but Christian missions faced many vicissitudes under the Ming and Qing regimes. Notably, in the early Qing, papal condemnation of Chinese rites angered Emperor Kangxi (r. 1661–1722), and the state issued a complete prohibition on Christian missions that lasted over a century. While these repressive measures did not entirely eliminate Catholicism, they forced it underground, where it became deeply embedded in the fabric of some rural communities, durably shaping the landscape of Catholicism in China today.[45]

The modern history of Christianity in China begins in the nineteenth century. The first Protestant missionary, Robert Morrison (1782–1834)—affiliated with the London Missionary Society (LMS)—came to Guangzhou in 1807, when the imperial state still strictly prohibited missionary activities. However, under the protection of the British East India Company, Morrison translated the Bible and conducted clandestine missionary work. His arrival signified a new era in Christianity in modern China.[46]

The first Protestant missionary to settle in Xiamen was David Abeel (1804–1846), who arrived on the island of Xiamen on a British warship on February 24, 1842.[47] Abeel pioneered the RCA mission in China. When the Treaty of Nanjing was signed, six months after Abeel's arrival, the forced opening of Xiamen as a treaty port made it quite independent of the Chinese state, and hence a comparatively relaxed space for the acceptance and spread of Christianity. The LMS and the Presbyterian Church of England (PCE) followed suit in 1844 and 1850, respectively.

In 1848, the RCA built a Protestant church for local worshippers in Xiamen, the New Street Church (Xinjie tang), reputed to be the "first holy church [building] in China" (*Zhonghua diyi shengtang*). Its title, conferred by the National Federation of the Church of Christ in China (Zhonghua Jidu jiaohui) in 1935, has been instrumental in situating the New Street Church and Christianity in Xiamen within China's Christian history. Xiamen has even been proclaimed the birthplace of China's Protestantism. Although this is something of an exaggeration, particularly since Abeel's arrival in Xiamen postdates Morrison's secret missionary activities in Guangzhou by a good third of a century, it is a useful peg for officials keen on promoting tourism and the city's international reputation.[48] More recently, locals have begun to insist that Xiamen, the second city in mainland China to receive Protestant Christianity, was the first place where missionaries preached openly, rather than clandestinely.[49]

The development of indigenous Christianity was a contentious issue in China from the mid-nineteenth century and throughout the twentieth century. By the 1850s, the prototypical indigenous Chinese churches had already formed in the Xiamen area. The missionaries held the first election of Chinese Christians to the position of church elders (*zhanglao*) and deacons (*zhishi*) by the early spring of 1856, when the combined church membership of the RCA-affiliated New Street Church and Bamboo Church (Zhushu tang) had reached 110.[50] A few years later, in a more significant step toward indigenization, two Chinese church workers named Luo Jiayu (1826–1870) and Ye Hanzhang (1832–1912) were ordained as pastors by the New Street Church and Bamboo Church on the morning and afternoon of March 29, 1863, respectively. Contemporary Xiamen Christians are still proud of being the pioneers of the independent movement in China's native church. They also claim that in the nineteenth century the Xiamen church had already adopted the "Three-Self" principles, nearly a century before it became the religious policy of the Communist Party (described below).

Hundreds of Western missionaries served in Xiamen up to the 1950s. Their work was not restricted to evangelization; they also became involved in health care, education, newspapers, and other public undertakings. In the early missionary era, the provision of medical facilities proved to be a valuable instrument of evangelism, described in further detail in chapter 2 in the history of Dr. John Otte, a medical missionary in Gulangyu whose statue now stands in front of the hospital he founded. The missionaries' medical activities were particularly helpful to the poor who were unable to afford treatment and did much more than relieve them of their ills. As Reverend Abeel wrote, "The gratuitous practice [has] made a good impression on all classes of the community. The number of cases treated during the past year has been about five thousand, and everywhere we learn how the hearts of the people are opened by the good done to their bodies. They see that foreigners can come with disinterested motives, as well as for the sake of gain. In this way, gratitude is won and confidence gained. The people are induced to respect us as friends, and are prepared to bear more readily the truths that tend to the healing of the soul."[51]

Whereas medical services were the magnet that attracted many poor people to Christianity, the missionaries' knowledge of the world was what interested members of the upper class. Western science appealed to the educated and opened the door for them to a kind of new cosmopolitanism. Chris White's historical research shows that Christianity in the Xiamen region successfully attracted those who were prominent and influential in local affairs.[52] Although the missionaries had very few opportunities to discuss religious matters with the members of the upper class, special efforts were made to cultivate good relations. They later realized that they would have to begin their proselytizing among "the lower orders and rise by degrees to the higher."[53] It was a strategic shift that showed that Christianity was no longer a religion of the needy but also one of the upper class.

Christian Education and the Development of Xiamen Society

After the establishment of the first primary school on Gulangyu by LMS missionary John Stronach (1810–1888) in 1844, church school education mushroomed on the small island. Mission schools ran the gamut from elementary education, through middle and vocational schools, and on to a theological seminary. The teaching in these schools was not restricted to the propagation of the Christian doctrine; it was also the vehicle for introducing locals to Western science and technology. The church-run institutions that featured a Western-style education or training provided converts with important routes to social mobility. As Ryan Dunch has argued, although the first generation of converts in Fujian often originally came from the lower echelons of society (such as villagers who had not received an education), their offspring rapidly moved on to professional jobs in urban areas.[54] The Shao family of Tong'an origin, whom I got to know during my research, is a very good example of this: Shao Zimei, the first convert of the family, was driven out of his home village by his lineage members, who were hostile to his conversion. When he moved to Gulangyu, his children were able to receive Western schooling. In only two subsequent generations, his descendants have included ten school, college, and seminary principals. The Shao family consequently became highly influential in Xiamen society.[55]

Among Christian schools in Gulangyu, some, such as the secondary-level Anglo-Chinese College (Ying Hua zhongxue) and Talmage College (Xunyuan zhongxue), established a notable reputation. Church-run schools offered children from poor families the chance to be educated, while for wealthy families, the more renowned schools supplying a Western-style education presented an attractive proposition. Missionaries recommended many outstanding graduates for study abroad, in the United States and Britain in particular, and quite a few of them later became famous scholars, scientists, and musicians.

The long list of noted graduates of the pre-1949 Anglo-Chinese College includes several prominent fellows of the Chinese Academy of Sciences (CAS) and Chinese Academy of Engineering (CAE), China's top two national research institutions, such as Huang Zhenxiang, Gu Maoxiang, Zhuo Renxi, Hong Boqian, and Wang Yinglai, who received his doctorate from Cambridge. Alumni of the same college also include archaeologist Zheng Dekun, who received his PhD from Harvard and taught at Cambridge; Zhu Xiaoping, who completed a PhD at Cambridge and became a professor there; as well as economist Wu Xuangong and biochemist and theologian Chen Weizhong.

Talmage College also trained outstanding students such as world-renowned writer Lin Yutang, who went on to study at Harvard and Leipzig and was nominated for a Nobel Prize in literature; astronomers Yu Qingsong and Dai Wensai, who obtained his PhD from Cambridge; horticulturist Li Lairong, who received his doctoral degree from the Pennsylvania State University; and marine biologist Zeng Chengkui, who studied at the University of Michigan and was elected to the CAS. Apart from these notable figures, the church schools also produced many other excellent graduates in medicine and physical education, including Lin Qiaozhi and Ma Yuehan.

These educational institutions have exerted important long-term effects. Many elderly residents of Xiamen today are still appreciative of their education in Christian schools prior to the establishment of the People's Republic. Graduates of mission schools, who were often Christians, became elites in all walks of life, enhancing the image and status of Christianity.

In addition to the role that missionary education played in the development of Gulangyu society, the missions' focus on musical ministry helped to cultivate the artistic temperament of Gulangyu. By the beginning of the twentieth century, Gulangyu had begun to enjoy a reputation for music, and almost all church-run schools offered music lessons and founded choirs or brass bands. It was at this time that the sound of pianos could be heard in every corner of the island, lending Gulangyu its reputation as "Piano Island." The musical tradition continued during the Republican and the Maoist period, when the island produced a number of pianists and music educators such as Zhou Shu'an and Xu Feiping.

From the 1840s until the Communist takeover, missionaries supplied most of the Western medical services in the Xiamen region. John Otte opened Xiamen's first modern Western hospital on Gulangyu in 1898, as discussed in the following chapter, and medical missionaries trained the first group of Western-style medical doctors. The Xiamen church also launched a series of campaigns against problems such as opium use, infanticide, foot-binding, and the keeping of slave girls.[56]

Protestant missionaries in Xiamen developed a romanization system based on the Latin alphabet to translate religious texts into the local dialect. In 1852, John Van Nest Talmage (1819–1892), an RCA missionary, published a fifteen-page "Introduction to the Amoy Alphabet" (*Tanghua fanzi chuxue*) to help locals read the Bible, which had been translated into the romanized dialect of Xiamen. Two decades later, Scottish missionary Carstairs Douglas (1830–1877) compiled and published the *Chinese-English Dictionary of the Vernacular or Spoken Language of Amoy* (Xia Ying da cidian). The romanization of the dialect significantly reduced the amount of time it took for locals to learn to read religious texts and also made it easier for later missionaries to learn the local Chinese dialect.[57]

Western missionaries and Chinese converts also translated or composed a handful of songs in the Southern Fujian dialect. After subsequent compositions and several compilations, there are now more than five hundred hymns in the current version of the *Amoy Hymnal*.[58] As Jenkins notes, producing scripture and hymns in the local language was an important move toward making local churches independent.[59] By translating the scripture into Xiamen vernacular and creating the *Amoy Hymnal*, Western missionaries were making a profound concession to indigenous culture, producing Chinese Christianity for a Chinese audience.

Adapting and Organizing the Church

To understand the landscape of Christianity in Xiamen today, it is important to look at how missionary organizations adapted to local society.

The traditional view of the RCA was that any churches and associations of churches organized by its missionaries abroad should be consistent with those in the United States in all essential matters. However, RCA missionaries in China had rather different ideas. They believed that Chinese churches should be established as one denomination, and that it was necessary to form a close association with other missions. Talmage stated that churches in Xiamen should unite and form one denomination.[60]

After a long debate, the missionary view prevailed, and a formal partnership between the RCA and the PCE was established in 1862. The two organizations could thus coordinate their activities while maintaining their own identities and a degree of denominational independence, allowing each mission to keep its financial matters relatively separate. Missionaries from each organization continued to act under the commissions of their own denominational boards. Furthermore, the union enabled the missions to join forces in such common pursuits as medical and educational work, publishing, and relief of the poor. The partnership allowed the missionaries, Chinese pastors, and converts of the various churches to consider themselves as part of a single church rather than two competing ones and meet to discuss their common problems.[61]

In the achievement of such a union, a major facilitating factor was denominational compatibility. Specifically, both the RCA and the PCE missions were adherents of Reformed/Calvinist theology and Presbyterian polity, allowing them to share liturgical forms.[62] As Reverend Talmage wrote, "[The two churches] hold to the same doctrinal standards, and they explain them in the same manner; they have the same form of church government and their officers are chosen and set apart in the same way; they have the same order of worship and of administering the sacraments; all their customs, civil, social, and religious, are precisely alike, and they love each other dearly."[63]

This denominational closeness strengthened the bond between the RCA and the PCE. Later, however, the LMS also joined their union, working toward the establishment of an indigenous Chinese Christian church.

An early agreement known as the "comity of missions" illustrates the efficient cooperation of the Three Missions (San gonghui). Under this agreement, the Southern Fujian region was divided into three approximately equal parts: the RCA had most of the western area plus a small amount of territory to the north, the PCE the south and part of the east, and the LMS the north and the remainder of the east.[64] The agreement was designed to avoid duplication of missionary activities and unnecessary expense. The headquarters of the Three Missions were initially built on Xiamen Island and later moved to Gulangyu. They displayed a high degree of harmony and cooperation and in 1927 joined the Church of Christ in China, an organization consisting of many large and denominationally affiliated church bodies across China. However, this body did not include minor denominational churches such as the Seventh-Day Adventist Church, the Christian Assembly, and the True Jesus Church.

In 1958, the Communist state instigated united worship (*lianhe libai*), a policy that forced Christians to unite and worship under the same roof regardless of their denomination. Despite the fact that both the state and official church organizations have declared that Chinese Christianity has entered into a "postdenominational" era,[65] the denominational differences have never been eradicated in Xiamen.

In recent years, a growing number of Christians in Xiamen have professed their denominational background to be the Church of Christ in China or the Three Missions. Since the 1990s, there has been a resurgent interest in Calvinism among the well-educated in the big cities of eastern and central China.[66] This growth in interest is largely attributable to the influence of overseas Chinese Christian leaders, among them Jonathan Chao (Zhao Tianen, 1938–2004), founder of the Chinese Church Research Centre and China Ministries International in Hong Kong, and Stephen Tong (Tang Chongrong), an evangelist from Indonesia who was born on Gulangyu Island. In Xiamen, though many educated Christians might describe themselves as adherents of Calvinist teaching, very few would know how to elucidate the connections between Calvinism and their faith. Calvinism, the theological foundation of the Three Missions, helps the local Christians to understand the close cooperation of the early missionary societies and to retain their identity as a united denomination. Other minor churches are naturally excluded from this process.

Today, religious governance is assured by the United Front Work Department (UFWD), the Communist Party organ responsible for uniting non-CCP elements in society. Various levels of the RAB, which used to be affiliated with the government, have been transferred to the Party system since the 2018 restructuring of the Party and state apparatus. The UFWD is responsible for formulating religious policies and rallying religious leaders around the Communist Party; whereas the RAB runs the day-to-day administration of religious affairs. On provincial, prefectural, and county levels, the RAB is sometimes combined with the Ethnic Affairs Commissions. The person who is the provincial- or lower-level RAB chief is frequently also a deputy director of the UFWD on the corresponding level. In Xiamen, the official name of this bureau is the Bureau of Ethnic and Religious Affairs of Xiamen. In this book, this is shortened to the Xiamen Religious Affairs Bureau (or Xiamen RAB). The dual handling of religious and ethnic affairs by the local Religious Affairs Bureau was promoted in the 1980s and 1990s in an effort to consolidate administrative activities. The same personnel deals with both religious and ethnic affairs.

The State Administration for Religious Affairs (SARA) and lower-level RABs usually exercise their control through what are known as patriotic religious associations.[67] Two Christian organizations are sanctioned by the state. The first of these is the National Committee of the TSPM, founded in the 1950s as a nondenominational Protestant organization. It is founded on the "Three-Self" principles: "self-governing" (*zizhi*), "self-supporting" (*ziyang*), and "self-propagating" (*zichuan*). The TSPM functions as a liaison between the state and registered (and therefore officially recognized) churches.

The second government-acknowledged Christian organization, the China Christian Council (CCC), was established in 1980 as a partner to the TSPM and is tasked with overseeing theological activities and training church leaders. The leaders and missions of these two organizations have often overlapped. On account of their close relationship, they are referred to as the Lianghui (literally meaning "two committees").[68] The provincial-level Lianghui is vested with the power to approve the ordination of ministers, although no one can be ordained without the prior approval of the provincial RAB.

In the restructuring of government functions, the Siming RAB, originally a deputy division-level (*fu chuji*) agency, was promoted to the chief division level (*zheng chuji*). Under the Regulations on Religious Affairs, which came into effect in 2005, a religious body was required to report to the RAB on the county or district level of the place in which it is located. In Xiamen City, however, the four major churches (the New Street Church, the Bamboo Church, Trinity Church, and the New District Gospel Church) are directly administered by the RAB on the city level rather than on the district level. For example, on the occasion of the eightieth anniversary of Trinity Church in October 2014, an official from the Xiamen RAB was invited to attend; however, no one from the Siming district RAB was invited.

As discussed in later chapters, the administrative organization of the church is important because of the pervasive importance of government policy and oversight in everyday life in China. And while the church is officially under state control, Christians and others in the Xiamen region engage in complex negotiations with representatives of the state in order to foster their vision of Christianity in social life.

Growing Roots

In the early years of Protestant missions in Xiamen, the region was regarded as a paragon of effective evangelism. In the 1870s the LMS described the thriving mission in these words: "In direct result, mission work in the Amoy [Xiamen] district will compare favorably with that carried on in any part of China. In the number of converts, the organization of churches, in evangelistic effort, and in contributions for the spread of the Gospel, the records of the Amoy mission afford conclusive evidence that the grace of God has not been received in vain."[69]

Xiamen enjoyed an excellent reputation in Christian circles as an area of pioneer activity and hosted the third General Conference of the Church of Christ in China.[70] Yet in the twentieth century, as more regions of China were increasingly evangelized, mission centers moved away from Xiamen to larger and more influential cities, mainly Shanghai and Beijing. In spite of this, Xiamen continued to be recognized as an area of pioneer activity. Christianity exerted a powerful influence on secular life in Xiamen right up to 1949, becoming deeply embedded in local cultural and social life.

Lineage ties constitute an important feature of the social structure of Fujian.[71] The conversion of several local lineages to Catholicism explains why Christianity successfully took root there during the Ming and Qing dynasties.[72] Subsequently, Protestant evangelists also turned the importance of lineage families to their advantage in missionary activities. The Christian tradition of marrying people of the same faith led to decades of intermarriage between Christian families with different surnames, particularly a few influential families. The upshot is that it is not easy to untangle the complicated family trees in the Xiamen Christian community today.

Under Maoism, the Xiamen church suffered. Widespread criticism of missionaries was evident in many of the city's political movements. In the 1950s, all remaining Western missionaries were either expelled or left Xiamen of their own accord. Some missionaries were prevented from leaving until after they had suffered public accusation or humiliation. At the time, the heritage left behind by Western missionaries was fading fast.

During the Cultural Revolution (1966–76), public religious activities of any kind were banned. All churches were shut down, and many were repurposed for uses serving collective production. On one occasion church workers were forced to kneel inside a circle of fire and watch the destruction of Bibles and faith-related books. One of the workers jumped from a building shortly after this event, the first Cultural Revolution suicide in Xiamen (described in chapter 4).

Yet in the absence of Western missionaries, Christianity grew deep roots in Xiamen, surviving the series of violent Maoist political campaigns that followed. As soon as political space was opened to religious practices, Christianity reentered public life.

Churches reopened only in 1979, after China entered the era of "reform and opening up" under Deng Xiaoping (1904–1997). The New Street Church and Trinity Church were among the first group of churches to be restored. In contrast to Maoist dogmatism, the reform-era policy sought to give room for divergent ideas, allowing a greater freedom of expression. Along with these changes came a form of freedom of religious belief. The noted 1982 directive entitled "The Basic Viewpoint and Policy on the Religious Question during Our Country's Socialist Period," more commonly known as "Document 19," was a seminal document in this regard, providing basic protection for religious beliefs but giving atheism preferential treatment.

Currently, there are forty-four officially sanctioned churches and gathering points (*juhuidian*) in Xiamen, and dozens of unregistered congregations or churches. Among these, two major groups have congregations of more than one thousand members each. There are no reliable figures for Xiamen Christians today. A leading pastor of Xiamen Lianghui conservatively estimated that there are thirty to forty thousand Christians in Xiamen City, making up 1.5 or 2 percent of the city's registered inhabitants. However, immediately after hearing the pastor's estimate from me, a preacher from an unregistered church gave me a number twice as high.

Southern Fujian and neighboring regions such as Putian have vibrant communities of Buddhists, Daoists, and followers of various popular religions, all of which have attracted extensive academic attention.[73] In Southern Fujian, most of the families possess carved wooden shrines that occupy the most prominent position in their living room. People typically worship several deities belonging to different categorized religions at the same time. A typical shrine houses statues of Buddha, the Goddess of Mercy (Guanyin), the Heavenly Empress (Mazu), the Great Emperor Who Preserves Life (Baosheng dadi), and the Earth God, all simultaneously enjoying the burning of red candles and incense sticks.

Compared to the large number of adherents of other religions, Christians constitute only a small part of Xiamen's religious population.

Statistically speaking, therefore, Christianity is definitely a minority religion. Nonetheless, the people of Xiamen undoubtedly consider Christianity a part of their local culture and history. Wander through the streets of Xiamen, the legacy of Christianity is evident in its prominent landmarks: old churches, hospitals, and school buildings. For the people of Xiamen, Christianity is an integral part not only of the city landscape but also of their everyday life.

Since the 1980s, the church has once more resumed its overseas ties, in particular with the Chinese diaspora church of Southeast Asia. Members of the Xiamen church who fled abroad prior to October 1949 have built bridges with overseas Chinese Christian communities and contributed huge amounts of money to the Xiamen church during tough times. For instance, when the New District Gospel Church (Xinqu fuyin tang) was built in the mid-1990s, one million RMB (USD120,000 according to the 1995 exchange rate) came from local contributions, but seven million (USD840,000) were donated by Chinese diaspora churches in Southeast Asia.

Financial contributions have decreased in recent years as overseas Christians moved from helping to (re)build churches in the 1980s and 1990s to funding theological training for Chinese people, in both China and Southeast Asia. The sentimental ties of overseas Chinese to their ancestral hometowns have faded over the generations, yet overseas Chinese Christians have remained involved and concerned with churches in mainland China. Their weaker ties to the villages and towns their ancestors left behind have freed them to provide training not just in their ancestral homes but throughout the country.[74]

Andrew Walls describes Christianity as "infinitely translatable," denoting that Christianity became enculturated in different societies where the package of Christian beliefs expanded because of contributions from various cultures.[75] Christianity, once a Eurocentric religion, has been "received and transformed into contextualized Christianities, with their own ecclesiastical structures, liturgy and prayers, spirituality, theology, art and architecture, music and songs and dances, etc."[76] The history of the Xiamen mission illustrates how a primarily non-Christian area was reshaped by global missionary movements and in turn contributed to broader Christian culture within and beyond China.

While the Xiamen church played an important role in the historical development of Christianity in China, it has attracted scant academic attention until now. Apart from a few early autobiographical works by Protestant missionaries, there are very few historical studies of the development of

Christianity in Xiamen. David Cheung's research focuses on the origins of Protestantism in Southern Fujian (in particular in Xiamen), delving into the development and progress made by the churches that pioneered the crucial processes of indigenization and ecclesiastical union in China in the second half of the nineteenth century.[77] Gerald de Jong's study specializes in the history of the RCA mission to Southern Fujian from its beginnings to its closure in 1951.[78] Chris White explores the lives of Protestants in Southern Fujian, mainly in the Xiamen region, in the late Qing and Republican periods, arguing that the new faith did not deracinate Christians; instead, they embraced and utilized both their Chinese and their Christian identities. White specifically addresses the topic of such elite Christians as Xu Chuncao (1874–1960) who were influential at the local level and actively engaged with society at large.[79]

Studies of Xiamen Christianity have recently moved to contemporary issues. A very recent edited volume, *Protestantism in Xiamen*, brings together the history and current outlook of Christianity in Xiamen, shedding light on mutual influence and the transformation of Christianity and the city.[80] Herman Colijn's anthropological research in Xiamen and surrounding regions attends to "pluriprax households" where a plurality of ritual practices can be observed. His insightful study challenges the prevalent idea that conversion often leads to Christians disintegrating from their families of origin, who are overwhelmingly non-Christians, and reveals that instead, negotiation and reconciliation are important aspects of their relationships.[81]

The starting point for this research is that Gulangyu Island was once the center of the Three Missions and a witness to the golden era of Christianity, but Christianity there was doomed to decline because of state-led tourism development and the subsequent commercialization of the island. The center of gravity of Christianity has shifted to Xiamen Island, which has thus experienced an upsurge in the number of Christians.

Chapter 2

DISCURSIVE REVERSALS ON
WESTERN MISSIONARIES

A Memorial Service Revisited

It was a sunny afternoon on April 10, 2010, a few days after the annual Grave Sweeping Festival (Qingming), before the white chrysanthemums people lay for the deceased on their gravestones had lost their bloom. On the island of Gulangyu a group of people had gathered in the square in front of the original site of the Hope Hospital (Jiushi yiyuan) to commemorate the centenary of the death of its founder, Dr. John A. Otte (1861–1910), a medical missionary who died and was buried on the island. Like so many other public events in contemporary China, the ceremony opened with a speech delivered by the convener on behalf of the organizing committee. Then several prominent local figures addressed the crowd before the organizers and key guests unveiled a specially commissioned bust of Otte. One after another, people came to lay flowers at the foot of the bust. The choir of the Xiamen YMCA opened and closed the ceremony with Christian hymns, "Ye Christian Heralds, Go, Proclaim" and "Ai de zhendi" (The true essence of love) in English and Chinese, respectively.[1]

To an observer, it might have looked like a fairly standard ceremonial event, similar to many other formal events in China. Behind the surface, however, the event was made possible by a series of complex negotiations involving members of a local history group, Party members, local officials, and foreign diplomats. A few years earlier, it would have been impossible to publicly celebrate a missionary in this way, particularly a foreign missionary whose name had been "blackened" under Maoism, accused of serious crimes as part of the CCP's efforts to denounce those associated with foreign powers and the church. The events that made Dr. Otte's rehabilitation possible are particularly informative because they reveal how these negotiations work in practice, and in what contexts and circumstances it is possible to make room for Christian history. In this chapter I look at how local people employed informal channels to counter official erasure and rewrite the history of missionaries to incorporate a positive vision of Christianity.

John Otte was born in the Netherlands on August 11, 1861, and migrated to the United States with his family in 1867.[2] He attended Hope College in Holland, Michigan, graduating in 1883. In the fall of that year he entered the University of Michigan to study medicine and obtained his MD three years later. Unfortunately, three consecutive attacks of diphtheria seriously damaged his voice. Rather than entering an evangelical profession that would have required preaching, his attention turned to the medical mission, a field of missionary work that was then in its infancy.

Otte joined the RCA and was appointed a medical missionary in China. However, there were neither the funds to send him to the field nor any hope of collecting a sufficient amount to build a hospital. Therefore, instead of going to China immediately, Otte returned to the Netherlands, where he continued his medical studies from 1886 to 1887. This allowed him to develop his medical expertise and secured financial support for his missionary work from some Dutch donors.

On January 13, 1888, Otte and his wife arrived in Xiamen. Otte spent the greater part of his first year studying the Southern Fujian dialect and making plans to set up his medical missionary work on a proper footing. Initially he opened the Neerbosch Hospital in Xiaoxi,[3] a village in the backwoods of remote Pinghe County, where there was a small but thriving church under the care of Chinese minister Ye Hanzhang. After six years of hospital work, Otte took his first furlough, returning to America with his wife and children. There, he succeeded in raising almost USD10,000 toward the construction of a men's hospital in Xiamen, which was to be named the Hope Hospital in honor of his alma mater. During this furlough, Otte also paid a brief visit to the Netherlands, where he raised funds for a women's hospital building that was to be named the Netherlands Women's Hospital.[4] In the autumn of 1897, the Otte family returned to Xiamen. Before his departure, Otte was ordained a minister by the classis of Michigan.[5] After

Fig. 1 The memorial service for John Otte on April 10, 2010. Courtesy of the Gulang Voice Group.

Fig. 2 People laying flowers at Otte's bust. Courtesy of the Gulang Voice Group.

Fig. 3 The Hope Hospital in Gulangyu. Courtesy of the Joint Archives of Holland at Hope College.

returning to Xiamen, he assumed responsibility for the construction and management of Hope Hospital, which opened in Gulangyu in April 1898.

Otte made his last trip to the United States in June 1908. Four months later, he returned to Xiamen and resumed his duties until his death on April 14, 1910, from pneumonic plague, which he had contracted from one of his patients. His last words were neither in English nor in Dutch but in the Southern Fujian dialect. He was buried in the island's missionary cemetery. At his funeral service, nearly one thousand people, natives and foreigners alike, gathered to express their sorrow.

After the founding of the People's Republic in 1949, nationalism soared and the presence of missionaries sharply declined. Once the Chinese military entered the Korean War in 1950 and began fighting for North Korea against US forces, any Chinese person associated with American groups was in danger of being labeled a "running dog of imperialism" (*diguozhuyi zougou*). As one RCA missionary declared, "[The Korean War] had made us enemy aliens and that put us in a new category."[6] Around the mid-1950s the few foreign missionaries who had remained after the Communist takeover were either forced to leave or actually expelled from Southern Fujian.[7] Though Otte had been dead for half a century, in the turmoil engendered by

Fig. 4 Otte's grave with his Chinese medical students and friends standing behind it. Courtesy of the Joint Archives of Holland at Hope College.

the extreme political movements of the time, he was made into a symbolic figure of denunciation. The first issue of the official *Xiamen Historical Materials* (Xiamen wenshi ziliao) published in 1963 included a critical article that attacked Otte specifically. In it, the authors accused Otte of bullying the weak, extorting patients' money, and committing indecent assaults on women. Otte was derided as a "hypocrite with an extremely ugly soul" and an "imperialist rogue riding on the Chinese people's heads."[8] Even more sadly, his grave was destroyed, and to this day his remains have never been found.[9]

During the memorial service in 2010, Otte's name was unofficially cleared, and he was even highly commended as "Xiamen's Bethune," after Canadian physician and antifascist Norman Bethune (1890–1939) whose service with the Eighth Route Army during the Second Sino-Japanese War (1937–45) made him a celebrated figure in China. Generations of Chinese students committed to memory Mao's 1939 article *In Memory of Norman Bethune*. The memorial event reached its climax with a speech by Zhao Tianyi, a retired Communist cadre and the former director of the Xiamen

Culture Bureau. Zhao's address, entitled "Dare to Rehabilitate Those Who Were Blackened" (*Ganyu wei bei mohei de ren fanbai*), deeply impressed the audience, enumerating all the accusations against Otte and refuting them one by one. Some participants were unhappy about the comparison with Bethune, as they felt that because Otte's dedication transcended class, wealth, and politics, Otte was a much greater man, the breadth of his humanity contrasting with the narrower path trod by Bethune, who only served the Communists. Be that as it may, the analogy between Otte and Bethune was a powerful way of granting the missionary recognition and acclaim.

The memorialization of John Otte in the ceremony operated a total discursive reversal from "imperialist rogue" to "Xiamen's Bethune." Yet official attitudes ostensibly have not changed: Western missionaries are still associated with "national humiliation," an association that has not been radically revised in official narratives. This begs the question of how and why this complete discursive reversal was possible in Otte's case.

Re-creating a Historical Figure

A brief sketch of the grassroots group that organized the activity is essential to understand the full significance of the memorial service. Gulang Voice (Gulang yu) is an informal group that began in 2009 on the QQ instant messaging app and was originally named the Gulangyu Cultural Conservation and Research QQ Group.[10] The group's goals are easily deduced from its original name: to research and preserve the cultural and historical heritage of Gulangyu. After the original QQ group was founded, in next to no time its membership swelled to over three hundred people from all walks of life, including scholars, writers, businesspeople, photographers, and documentary filmmakers. They were drawn together by a common purpose—their great affection for Gulangyu. This informal, fairly loose-knit group was convened by Cui Jiayu, an employee in a state-owned enterprise. Members address each other informally as "group friend." The stance adopted by the group is to insist that it adheres to open, independent, noncommercial, and academic principles. The group occasionally organizes cultural salons, invites domestic or foreign experts to speak at forums in Gulangyu, records eyewitness accounts of Gulangyu history, and regularly holds small concerts on the island. Every member is required to use his or her real name upon registration. No "unlawful issue" can be raised in the online group discussion, and members are often reminded to avoid politically sensitive topics.

Anxious to share their mission to preserve Gulangyu history and culture, the members had been waiting for a major opportunity to make their public debut.

Prior Collective Practice: Restoring the Union Church

Although the memorial service for Otte was their proudest achievement so far, the first action undertaken by the Gulang Voice group was the restoration of the Union Church (Xiehe libaitang). Qin Gaoyang, a documentary film-maker and active member of the group, posted an old picture of Gulangyu in the QQ group discussion in May 2009. Almost none of the members, even those who were long-time Gulangyu residents, recognized the building in the picture. In fact, the only person who could identify it was the son of an elderly local history expert. The picture was of the Union Church.

The Union Church was established in 1863. The funds for its construction were donated by Christian Westerners on the island, and it was initially named the International Church (Guoji libaitang). Since most of the people who attended the church were Westerners, services were conducted in English. It was renamed the Union Church after being rebuilt in 1911, but locals typically referred to it as the "Barbarian Church" (Fanzai libaitang) for reasons that will become clear.[11]

After Xiamen was taken over by the CCP in 1949, the church board was placed under the authority of the Southern Fujian Synod (Minnan dahui) of the Church of Christ in China. However, it ceased to be a functioning church in 1952. In the following years, the premises of the neighboring Xiamen Second Hospital were expanded, and the church building was appropriated for use as a storehouse. In 1974, the building was hemmed in by new structures and concealed from view. After churches were reopened in the reform era, the property rights of the Union Church were returned to the Xiamen Lianghui. However, the Lianghui lacked the considerable funds that would have been needed to restore the church, so for decades the dilapidated building remained invisible to the public.

When members of Gulang Voice "rediscovered" the old church, the beautiful architecture so clearly visible in the old picture was unrecognizable. They were distraught that the building had fallen into such disrepair, and that the historical and cultural significance of the landmark had gone unrecognized. This sense of frustration pushed the group to mobilize its resources and draw attention to the plight of this historic building. Group members called on acquaintances for support and arranged for television and newspaper coverage, presenting the church as a symbol of the need to preserve the history and architecture of Gulangyu. Some of the members drew on their personal relationships with the Gulangyu Management Committee, the Xiamen Lianghui, and other official agencies to plead their cause. A wealthy entrepreneur from a Gulangyu Christian family provided the full funds for the restoration costs. Thanks to the group's efficient cooperation and the social influence exerted by its members, the church building was eventually restored and reopened.

The restoration of the Union Church was a defining moment for Gulang Voice. Not only had the building been in a lamentable state; even more shocking was the fact that hardly anyone knew it existed. Their achievement in restoring the church made the group well known and boosted their self-confidence. More importantly, group members learned that arousing public concern was a good way to deal with authorities and make it possible for the project to move forward. This was the first time the group got involved in a project associated with Christianity. Shortly afterward, Gulang Voice seized another opportunity to make its voice heard.

The Rediscovery of John Otte

When Gulang Voice became interested in the figure of John Otte, there had been one previous attempt to commemorate him when a statue of Otte was erected on April 28, 2008, on the 110th anniversary of the founding of Xiamen Second Hospital, the successor to the Hope Hospital. On that occasion, John de Velder (1944–2016),[12] a hospital chaplain in New Jersey, was invited to represent Otte's family. Erecting a statue of Otte was a way for the hospital to distinguish itself through historical associations, evoking the positive reputation of the Hope Hospital to enhance its competitiveness. However, the figure of Otte, the founder of the Hope Hospital, played only a minor part in the celebrations. Otte remained largely unknown in Xiamen.

The breakthrough in the rediscovery of John Otte came in August 2009, when members of Gulang Voice were enthusiastically discussing historical celebrities from Gulangyu in their QQ online forum. One of the members posted a scanned letter from Otte's granddaughter to the Xiamen Municipal Government.[13] The letter describes his life in China and mentions the Hope Hospital and other major landmarks he designed, including the Eight-Trigram Building (Bagua lou). It immediately sparked an intense discussion online.

Forum members started posting comments on themes like Otte's "professionalism in saving lives regardless of his personal safety" and his

Fig. 5 Unveiling the statue of John Otte in front of Xiamen Second Hospital. Courtesy of Lan Yupei.

"dedication to the people of Xiamen." Members of the group started refer-ring to Otte as "Xiamen's Bethune." Group convener Cui Jiayu noticed that the centenary of Otte's death was approaching and suggested commemo-rating this event. The idea resonated with other members. Filmmaker and group member Qin Gaoyang floated the idea of holding a photo exhibi-tion and memorial service for Otte with the title *Love Never Ends*. Other members also proposed renaming the road around the hospital complex after Otte and erecting a second statue. Within a short time, a rough plan was submitted for discussion at the next cultural meeting. At the meeting the group reached a general consensus, which they called the *Three-in-One Program*: one photo exhibition, one memorial service, and one anthology of books and articles written in praise of Otte.

Reconstructing John Otte

Of the hundreds of missionaries who served in Xiamen from the 1840s to the 1950s, over 150 were sent into the field by the RCA.[14] Many of them died and were buried in the missionary cemetery in Gulangyu. However, apart from a handful of old buildings and tombstones, few material remains survived the series of political campaigns unleashed in the Maoist era. How, then, did Gulang Voice re-create the historical figure of John Otte?

When Pastor Zhou mentioned to me that Otte was unfamiliar to the people of Xiamen before 2010, even to Gulangyu residents and churchgoers, my curiosity was piqued. I thought it strange that such an influential historical figure had all but completely vanished from collective memory. I challenged this statement in my interviews with church clergy and lay believers. I repeatedly asked the same question: "Do you know of Dr. Otte?" Nearly all the people I talked to said they did not know about Otte or, if they did know now, they had not been aware of him before the 2010 memorial service. In short, Pastor Zhou's comment seems to have been quite accurate. Even the key organizers of the memorial service, among them Cui Jiayu and Qin Gaoyang, admitted that they did not really know much about either Otte or missionary history, although they had been living in Xiamen for years.

Rather than commemorating a missionary, group members described themselves as having a social conscience. They were motivated by the desire to participate in a socially meaningful event in a broad sense. It is a long-standing Chinese tradition that, in order to avoid trouble, people refer to the past in a circumlocutory fashion, using it as a tool to speak about the present.[15] And this is precisely what happened with the figure of John Otte. Educated group members well versed in the history of late imperial and Republican Xiamen insist that this area was once the most prosperous place in South China. Today, comparatively speaking, Gulangyu has deteriorated into a tourist destination, and Xiamen has been overtaken economically by other coastal cities. In the view of group members and members of the Christian community, Otte represented the glorious past of the Xiamen region. As one of them told me, if Otte had not been there, sooner or later they would have commemorated another figure. Otte's memory reappeared at precisely the right moment for him to become a symbol of the past and a way of tacitly commenting on the present.

As soon as it was decided to hold the commemorative event, the first priority was to create a vivid image of Otte. The organizers were convinced that they needed to reconstruct Otte as a "real" historical figure who had lived and served in the Xiamen region for decades. To resolve the problem of how to go about this, the group convened in ten face-to-face discussions involving over one hundred members. Filmmaker Qin Gaoyang bought dozens of old photographs and postcards from abroad. Pastor Zhou shared a series of unpublished articles about Otte that had been collected by Otte's granddaughter. The program for a memorial service that the RCA held for Otte in Grand Rapids, Michigan, on June 16, 1910, became a key element in reconstructing his memory, buttressed by one of his old calling cards and the title deed for the hospital land. The campaign as a whole was helped enormously by another contributor, an American professor working at Xiamen University who provided historical collections that he had built up over a long period.

Of the documents collected by the group, the most valuable one was the hospital title deed, which was purchased from abroad by one of the group members. It actually consists of three documents: a survey of the hospital site by the Xiamen coastal defense authorities in 1887, the official permit for permanently leasing land for the construction of the Hope Hospital in 1889, and the 1905 land lease for the women's hospital. This title deed bears the seals of the Qing government and the American and Dutch consulates as well as Otte's signature. Its authenticity was confirmed by local history experts. People believed that the title deed was sufficient to prove Otte had acquired the land through legitimate channels. This legality contrasted sharply with the prevalent narratives that Western missionaries had used imperialist force to seize the rights to lease or buy Chinese land.[16] The documents effectively cleared Otte of any misdeed in the disgraceful history of imperialist aggression. The group members fervently hoped that he could be portrayed as a great man, his reputation cleansed of any historical blemish. In other words, they expected that organizing an event of this kind for a noncontroversial figure would avoid political problems.

When all these items were displayed, group members were delighted to see the materialization of so many fragments that revealed Otte's life and commitment to Gulangyu. However, the group soon realized that a scattering of historical documents would not be enough to restore Otte's status in history. What the celebration was still lacking was the support of renowned historians. With this thought in mind, the group consulted and subsequently invited several local history experts to introduce Otte's life. Wang Yaode, former deputy director of the Xiamen Zheng Chenggong Memorial Hall, is a renowned expert on Xiamen history and, because of his exposure in the local media and participation in many local cultural events, has become a well-known public figure. Regarded as an Otte expert principally on account of his translation of A. L. Warnshuis's *A Brief Sketch of the Life and Work of Dr. John A. Otte*, he was invited to give the group an introduction to the doctor's life. This meant he was seen as the main authority on Otte compared to other elderly local history experts, though he did not know much more about Otte beyond the contents of the biography he had translated. In fact, this limited information was quite sufficient, since what the group needed was Wang's reputation rather than his knowledge.

The group's deliberate use of expert authority to sanction its activities resembles the process by which folk religious practices are legitimized in reform-era China. During the Maoist period, popular religions were labeled "feudal superstition" (*fengjian mixin*) and violently suppressed. Yet some are now being revived with the explicit or tacit approval of local authorities, and intellectuals play a key role in the process. In events that Kenneth Dean dubs "conferences of the gods," temple committees and local governments invite intellectuals to participate in temple-sponsored academic conferences so that their scholarly credentials can be used to endorse claims to antiquity or cultural significance in order to legitimize a particular deity cult or religious festival.[17] In a similar process, the Gulang Voice group consciously drew on the reputation of Wang Yaode more than his work itself.

On the basis of Wang's guidance, group members drew up a detailed chronology of Otte's life, and no time was lost adopting this as the standard version. Group members involved in the memorial event attended several lectures and were acquainted with the historical "truth" embodied in Otte's chronology. Even though the chronology contained some mistakes, they were not concerned about seeking clarification and quickly circulated it within and beyond the group. Their efforts to counter the official ruination and erasure of Otte's memory were gaining momentum.

The central figures on the organizing committee understood that, if the memorial was going to be held, it was crucial to make Otte a less politically sensitive figure. Otte was a man with multiple identities: he was a missionary, a doctor, and an architect. The group reached a consensus that Otte's missionary background should be touched on only lightly and his identities as doctor and architect should be highlighted instead. His contributions in these fields were undeniable, concretely manifested in the hospital he founded and the Eight-Trigram Building, a landmark not just of Gulangyu but of the Xiamen region as a whole and a testament to his great talent as an architect.

Qin felt that Otte should also be celebrated as a photographer. He had purchased four sets of old postcards issued by the RCA in memory of Otte. On the bottom of the cards, Qin was excited to find that some of the photographs had been taken by Otte personally. Nothing could have brought him more pleasure than learning that the great Otte shared his love of photography. Hence he regarded his findings as a major discovery. However, some group members doubted Otte's newfound identity as a photographer and believed that he was, at best, an enthusiastic amateur. Qin insisted that these beautiful pictures could not have been taken if Otte had not mastered a high technical proficiency. Besides, he added, as a doctor Otte must have learned about X-ray technology, for which photography and film processing skills were both required. In fact, it was not until 1895 that German scientist Wilhelm Röntgen (1845–1923) discovered X-rays, which were only later applied in medicine. The Hope Hospital bought its first X-ray machine from the United States in 1932.[18] Otte could not have had any experience with radiology before his departure for China in 1887. Furthermore, there is no evidence suggesting he learned anything about X-ray technology during his furloughs. Nevertheless, since Qin's "discovery" could enhance Otte's image and contribute to balancing his missionary background, fellow group members finally agreed to accept Otte's identity as a photographer.

The group determined that Otte would primarily be represented as a doctor, then as an architect, and finally a photographer. Otte's missionary background was not mentioned publicly at the memorial service, though no one denied Otte's position in the Christian history of Xiamen. To depoliticize Otte's legacy, the organizing committee decided that Gulang Voice should nominally be in charge of the event. As a grassroots group, it would help to highlight the secular aspects of the event. It was understood that the Xiamen church and the Christian community could not adopt a high profile in such an uncertain political situation.

It is worth comparing the careful reconstruction of Otte as an acceptable subject of memorialization with the tactics employed to legitimize popular religious practices in contemporary China. Such undertakings include the construction of museums or the "new socialist countryside" (shehuizhuyi xin nongcun), intangible cultural heritage, places for elderly people's activities, or even a reforestation project.[19] In contrast to popular religions, Christianity has to maneuver to gain space for its survival and development through other channels. Thus, numerous studies show that popular religions can be legitimated and given official space by presenting them as acceptable subjects, while Christianity must rely on other tactics. The prosperity of Christianity in contemporary Wenzhou, for instance, as Nanlai Cao points out, is based principally on the economic success of this area and the fame of the "Wenzhou model" promoted by the reformist state; economic progress makes Christianity less politically sensitive and wins Christian entrepreneurs negotiating room with local authorities.[20]

Former Rightists: Remembering the Dead, Grieving for the Living

In China and elsewhere, mourning ceremonies offer a special arena within which individual suffering can be accorded a public or cultural significance.[21] A funeral or memorial service, whether for an individual or a public figure, can serve as an occasion not only for grieving but also for challenging the political order.[22] The memorial service for Otte supplied an opportunity for some participants to present their grievances about their decades of suffering and the Party's refusal to admit the traumas it inflicted on ordinary people.

Among the group members were four well-acknowledged experts on Xiamen history who had once served as government officials or quasi-officials. An immediate question was who, of these four, should be invited to give the keynote speech? In the end, two members were chosen, Kong Qinmai (1928–2019) and Zhao Tianyi. Kong, in his eighties, was the oldest expert. He had once held leading positions in the Xiamen Federation of Social Sciences, the Xiamen Committee of the Chinese People's Political Consultative Conference (CPPCC), and the Xiamen Local Gazetteer Office and had long worked as the editor-in-chief of *Xiamen Historical Materials*. Because of Kong's long-term involvement in the compilation of local gazetteers, he is often referred to as a "living map of Xiamen" or a "living encyclopedia of Xiamen." He is regarded as an authority on historical matters and has frequently appeared in the media. Kong has a talent for dealing with state organs and is balanced in the views he expresses, a skill he probably acquired in his many years of experience writing and researching local history. When speaking on missionary history, he mentions their contributions but avoids any politically sensitive issues.

The second keynote speaker was Zhao Tianyi, a retired Communist cadre who was head of the Xiamen Culture Bureau. Both Kong and Zhao were labeled "rightists" (*youpai*) and therefore became nonpersons during the Anti-Rightist Campaign of the 1950s.[23] In comparison to Kong's judicious prudence, Zhao was much bolder in his comments. In view of his Communist background and courage in speaking up, the group believed his speech would exert the greater influence and therefore made Zhao the primary keynote speaker. Zhao, like Kong and the others, knew very little about Otte, but he was delighted to accept the invitation to give a speech at the memorial. He knew what the audience expected and his speech did not disappoint. He carefully read the article targeting Otte in the first issue of *Xiamen Historical Materials* and analyzed the accusations against him. Unlike Kong's measured tone, Zhao expanded on his theme more broadly

76

and advocated the rehabilitation of once stigmatized people. In the late 1970s and early 1980s, redressing (*gaizheng*) those who had been deeply wronged in the Maoist period was a central political concern. Consequently, Zhao's speech made an easy segue to political matters. As Pastor Zhou said to me, "Zhao opened fire on the government."

In my conversations with those who were accused of being rightists, they often lamented that they had been redressed but not completely rehabilitated (*pingfan*). There are significant differences between these two corrective actions. In the late 1970s, the Chinese leadership launched its work of righting past wrongs under the slogan "bringing order out of chaos and returning to rectitude" (*boluan fanzheng*). The upshot was that in the early 1980s, those who had been wronged were allowed to resume their former positions; neither a public apology nor national compensation was forthcoming. Hence in their addresses Kong and Zhao repeatedly stressed that they had never been rehabilitated. Neither for them nor for these stigmatized missionaries had any corrective action been taken. In my interviews with Gulang Voice leaders, even though almost none of them are Christian, I sensed a great deal of gratitude and respect for the missionaries who had suffered a fate not far removed from their own experiences.

Although the political atmosphere has grown more liberal, so far there has been no official reevaluation of missionaries. In other words, missionaries, unlike numerous Chinese wronged during the Maoist era, have never been officially redressed. "Tactics were therefore necessary," said Zhao Tianyi. He gave me a proud smile and continued, "I spoke from the Marxist perspective of historical stages. Specifically, they [the Party's Marxist theorists] said the late Qing was [an era of] feudalism. Without a doubt, the Western capitalism represented by missionaries was an advanced [social] stage; their arrival in China was [therefore part of] a [process of] historical progress." Zhao even quoted the Party's former leader Liu Shaoqi's (1898–1969) remark—"History is written by the people"—in support of grassroots efforts to reevaluate Otte.

Zhao's speech resonated with the audience. Some grassroots officials even privately praised him for his courage. However, the newspaper report the next day did not mention a word about the contents of his speech (although it mentioned him by name). Zhao was quite proud of his courage and regarded it as a breakthrough in freedom of speech for intellectuals. He feels that the term *rightist*, once a stigmatized political label, is now being reinterpreted and employed as a positive symbol. In his eyes, the suffering he experienced as a rightist was proof of his right-minded, honest character.

World Heritage and Local Politics

Pragmatism and the Principled Stance of the Local State

In 1987, UNESCO endorsed the Chinese government's applications for six sites to be listed as World Heritage Sites (WHS). Currently, according to official statistics, there are fifty-five sites in China inscribed on the WHS list and another sixty sites on the tentative list.[24] In recent years the government has actively promoted cultural and religious sites both as a means of earning tourism revenue and as an expression of nationalistic pride in China's past.[25] As China rises in global status, the government is striving to increase its "soft power" (*ruan shili*), and WHS status is regarded as one means to project Chinese culture and history on a global stage. For local governments, entering scenic spots on the UNESCO list has become a coveted asset.

Gulangyu, an officially recognized National 5A Scenic Area, was formally placed on the agenda to apply for WHS status in 2009. This move was not universally popular, immediately incurring both silent and vocal opposition for a variety of reasons. Gulangyu officials were reluctant to be responsible for the application, as they were well aware that the process was an uphill battle. Some university scholars opposed the application as a "matter of principle" (*yuanze wenti*): Gulangyu used to be a colony forcibly occupied by foreign powers, and therefore celebrating this heritage would be tantamount to celebrating imperialism. Among the consultants, for instance, a professor of history at Xiamen University who had once published a book criticizing the Gulangyu International Settlement firmly opposed the proposal for the WHS application.[26] Scholars argued that the Chinese people in Xiamen should not be "doubly humiliated." However, their objections went unheard as the main municipal leaders had already pledged their commitment to their provincial superiors, so the expert consultation was merely a formality. Whatever their discomfort about proceeding with the application process, subordinate officials were not prepared to risk their political future by opposing their seniors. The university professors who disagreed with the plan were labeled excessively academic (*xueyuan pai*). In this semantic context in Chinese, *academic* usually carries a negative connotation, indicating a pedantic, overly conservative attitude or an inflexible stance. The university professors were not subsequently consulted and were in fact completely marginalized in the decision-making process.

In present-day Xiamen, the rewriting of local history is a popular pastime among both civilians and authorities. In the process of knowledge production, the reconfiguration of power relations never stops. Local history experts without any academic training in history have seized the higher ground. Simultaneously, university historians have seen their voices ignored, in part because of their reluctance to cooperate with such efforts. Paradoxically, their names are still listed as consultants in the official application documents. Rather than being concerned about their opinions, what the government apparently needed were their academic credentials and the distinguished reputation of their affiliated institution, Xiamen University. Unsurprisingly, regardless of academic opposition, no time was lost in submitting the big-budget (over USD100 million) program to formally apply for WHS status.

The GMC officials understood that for the application to be successful, it was essential to redefine Gulangyu's past. This tactic was essential for two reasons: first, to fulfill WHS criteria, but second, to sway opposition. In its quest to distinguish Gulangyu from other competitors around the world, the application committee conducted a comparative study and determined that Gulangyu's superiority lay in its architectural and cultural diversity. "There are numerous colonies around the world, how can we convince UNESCO experts?" Xu Mingde, one official in charge of the WHS application, said, "The most outstanding feature of Gulangyu was that the KMC, made up of representatives from different countries, was established to manage the island. These Westerners therefore lived together in peace and harmony [with the Chinese]." In this sense, as far as the officials were concerned, Western countries represented diverse cultures rather than colonial powers. A design team affiliated with Tsinghua University in Beijing, one of the most prestigious universities in China, was invited to draft the application documents, and the officials specifically instructed them not to mention the island's colonial background; instead, the description had to be "neutral" and avoid such words as "imperialist aggression."[27] The true semantics of "neutral description" as used by local cadres was actually a positive reinterpretation of the past, reflected in a profile of Gulangyu on the World Heritage Centre list:

> With the opening of Xiamen as a commercial port in 1843, and Kulangsu as an international settlement in 1903, the island of the southern coastal areas of the Chinese empire suddenly became an important window for Sino-foreign exchanges. Its heritage reflects the composite nature of a modern settlement composed of 931 historical buildings of a variety of local and international

architectural styles, natural sceneries, a historic network of roads and historic gardens.

Through the concerted endeavour of local Chinese, returned overseas Chinese, and foreign residents from many countries, Kulangsu developed into an international settlement with outstanding cultural diversity and modern living quality. It also became an ideal dwelling place for the overseas Chinese and elites who were active in East Asia and South-eastern Asia as well as an embodiment of modern habitat concepts of the period between [the] mid-19th and mid-20th century.[28]

The Gulangyu International Settlement had long been denounced as a base of imperialist aggression against China's southeast coast. The KMC was also criticized for allowing imperialists to seize lands, for trampling on China's sovereignty, and for degrading the Chinese people. The third (1980) and sixteenth (1990) volumes of *Xiamen Historical Materials*, focusing on the Gulangyu International Settlement, lay bare the darkness that enshrouded the island under the imperialist occupation and praise the anti-imperialist struggle of local people. Now times have changed. The new official narrative reinterprets the International Settlement as "a modern, international, public community housing multiple cultures"; it even describes the KMC as "a self-administered agency with modern attributes."[29] The rewritten history of the island elides historical shame to make the WHS application more palatable. The so-called "matter of principle" the university scholars had railed against was no longer an issue.

This transformation of Gulangyu's history is remarkable given the significance of "*lieux de mémoire*" (realms of memory), proposed by French historian Pierre Nora in 1989, in Chinese political practice. Nora's idea is that memory needs to take root in a concrete object or site and should be nurtured by anniversaries or celebrations; otherwise it is overtaken by, or lost in, the authority held by universal claims of history.[30] Nora's concept helps contribute to our understanding of why the Chinese state at all levels is so busy establishing patriotism education bases and red tourism destinations (Chinese Communist revolutionary sites).[31] However, pragmatically, in the process of the nation's modernization, meanings bestowed by the state have always been movable feasts.

Writing about Humen, Guangdong Province, where the Opium War broke out, James Flath notes that the city became a symbol of resistance to imperialism during the Maoist era. In the reform era, Humen was "further articulated as the place where China's 'Century of Humiliation' began. But paradoxically," today, "as the Pearl River Triangle takes a leading role in Chinese commerce and manufacturing, the site is just as likely to be associated with global export, high fashion, and high technology."[32] The present-day Old Summer Palace is another case of creative reinvention in a similar vein: sacked and burned down by Anglo-French allied troops at the end of the Second Opium War (1856–60), this former summer retreat of the Qing emperors was officially designated a patriotic education site under Mao. However, it was subsequently made into a scenic public park and is a major tourist attraction in Beijing. The transformation of national wounds into tourist destinations boosts local revenues, yet remarkably, it renders the designated role of patriotic education null and void.[33]

Neither the Xiamen authorities nor ordinary citizens are willing to define Gulangyu as a site of historical shame. Gulangyu basks in a romantic image created by its architecture, sandy beach, and its reputation as an islet of pianos; features that every year attract millions of domestic and international tourists to the island. If this lucrative image is to be preserved, the rewriting of Gulangyu's history must take a positive direction; in other words, it would simply not do to highlight the humiliation of its colonial past. For Gulangyu, both the former discourse of imperialist humiliation and the current narrative of harmonious multiculturalism are products of official efforts to reframe history in keeping with overarching political narratives of the times. They vividly illustrate the ways that history is strategically deployed for political ends, though some histories are more factually accurate than others.

Church Legacies and World Cultural Heritage

Instead of following a policy of sporadically trying to eradicate all religions, the post-Mao government acquiesces in a trade-off that permits limited freedom of religious expression in exchange for continued political loyalty.[34] In Gulangyu, a recent event transformed the local government's attitude toward Christianity.

In 2002, Xiamen was entered into the international competition for the most livable communities award, hosted in Germany. An American member of the Xiamen delegation suggested that the New Street Church should be incorporated in the Xiamen document. As China's first Protestant church, the New Street Church could make the city stand out against the competition. Initially the heads of the delegation disagreed with making any reference to Christian elements, but they changed their minds when their American colleague explained that Xiamen's association with Protestantism could contribute to its chances of winning the gold medal, given that the competition was being hosted by the country that was the birthplace of Protestantism.

"There are two forms of renovation of historical relics," Xu Mingde said, "namely: either the restoration of the architecture or of the function." The officials understood that the restoration of function (for example, hospital, school, or consulate) was beyond the bounds of possibility. The heavy loss of cultural elements, Xu complained to me, was a thorny issue for GMC officials. The group presenting the WHS application was faced with a dilemma: the departure of foreigners before the Communist victory left behind only tangible buildings and not intangible cultural heritage. Ravaged by the forces of commercialization, in the locals' eyes Gulangyu has quickly "deteriorated into a resort island and seafood market." Only a very small number of foreigners still live there. This present situation is in stark contrast to the current official narrative about its past—"a modern, international, public community housing multiple cultures."[35]

In the application for WHS status, fifty-three core heritage sites (*hexin yicun dian*) were identified in Gulangyu, over ten of which were related to Christianity, including the Christian cemetery, a church-run hospital, and Christian schools. In the past Gulangyu was a major mission base that was home to approximately one-third of the missionaries in Fujian. It was separated from Xiamen by less than a kilometer stretch of water, making it a useful base to reach the growing population and churches there. The presence of the RCA, LMS, and PCE members on Gulangyu encouraged easy contacts among the Three Missions. Moreover, as one of China's best deep harbors, it was a convenient place from which to travel and communicate with the outside world.[36] From 1903, the Gulangyu International Settlement enjoyed certain self-governing privileges that were designed to protect foreigners and Christianity. Certainly, no one would deny the role of Christianity in the historical modernization of Gulangyu.

If truth be told, authorities paid little attention to Christian sites before Gulangyu was placed on the WHS application agenda. In 1992, the authorities had even toyed with the idea of taking over the Christian cemetery to expand the island's large botanical garden. As I describe in the following chapter, the plan provoked an outpouring of protest and outrage by local Christians and Chinese Filipinos in the pages of overseas Chinese-language newspapers. Local authorities eventually backed out of the plan to

Fig. 6 The Union Church before repairs. Courtesy of Chen Yongpeng.

Fig. 7 The Union Church after repairs. Courtesy of Wang Shitai.

avoid offending the overseas Chinese who tended to invest in the Xiamen area, their ancestral homeland, and many of whom had relatives who were buried in the cemetery. Furthermore, Xiamen, a state-designated Special Economic Zone, needed to establish a good international image (*guoji xingxiang*) vis-à-vis the outside world, in particular in Taiwan, just across the strait.

Another incident occurred in 2004 when the original Hope Hospital building was scheduled for demolition to make way for real estate development. Concerned local residents alerted John Otte's granddaughter, who immediately wrote to the municipal government. The letter, underlining the site's historical significance, was submitted to the Xiamen government through the Xiamen Second Hospital—the Hope Hospital's professed successor—and drew the attention of local authorities, who eventually abandoned the plan.

However, the decision to go ahead with the WHS application meant authorities could no longer overlook Gulangyu's "religious issue"—its connection to Christianity. As Xu told me:

> Christianity constitutes an indispensable part of Gulangyu's cultural heritage; therefore we must pay attention to it and include it in our WHS application. If there were no Christian culture, there would have been no modern Gulangyu civilization or any possibility of submitting the present WHS application. Few things would be left if Christianity were excluded, since these core sites—the hospital, schools and churches—were all related to it. It was Christianity that led the way for the modern civilization of Gulangyu. Following the introduction of Christianity, Western thought, culture, music and lifestyles arrived. As the presence of foreigners increased, more Western cultures were introduced and interacted with Chinese culture. Gulangyu prospered soon after.

Hu Weikang, deputy head of the GMC, also noted, "Christianity exerted a great influence not only on Gulangyu, but also on Southern Fujian and the whole of China, in the fields of medicine, the arts, and sports. It changed the Xiamen people's way of thinking and their lifestyle; it affects the way people live even now. The people of Gulangyu have a unique character precisely because of Christianity. They love music and sports because of Christianity."

The original restored Hope Hospital building was altered by authorities to make it into a musical instrument museum, a plan that also attracted widespread criticism. The government balked when faced with dissatisfied citizens' critique that it was "uncultured" (*mei wenhua*). However, as local officials revealed in our interviews, the emergence of Gulang Voice inspired them to take a greater interest in the Christian history. Because of their affection for Gulangyu, the group members made a concerted effort to rescue its once flourishing culture from the detrimental trends introduced by tourism. The group members regarded their efforts as "civic engagement in the WHS application" (*minjian shenyi*)—a form of volunteer assistance. The authorities were pleased to welcome the group's participation and enthusiasm. Hence, when Cui Jiayu paid them a visit to discuss John Otte, officials were receptive.

The value of Otte's legacy is immediately apparent in the description given by Hu Weikang: "When the world heritage experts come, we shall lead them to see Otte's bust. Hopefully when that happens there will be flowers laid there by Chinese people in his memory. Even if the flowers are withered, it will show that the Chinese people have not forgotten Otte." Hu sat quietly sipping tea. He probably realized he had said something ambiguous that might suggest some kind of staging on his part, so he hastened to add, "It would not make sense if I deliberately arranged for withered flowers past their prime to be placed at the bust." Although I do not know if this is something he really plans to do when the visit occurs, from the local officials' point of view, his attitude makes Otte's role in the heritage project abundantly clear.

The Invisible Presence of the State

The State as a Silent Partner

As the members of Gulang Voice started planning the memorial for John Otte, one of their chief concerns was how to obtain the support, or at least the tolerance, of local authorities. The Hope Hospital complex and the square in front of it are government property. Group members were well aware that the memorial service could not be held without official approval, and they would have been hard put to find another spot on Gulangyu to host this kind of event. More importantly, they were all highly aware that the event would be politically sensitive, in spite of their efforts to neutralize Otte's tarnished legacy and re-create a positive image of him.

Group members come from all walks of life and many of them have contacts among high-level authorities. One of the group members is Zhang

Haiqin, a staff member at the Xiamen Federation of Social Sciences, a think tank for the Xiamen government that also conducts research on Gulangyu and offers consultancy on heritage conservation. More importantly, as a semiofficial institution "within the system" (*tizhi nei*), its status in the administration is equal to that of the GMC (deputy department level, *fu tingji*). Even if Zhang acted in an informal capacity, without the official backing of her work unit, her state-recognized background would still make her an effective go-between. Zhang's introduction helped to ease the way with government officials, making them more welcoming to group members. Hu Weikang, a Gulangyu official, showed great interest in the group's activities, though he received them privately rather than as a representative of the GMC. Hu was happy to give permission for the event and even sent a subordinate to attend the group's memorial planning meetings on his behalf.

Although the venue no longer presented a problem, there were still some persistent concerns about the politically sensitive nature of the event. As it drew closer, Cui perceived slight changes in Hu Weikang's attitude. At first, Hu had been strongly supportive, but now he was becoming quite circumspect. When I interviewed Hu, I also sensed his caution. I mentioned to him that the GMC's involvement in the recovery and preservation of church heritage had "made its mark on the WHS application, and indirectly helped the church." He immediately interjected, "This is not about help. You should not put it in those terms. . . . When church [buildings] are restored, it does seem superficially like protection of the church. But in fact, the reason [it's done] is to ensure that tourists can experience religious culture and that this will enhance the quality of their tourism."

Just three years after Otte's commemoration, the authorities held a grand ceremony for renowned Buddhist Master Hong Yi (1880–1942) on the theme of republishing his transcribed scriptures on Gulangyu. The event drew over two hundred guests, including Communist Party cadres, Buddhist clergy, and laypeople as well as various local celebrities.[37] The event had a self-evident connection to Buddhism. Cadres declared that it was a "cultural event" rather than a religious activity. Nevertheless, as an event related to Buddhism, it was a much less sensitive issue.

In contrast, no official was willing to risk jeopardizing his or her political future by becoming directly involved in the memorial for Otte. Hu Weikang explained to me, "The [Xiamen] government has not carried out any research on John Otte's value; there is no unit to undertake a professional study of this kind. Therefore no historical evaluation has been formulated. The [local] government is not permitted to put forward foreigners [for official recognition], certainly not their systemic glorification, until it has been supplied with a scientific appraisal based on studies conducted by relevant departments."

With both sides aware of these limitations, all exchanges between the authorities and Gulang Voice took place through informal channels. In reference to their negotiations with the government, Cui Jiayu looked proud and said, "We did serious things in a non-serious [informal] way" (*Women yong bu renzhen de fangshi ban renzhen de shi*). What Cui meant was that the group was deeply committed to holding the memorial event, but to do so they had to use informal, roundabout means. He continued, "Government officials, in particular those who are natives, supported us in private. However, they were all aware of the potential for trouble and did not dare acknowledge their endorsement in public. All negotiations took place privately, while in public they turned a blind eye to our activities."

In the bureaucratic system, whether the government "knows" or "does not know" something at any level depends on whether a written report has been filed. Even if individual officials know about something in private, the absence of a written record allows the government to formally deny its awareness of a particular event. Therefore, Gulang Voice members communicated with officials without using written documents, and private meetings were preferred. The GMC did not report the event to its superior authorities. If any blame had been forthcoming from senior government officials, Gulangyu officials had plausible deniability to evade any responsibility for the event.

Gulang Voice is a grassroots group that lacks an official status. This meant that as far as government officials were concerned, cooperation with Gulang Voice could easily land them in hot water. Before the memorial event, officials suggested that the group should register with the civil affairs department, arguing that the government could not financially support the group because its lack of a legal status meant it did not have an official bank account and seal. At the time, the group was short of funds to support its activities, and some of the main members hoped to obtain government financial support. However, they eventually gave up the idea. Their reasoning was simple: once they registered with the government, they would be supervised by authorities, which would run contrary to their initial position. The upshot was that the authorities failed to co-opt the group. In fact, the grassroots nature of the group is what made the event possible because members did not need to obey official regulations or follow cumbersome reporting procedures. In reform-era Chinese society, the "system" tends to constrain those who are within it. In contrast, those who are outside are able to be more flexible in a freer space. By establishing relationships that transcend the boundaries of the "system," particular state-society relations can be formed.[38]

87

Local officials often complained to me that the group was moving too slowly. They indicated that they were much more open-minded than group members thought. Yet their strategic caution gave them the flexibility to modify their stance as needed. This is evident in their "flexible participation" in the event itself: none of the officials whom Gulang Voice had invited to the event showed up, but since the memorial did not elicit any negative response from their superiors, Gulangyu officials—even officials who hadn't been invited—were pleased to publicly claim their support and participation in retrospect. Hu Weikang, the deputy head of the GMC, told me, "We supplied the site for them. They invited us to attend the event. I was there." However, all the group leaders I interviewed denied his presence. If he had been there, he would have been invited to give a speech by the organizing team as a mark of respect. I could not identify the officials who claimed to have been present on any of the photos taken that day. Only the officials themselves know if they were really there. "They are all cowards," Pastor Zhou told me.

Incorporating State Authority

Although officials themselves did not attend the memorial for John Otte, the state was present in this civic event nevertheless.

Despite the success of the memorial service, disagreements inevitably arose during the planning process. The first source of tension was that not all members of Gulang Voice agreed on the program, feeling that such a high-profile memorial event for a historical missionary would probably be banned by the government. However, the concerns of a few members did not dissuade the majority of the group. On the contrary, opponents of the plan were disparaged as "the left" (*zuo de*). Although the concept of "left" is not fully elaborated, Chinese intellectuals tend to use it to refer to conservatives who "prefer authoritarian rule and support nationalism, state intervention in the economy, and traditional social values."[39] In such a self-proclaimed nongovernmental group, this was tantamount to negative labeling, a disparaging remark leveled at those willing to accept authoritarian single-party rule. The dissenting voices were quickly silenced by the louder majority.

Using a network of personal relations, Qin Gaoyang contacted the United States consul general in Guangzhou, who expressed his appreciation for their efforts to commemorate an American citizen and promised to attend the ceremony. The prospect of a big name appearing at the event was a great source of excitement for members of Gulang Voice, who considered that the presence of an American diplomat would give it a greater impact. Qin was quite proud of his personal connections and excitedly mentioned their support in group discussions: "The consul general asked me how they could be of assistance. I told them to ask Hillary Clinton to help us obtain some texts and pictures [related to Otte]." It all sounded as if he had a close relationship with the American embassy officials. By referring to the name of a leading American politician, Qin hoped to vaunt the contribution he could make to the event. However, he failed to convince the other members, who judged that he was exaggerating his avowed political connections.

To Qin's surprise, the plan he formally submitted to the organizing committee was met with fierce opposition. Even Cui Jiayu, who had formerly supported him, rejected his proposal. Opponents of the plan argued that inviting an American diplomat to the memorial service would lead to a diplomatic incident. It was reasonable to assume that if the US consul general in Guangzhou was in attendance, the municipal or even provincial governments would send officials from foreign affairs to escort the guest. This would elevate the commemoration to a diplomatic and political affair, inevitably politicizing the event and attracting the attention of the government. To avoid trouble, the government would probably ban it. The most likely scenario would be that local-level Gulangyu authorities would prohibit the program from going forward without even attempting to report it for municipal approval. Qin tried to set the members' minds at ease by explaining that he had mentioned the plan to the municipal Foreign Affairs Office; an official supported the plan and praised him as a "popular goodwill ambassador" (*minjian youhao dashi*). However, the organizing team could not be convinced that this private support was enough to obtain official approval. Qin finally had to withdraw his invitation to the American diplomat, asking instead for a congratulatory letter that was to be translated into Chinese and read out at the memorial event. The consul general was pleased to send them a letter expressing his gratitude for their efforts to recognize and commemorate the remarkable contributions of one of the early Americans in China.

Apart from Qin's informal communication with foreign affairs officials, nobody else raised the possibility of American diplomats attending the event to any government officials. Most members of the group were certain it would cause trouble. The group's internal discussion and Qin's eventual decision to scrap the invitation shows how group members incorporated the authority of the state. Not only here but throughout the whole planning process the specter of the state continued to hover in the back of people's minds, imperceptibly causing tensions to emerge from time to time. Paradoxically, the symbolic power of the state revealed itself in the form of an invisible presence, showing its effectiveness even without the direct intervention of local officials.

The Church Behind the Scenes

Stigmatized Missionaries and Official Amnesia

The first churchman the group contacted was Pastor Zhou, who was familiar to many of them. They had recently collaborated with Pastor Zhou to restore the Union Church building and hoped he would again offer the group his support. Zhou was pleased to see the plans and promised to be of assistance. However, Zhou did not formally report his and the YMCA's involvement to the Xiamen Lianghui, as he assumed the leadership would not give its approval. In fact, as it transpired, the members of the Lianghui clergy whom Zhou invited to the ceremony did not show up, proving his caution was justified. As Zhou said, it is wise to "play it safe" (*mingzhe baoshen*).

Very few people in the church knew anything about Otte before the memorial, a fact I confirmed in interviews with both clergy and lay Christians. More importantly, the clergy tended not to concern themselves with historical matters in general. "The teaching of Christian history was halted for decades, therefore many ministers do not have a sense of the past," Zhou said with a reluctant smile, then added, "From this year in the Fujian Theological Seminary I am going to teach a course on the Christian history of Southern Fujian."

Considering the Xiamen church as a whole, it is impossible to say with confidence what church people know about the past. Some are still aware of what happened to foreign missionaries during Mao's rule. In the 1950s, instead of being expelled immediately, some missionaries were obstructed on their way out of China. It was not uncommon to put members of a missionary group on trial before allowing them to exit the country. Rev. Henry A. Poppen (1889–1972), an RCA missionary, was singled out for trial, undoubtedly on account of having served in many capacities during his more than thirty years of service in the Xiamen region.[40] Poppen's trial, held on the athletics field of church-affiliated Talmage College in Zhangzhou in 1951, was attended by approximately ten thousand locals, Christians and non-Christians. The trial lasted about three hours, during which various accusations were leveled at Poppen. Two of his chief accusers were people he had befriended—one, a teacher whose education he had supported financially; the other, a student he had visited frequently in the hospital and whose medical expenses he had paid.[41] The main accusation was that he was an American imperialist. This sort of public criticism was deliberately voiced to discredit missionaries, intentionally distorting their image and stigmatizing Christianity as a whole. Missionaries were associated with Western (mainly American) imperialism, and the masses were mobilized in exercises of public humiliation to legitimize the newly established Communist regime.

In or around the mid-1950s, the few foreign missionaries remaining in Southern Fujian were expelled from the country. Items relating to missionaries became a potential source of serious political trouble for Chinese citizens. Photos with foreign faces were an invitation to danger, and some of my respondents possess old broken pictures from which the images of missionaries have been cut out. During the Cultural Revolution, numerous pictures were burned for fear of what would happen if they were found during raids by Red Guards (Hong weibing). Bibles and other faith-related books were also publicly burned. Thus, the quest to revive the legacy of John Otte may have carried with it the painful memories of past turmoil.

The Suez Canal protests were another painful memory associated with foreign missionaries. In June 1957, people throughout China, including residents of Gulangyu, held public marches in support of the Egyptian struggle for control of the Suez Canal against the British, French, and Israeli armies. In Gulangyu, as the procession passed by the "Barbarian Cemetery" (Fanzai mu), the crowd vented its wrath on foreign tombs, digging up the remains of 320 people buried in the cemetery.[42] John Otte's tomb was located in the missionary cemetery in Gulangyu and was probably destroyed around this time. The disturbance of graves was not an anodyne matter but held great significance in Chinese culture and was a profound and intentional affront.[43] The incident severely offended the sensibilities of older Christians, a fact that people mentioned several times during my field research.

In the Maoist era no exception was made for the Hope Hospital. The Xiamen Military Management Committee announced the expropriation of the hospital property in January 1951.[44] The provincial government officially approved the municipal government's request to take over the hospital

Fig. 8 Most of the cross-shaped gravestones were damaged. Courtesy of Chris White.

on October 30.[45] In December 1951, the Xiamen Health Bureau formally assumed control of the Hope Hospital and its affiliated nursing school,[46] and renamed it the Second Hospital of Xiamen. The Hope Hospital was condemned as a tool of imperialist aggression. American medical personnel were accused of adopting an "anti-Communist stance" and of being involved in "counter-revolutionary activities," of "deliberately distributing the wrong medicine to sick children," and of "carrying out tests on Chinese patients for experimental purposes."[47]

Although some Chinese academics now acknowledge the contributions of Protestant missionaries to the modernization of China, the Chinese government has not yet officially reevaluated their historical role. Thus John Otte has never been officially reevaluated, meaning his legacy remained a politically sensitive topic. Xiamen clergy were acutely aware of this and did not want to risk stirring up sensitive issues by getting involved.

State-Recognized Pastor: Coordinator in Local Politics

Pastor Zhou comes from a Christian family in Inner Mongolia. After graduating from the Nanjing Union Theological Seminary in 1994, he followed his girlfriend, now his wife, to Xiamen and served as a preacher in an officially sanctioned church. A few years after he began his ministry, the Fujian Lianghui sent him to study abroad. He obtained his master's degree in theology at Trinity Theological College in Singapore in 2003 and was ordained as a pastor the following year. He rose to head pastor (*zhuren mushi*) in 2008. Only a year later, he was promoted to the provincial and municipal Lianghui offices, allowing him to play a greater role in church affairs. Pastor Zhou now holds several positions within state-recognized Christian organizations, including the Xiamen YMCA and TSPM, the provincial TSPM, and the Fujian Theological Seminary. This endows Pastor Zhou with state legitimacy, and he enjoys a good relationship with the authorities, taking an active role in various social events. During the WHS application process, representing the Xiamen Lianghui, he assisted cadres in the restoration of church buildings as cultural relics, and in doing so won the trust of local officials. Pastor Zhou is always willing to bring in and make use of secular resources to serve church requirements. "These are connections [*renmai*]," he said to me proudly after hanging up a phone call in which he recommended me to a government official.

Some people both inside and outside the church call him a "social pastor" or even a "political pastor" because of his active participation in social activities and his close relationship with government officials. In dealing with authorities, he has the advantage of being familiar with the "bureaucratic culture" (*guanchang wenhua*) and specializes in communicating and coordinating with local politics. When he was consulted about the Otte event, Pastor Zhou made it clear that he should keep a low profile. Hence his coordinating role between Gulang Voice and the church attracted no undue attention. In the media coverage that followed, his identity as a pastor was deliberately obfuscated. Even so, his role should not be underestimated. Apart from the participation of the YMCA choir, as a member of the organizing team his presence definitely encouraged the group. All the people present were aware of Otte's missionary background. They would have been disappointed if the church had stayed away, since the memorial service was, to a certain extent, a celebration of Christianity.

Conclusion

In imperial China, there was a long tradition of voicing criticisms of the present in the form of discourse ostensibly about past nobles and dynasties.[48]

Elements of this discursive practice have remained in the way Chinese people think and speak about history in contemporary China. On the surface, the memorial event for John Otte was a commemoration for a medical missionary reinvented as "China's Bethune," a doctor, architect, and photographer who contributed to the development of Gulangyu. However, entwined in the memorial event were complex negotiations about the past. It was not only the place of a foreign missionary that was at stake. It was also the place of Christianity, and the desire to rehabilitate those whose names were "blackened" during Maoist political campaigns—not only Christians but others as well, such as some members of Gulang Voice.

The memorial allowed participants, including members of Gulang Voice, clergy, and local history experts, to proclaim their cultural and historical missions, and to let it be known that they expected a fair evaluation of historical figures. The event elicited strong and positive responses in the media. Several central figures boasted that it was the first time such a ceremony had been held for a missionary in postsocialist China. When I mentioned a much earlier monument and ceremony for another missionary—Eric Henry Liddell—held in 1988,[49] they showed no interest in learning more. The point here is not whether the memorial for Otte was truly the first one held for a Western missionary in the PRC but rather that locals believe it was. They are convinced that the event is a concrete example of their contribution toward the correction of the unfair treatment of missionary figures. By paying tribute to Otte and the work he did, group members were putting their sense of historical mission into practice.

What made the discursive reversals on missionaries possible was the local government's pragmatic and tacit approval. Authorities were willing to reappraise the value of a missionary figure, and of Christianity as a whole, in the context of Gulangyu's application for WHS status. However, the amount of social space the state allows for Christianity remained limited. Officials were cautious to avoid risking their political positions, playing a deliberately ambivalent role that gave them plausible deniability in the event.

As a religious organization, the Xiamen church kept a low profile at the ceremony. The memory of the church's suffering is still alive and prevents many church members from publicly participating in religious events. Even so, the success of the event contributed to rehabilitating Christianity and missionaries in local society, as well as stimulating a broader interest in the Christian history of Xiamen among history enthusiasts.

Two years after the 2010 memorial service, a memorial event for Otte on a smaller scale, attended by dozens of people, was held in the newly restored Gulangyu Union Church. Additionally, the Xiamen YMCA supplied a free medical diagnostic service for residents of the island to mark the 102nd anniversary of Otte's death. This time, it was the Christian community, rather than a secular group, that organized the event. Although government officials did not attend, they sent flowers in the name of the Gulangyu Management Committee. Compared to the 2010 memorial, holding a second event for Otte was a bold move on the part of the Christian community, expanding space for Christian history and heralding a change in official attitudes.

Chapter 3

THE PASSING OF GLORY

On the morning of October 25, 2014, I arrived at the Gulangyu ferry terminal on my way to attend the eightieth anniversary celebration of Trinity Church, the main church in Gulangyu. It was a Saturday, around eight o'clock, and although the Descent of the Frost (Shuangjiang, the last solar term of the autumn according to the Chinese calendar) had already passed, the weather was still as torrid as ever.

Unlike most weekends when I had been there before, Egret River Avenue (Lujiang dao), the road leading to the ferry port in Xiamen, was not at all crowded. Gulangyu is one of the Xiamen region's major tourist attractions, hosting millions of visitors every year, and around seventy thousand visitors a day pass through this terminal during the peak tourist seasons. The upshot is that in recent years, the road has been cursed with traffic congestion, causing problems for citizens and authorities alike. But on this day only small groups of people were wandering around outside the terminal or consulting the information desk. Precisely five days earlier, local authorities had adopted new measures to relieve traffic congestion: all non-Xiamen residents were now required to take ferries from another port 5 km away and pay newly adjusted fares, four times higher than before; the original terminal and fee were now reserved for local residents holding Xiamen identity cards.

On the surface, the newly implemented measure, one of the local government's projects to exploit the tourism potential of Gulangyu, did not

96

have much to do with religion. But in fact, it had significant repercussions for Trinity Church. As a tourism-oriented policy, it prevents non-Xiamen citizens from easily visiting the church, and the local government has never taken the church's needs into consideration. It was another indication of the church's decreasing power to determine its own future.

Trinity Church, built in 1934, survived the harsh repression of Mao's political campaigns, reopening in the late 1970s to witness the renewal of Christianity in Gulangyu. However, in recent years, state-led commercialization projects propelled by tourist development have doomed it to a gradual decline. The rapid social, cultural, and demographic changes in Gulangyu have inevitably affected Christianity on the island in general and Trinity Church in particular. Compared to the repressive and hostile Maoist state, the postsocialist state is multifaceted and diffused in its dealings with Christianity in diverse aspects of society. One of the most immediate results is that Christianity in Gulangyu has been thrust into state projects and it is now impossible to separate from the market economy.

This chapter delves into the significance and history of Trinity Church and the people dedicated to its mission. I first describe the eightieth anniversary celebration of the church, then explore the life story of Pastor Wen, an influential figure who has been key to the church's survival and success through successive eras in China's religious policies, before examining the church's decline and the change in its relationship with the government under its current leader. The chapter looks at both the broad and the subtle effects of shifts in government policy, and church members' nostalgic longing for a glorious church that no longer exists.

Celebrating Eighty Years

That October day, walking through the winding alleys of Gulangyu on my way to Trinity Church, I saw posters pasted on walls advertising the eightieth anniversary celebration. Members of the young reception committee carried placards aloft to convey an enthusiastic welcome to visiting guests and guided nonlocal participants through the busy pathways to the church. Ceremonial assistants wearing red T-shirts with badges, most of them middle-aged and elderly female church members, stood at the church gate and around the compound to welcome participants and escort honored guests, mainly overseas church representatives, respected senior Christians, and major contributors to the celebration. As I entered the gate, there were two reception desks on each side of the pathway. Honored guests were ushered to sign their names in the red book[1] and collect gift bags with badges and memorial coffee mugs bearing a picture of Trinity Church. Pastors, elders, and deacons/deaconesses were busy receiving visitors. Since Trinity Church does not encourage named donations, there were very few signs indicating contributors, in contrast with ceremonial events I attended in other church communities in Southern Fujian.[2]

The daylong event consisted of two parts, a morning ceremony and afternoon celebration. The morning ceremony was scheduled to begin at ten, but by 9:20 the church was already packed with believers, honored guests, and curious tourists. The wooden backdrop of the stage was covered with a crimson velvet cloth, with a cross prominently displayed in the middle. A big numeral "80" was on its left and the phrases "testament," "thanksgiving" and "glory" on the right. The backdrop was also embellished with decorative doves and waves above and below, and a painted night sky spangled with glittering stars above and on both sides.

The front rows of pews were reserved for honored guests; ordinary church members took their seats in the middle and back sections of the nave. Most seats were already occupied by people who had come to attend the ceremony, most of them in their sixties or above; a few attendees were even in their eighties or nineties and might have known the church in its earliest days, before the Communist revolution. Young people made up much less than half of the audience. Considering the church was full, I estimate that at least nine hundred people were there as participants or curiosity seekers.

As an invited guest, I chose a reserved seat in the third row near the middle aisle, a good spot for taking pictures. A camera crew hired by the church committee moved around the church videotaping the event. By my side, a photographer standing in the aisle videotaped the front stage throughout the event with a professional video camera supported on a tripod.

Around a quarter to ten, a female church worker walked onto the stage and led those gathered in singing a Southern Fujian–language hymn. People hurriedly stopped chatting and greeting the people they knew and seated themselves. At ten o'clock exactly as the church bell rang, the noisy crowd fell quiet. Choir members wearing white half-length surplices with blue-edged capes assembled in the choir loft in five rows. The ceremony opened with a hymn entitled "Zanmei Yehehua" (Praise Jehovah) under the guidance of the conductor. After this, the choir members sat down as Head

Pastor Han, the host of the event, mounted the pulpit and led a responsive reading from the Bible projected onto two screens hanging from the ceiling on either side of the stage. Reverend Han read the chapter displayed and the congregation followed closely behind. After several rounds the reading drew to a close, the assembled guests stood up and sang the hymn from the *Amoy Hymnal* announced by Han. Throughout the service the choir sang hymns alternately in Mandarin and dialect.

After the scripture reading and prayer, Preacher (*chuandao*)[3] Yu went to the pulpit to deliver the main sermon, entitled "Sustaining the Glory." The church was founded in 1934. Yu reviewed the achievements of Trinity Church since the very beginning and identified it as a successor to churches built in Jerusalem and Antioch at the time of Jesus and the Apostles. It had been one of the first churches to reopen in China after the end of the Maoist era, initiating a new chapter in China's Christian history.

To illustrate the church's pioneering role over the past three decades, he listed some of its groundbreaking accomplishments: Trinity had been one of the first churches in China to reestablish its young adult fellow-ship, youth fellowship, and children's Sunday school after 1979. Yu stressed that these seemingly ordinary activities were in fact bold and trailblazing in those particularly uncertain times. He said, "Under extremely difficult conditions, we took that courageous step. This had proved to be unimag-inable and too extreme for other churches three decades ago. Today, history is again pushing Trinity Church to the forefront. We are now experienc-ing difficulties that other churches will find themselves confronted by. We are crossing the river by feeling the stones (*mo zhe shitou guo he*) and will share our experiences and pathways with fellow churches, just as we did thirty years ago."

Rather than emphasizing the early years prior to 1949, Yu's sermon was focused on Trinity Church's experience since 1979 and on the present chal-lenges it was facing. Interestingly, the change in the ferry policy was one of the specific difficulties he mentioned. He concluded, "We need to change. This is a prosperous time but also a turning point. . . . The environment is forcing us to make changes. Our historic mission is to keep the torch of the gospel alight."

After Yu had completed his sermon, Pastor Han briefly mentioned the situation in which Trinity Church found itself, using the words "change," "challenge" and "crisis." Her words reflected a self-evident problem facing the church: "The elderly [members] have moved to Heaven and the young [members] have moved to Xiamen [Island]."

Fig. 9 Old photos of Trinity Church in the showcase. Photo by author.

The morning ceremony closed with a prayer by the chairwoman of the Xiamen TSPM and a benediction given by Pastor Wen Yihan, a retired but still widely respected pastor of Trinity Church whose life story is described below. The church committee had prepared a simple lunch for each participant: one bottle of Coca-Cola, a steamed stuffed bun, and a rice cake. One by one, people collected their lunch from the church workers and ate as they stood in the yard or sat in the church. Many people gathered in groups to chat with visiting relatives or friends who had traveled from far away to attend the service. I came across a few people I knew and had a quick lunch with them as they discussed recent events in the Christian community.

An exhibition of old photographs had been set up in the basement as part of the event. It apparently reveals the suffering of Trinity Church and its members during the Cultural Revolution. It includes photos of Lu Zhuying, the first head pastor of Trinity, who died in 1966, a turbulent year; Bibles preserved by Reverend Chen at the risk of being persecuted during the Cultural Revolution; photos of Ms. Wen, a nurse, with children; and of the faithful who, in their youth, had taken part in clandestine gatherings together at Ms. Wen's place, reunited for a photograph to commemorate their years of hardship; Preacher Shao Youwen after her release from prison in 1974. People milled around the showcases displaying pictures of the church in the early Communist era.

Around 1:30, after lunch, the praise service commenced with a hymn and a prayer. People had a little more room to make themselves comfortable as some had left. Performers already made up and in costume were sitting in the front rows. During the prayer a religious affairs official, escorted by Head Pastor Han, took his place in the first row, to my front left. He and all the people in the nave stood until the prayer was finished.

The first guest to give an address was an American representative of the RCA. A deaconess translated his short message into Mandarin Chinese. On behalf of the RCA, the American guest of honor presented the church with a gift, a tablet bearing the inscription "The Reformed Church in America celebrates with Trinity Church God's faithfulness in its 80 years of witness and service." The audience clapped respectfully when he finished.

When the religious affairs cadre was led onto the stage, some of the audience murmured their displeasure. I checked the program but could not find his name. He had not been expected and his speech was added to the schedule at the last minute. I was quite aware that, after being reopened in 1979, Trinity Church was wary of inviting government officials to attend any public event. Nevertheless, the official's speech proved to be quite welcome; in fact, some of the Christians in attendance even characterized it as "spiritual" (*shuling de*).

In his five-minute speech, given without any notes, the official cited Bible verses or used a Christian vocabulary (key words or sentences underlined below) at least ten times. Moreover, he did not focus on the role of the state or religious regulations; instead, he emphasized faith and fused state narratives and Christian beliefs into a natural whole. For instance, by interpreting the verse "But everything should be done in a fitting and orderly way," running the church according to the laws and regulations, he deliberately mingled biblical teaching and the state narrative of religious governance.

> The status and role of Trinity Church is irreplaceable in Xiamen Christian circles. The reasons for its fruitful accomplishments are three-fold. First and foremost, it is the care of the faithful by the dedicated clergy. They distribute timely spiritual sustenance (*ling-liang*) and always offer fragrant manna (*xinxiang de ma'na*)[4] from the pulpit. Secondly, [the church committee] organizes religion in

accordance with laws and regulations (*yifa yigui banjiao*), and with the teaching, "But everything should be done in a fitting and orderly way."[5] To satisfy the need for self-reliance, Trinity Church establishes and improves various aspects of the regulations and rules, and organizes religion according to legal requirements. This guarantees an orderly operation of the whole church. Thirdly, Trinity Church serves society. Apart from the [church-management] work, we should be actively engaged in social welfare charities,[6] following the teaching of Scriptures: "Be careful to do what is right in the eyes of everybody."[7] Our Trinity Church has been engaged in charity work for years. There is a verse from the Bible: "Is not wisdom found among the aged? Does not long life bring understanding?"[8]

Our Trinity Church has eighty years of rich historical experiences and a wealth of understanding of how to organize religion. In the future, on the foundation of its experience and achievements, may Trinity Church follow the principles of self-governing, self-supporting, and self-propagating. May it carry forward the fine tradition of "loving the country and loving religion" (*aiguo aijiao*) and act as the light and salt (*zuo guang zuo yan*) of the world. We should continue to guide the faithful in dealing with the heavenly mission (*tianguo de shiming*) and with citizenship in the proper way, with spiritual life (*shuling de shengming*) and with real life, hope of the afterlife (*laishi de panwang*) and responsibility in this life, and the themes of faith and life. We should guide the faithful better to serve and contribute to society. We should also promote the positive functions of Christianity, counting among them humane care, ethics and social responsibility, alongside economic development, cultural prosperity and social harmony. Finally, I wish you all, the pastors, the faithful and friends, peace and joy (*ping'an xile*). I hope Trinity Church will stay young forever. Thank you all.

A 298-page history book entitled *Trinity Church 1934–2014* was featured in the anniversary celebration. Although it is nominally a collective work by the church, the actual author is Ma Zhenyu, a retired engineer and member of the church's literary group, who shared his experiences during the writing process with those attending.

Following Ma, Pastor Wen Yihan opened his speech on a very high note: "Today I am filled with thanksgiving and joy." Even though he is now in his eighties, Wen's voice is quite resonant. His opening received a big round of applause, and during his address the audience broke into rapturous applause several times. His account of the history of Trinity Church and its former prosperity touched the audience, bringing memories to life.

During the remainder of the afternoon, the church's Sunday school children, youth fellowship, Enoch Choir, and other groups performed as billed on the program. After the celebration, those attending were called to join in a group photo, standing on the doorstep of the main church building. Afterward people drifted away one by one and the compound gradually emptied. Honored guests were invited to enjoy a feast in the company of some members of the church committee.

To make sense of church members' nostalgia for Trinity Church's glorious past, I will elaborate on the church's history, especially the difficult years of the Maoist period, and the church's influence in the reform era.

The History of Trinity Church

After Christianity arrived in Xiamen in 1842, churches were built throughout the city, among them three of the main churches, the New Street Church, the Bamboo Church, and the Xiamen Port Church (Xiagang tang). In the early 1930s, the New Street Church had a congregation of more than three hundred members, the Bamboo Church had four hundred, and Xiamen Port Church had a few hundred.

At the time, more than three hundred members of these three churches resided in Gulangyu.[9] The Gospel Church (Fuyin tang) had been built specifically for Chinese believers on the small island in 1903, but it could not accommodate the growing Christian population. Furthermore, from an ecclesiastical perspective, the New Street, Bamboo, and Xiamen Port churches were all part of the RCA and PCE union, but the Gospel Church was established by the LMS. Christians living in Gulangyu were rather reluctant to attend the Gospel Church, in part because of its different church structure and history.[10] Those who retained an affiliation with the other three churches had to take sampan boats to Xiamen Island for church services at the weekend. Sampans were the most common means of transport between Xiamen and Gulangyu islands until the ferry terminal opened in 1937, and the commute was extremely inconvenient, particularly in windy or rainy weather.

In 1928, the Bamboo Church invited New Street and Xiamen Port to establish a joint church on Gulangyu to cater to the ever-increasing needs of church members there.[11] Shortly afterward a church building committee was founded. The new church under construction was named Trinity Church, both to indicate that it was being built by the three churches together and as a reference to the doctrine of the Trinity.

After years of fund-raising, the building committee collected eighty thousand Chinese silver dollars (*yinyuan*) in donations toward the construction of the new church, only eighteen thousand of which came from foreign missions. Ground was finally broken on October 24, 1934. Architect Lin Rongting (1901–1998) had initially drawn up a blueprint for a building that would seat five hundred people, but after he left for the United States, members of the church building committee—whose architectural knowledge could have fit on the back of a postage stamp—recklessly expanded the scale of the foundations without Lin's knowledge in order to accommodate a congregation of up to one thousand people. After some speedy construction work, the main structure was finished in March 1935, but the roof was not completed until the summer of 1936.

One month later, Trinity Church hosted the month-long Second National Bible Assembly, where more than two thousand participants studied the Old and New Testaments under the guidance of Dr. John Sung (Song Shangjie, 1901–1944).[12] In spite of its reckless expansion, the building survived, and even today Trinity Church is renowned for its magnificence and grandeur.

In May 1935, Lu Zhuying (1880–1966), the principal of a Christian school on the island, was elected the first head pastor of the church. Before the main building was roofed, he preached to the congregation in the assembly hall of the Lok Tek Girls' School (Yude nüzhong). In the early years three to four hundred Christians would attend Sunday services.[13]

Before the ceiling and decoration of the main building were completed, the Japanese occupied Xiamen Island on May 10, 1938. Tens of thousands of refugees fled to the Gulangyu International Settlement seeking shelter. Trinity Church became a sanctuary for a large number of refugees. However, on December 8, 1941, after the outbreak of the Pacific War, Gulangyu as well was invaded by Japanese troops, and Pastor Lu Zhuying was jailed for ninety-three days.[14]

In October 1945, Xiamen and Gulangyu islands were both retaken by the Nationalist government. The church committee decided to raise money to continue construction, the ceiling and the walls requiring the most work. The civil war between the Communist and Nationalist parties was in full swing and Nationalist rule crumbled in mainland China. The war inched

104

closer to Gulangyu, and eventually Xiamen became one of the final battle-fields between the two forces. Aware of the Communists' attitude toward Christianity, church members were concerned that the dedication would not be possible after a Communist victory. Consequently, on the morning of July 10, 1949, thirteen years after the church had first been used, they held a hasty dedication ceremony. Their tense joy was punctuated by bursts of gunfire not far away.

During this period, hundreds of Gulangyu church members fled abroad in fear of the Communists and later became an important source of financial aid in the reform era. Though the Communist revolution ended in 1949 with the establishment of the PRC, the suffering of Trinity Church was only beginning.

When the Communist victory was achieved in Xiamen, Pastor Lu Zhuying had just turned seventy. Pastor Zhang Hanqing (1903–1992), Lu's assistant, was in fact responsible for church affairs. At first, compared to the corrupt Nationalist Party officials, the highly disciplined Communist army and cadres made a positive impression on the church members, who did not yet suffer any obvious oppression. Trinity Church held Christmas and Easter concerts in 1949 and again the following year, reports of which even appeared in local official newspapers. Every Sunday some 440 believers came to the service.

With the outbreak of the Korean War, a nationwide Christian Three-Self Reform Movement (renamed the Three-Self Patriotic Movement in 1954) significantly reshaped the development of Christianity in China, drawing it into a patriotic and anti-imperialistic united front. When the movement's Xiamen preparatory committee was set up, Zhang Hanqing became a part of it. Shortly afterward, a series of rigorous investigations into churches was launched. Lu Zhuying and Zhang Hanqing were required to fill in a great number of forms on behalf of Trinity Church dealing with political censorship as well as reporting progress in work and political thought. Over and over again, they were instructed to confess their association with imperialism and disclose "reactionary elements" (*fandong fenzi*) hidden in the church.[15]

In early April 1952, the cross was removed from the church's central stage. It was replaced by the national flag of the PRC, which was hung up under official instructions to "love the country and love religion." As of July 1957, during Sunday services, pastors were required to read materials assigned to improve the congregation's "political consciousness" (*zhengzhi juewu*). This aroused widespread discontent and embarrassed the clergy.

Fig. 10 The Easter celebration in Trinity Church in 1957. Note the PRC's national flag.
Courtesy of Xiamen Trinity Church.

The church building was often used for mass meetings. Its report to the authorities in 1951 shows that the number of regular churchgoers was over 600; 328 of those members did not reside in the Xiamen area (mainly abroad).[16] According to a brief report by then incumbent Preacher Wen Yihan, published in 1957 in *Heavenly Wind* (*Tianfeng*), the official journal of the national TSPM, there were over 800 adherents registered with Trinity Church and more than 400 people regularly attended Sunday services.[17] In half a decade, nearly 200 members had gone, mainly for political reasons.

After the Anti-Rightist Movement, two decades of suffering engulfed Trinity Church. As described further below, Pastor Wen Yihan (then a young man), two church committee members, and four lay Christians were labeled rightists. During that period, pervasive government surveillance stretched people's nerves to the limit.

In 1958, the authorities promoted united worship, forcing Christians of different denominations to merge. The Gulangyu government initially intended to merge Trinity Church and the Preaching Church (Jiangdao tang), another small church on the island, with the Gospel Church. By all accounts, there were two reasons for this: on the one hand, the government was seeking a way to expropriate the huge Trinity Church building to use it as a people's assembly hall; on the other hand, it was located near the seat of the district government, and the peal of church bells irritated the atheist cadres.

However, in September 1957 Head Pastor Zhou Qingze (1916–1964) of the Gospel Church was criticized as a rightist for publicly condemning the government's religious policy.[18] With the head pastor labeled a "reactionary," in the eyes of officials, the church he led could not be innocent. In contrast, Zhang Hanqing was unobtrusive and barely uttered a word in public against cooperation with the government. Furthermore, authorities were aware that they still needed Zhang, then vice-chairman of the Xiamen TSPM, to unite the Christian communion. Thus, instead of being incorporated into the Gospel Church, Trinity Church expanded to host the other two congregations.

The size of the congregation should have grown as members of the two other churches joined Trinity, but instead, many members left in fear of persecution, and the church became virtually economically unsustainable. In 1966, as the Cultural Revolution swept over Xiamen, Red Guards targeted Trinity Church under the slogan of the "complete elimination of any traces of imperialist aggression." The church was shut down, and the building was confiscated to serve as an assembly hall for the Gulangyu District People's Government. While Red Guards attacked and destroyed religious buildings in many other parts of China, the appropriated Trinity Church building escaped nearly unharmed, although Red Guards did smash the three large characters giving the church's name above the main entrance and foundation stone. In stark contrast to Trinity Church, the compound of the Gospel Church was turned into a factory workshop and gradually fell into disrepair. Its property was not restored until 1987.[19] Lu Zhuying died on October 8, 1966, several months after the launch of the Cultural Revolution, his file still under a cloud of suspicion for "reactionary thought" (fandong sixiang).

After Mao's death, when Deng Xiaoping announced the beginning of the new reform policy, Christians throughout China began to form congregations and hold public services once more. On October 28, 1979, the reopened Trinity Church held its first Sunday service; the nave was packed. Although any kind of public announcement was forbidden, the news spread rapidly by word of mouth. It was clear that people had not abandoned their Christian beliefs. During the turbulence of the Cultural Revolution, their worship actually went underground, only to surface as soon as more relaxed religious policies were implemented. History tells us that repression does not necessarily cause the decline of Christianity; on the contrary, it can lead to its growth.[20]

On the basis of the religious market theory, Fenggang Yang has proposed a triple-market model indicating that the heavy religious regulation in Chinese society cannot necessarily eliminate or reduce religion. In fact, he argues that extremely strict regulation might make the religious scene more complex by forcing religious groups and believers to take refuge in the "black and gray markets" for religion, akin to a black market in contraband goods during times of rationing and shortages.[21] Another consequence of harsh government repression in China, still understudied, is the way it has shaped the collective memory of a generation, profoundly affecting their religious practices and church-related politics.

In the early reform years, the climate changed from eradication to limited tolerance, yet government policy largely confined the church to reinstating church activities, in particular those for young adults. Although the post-Mao state nominally reaffirmed freedom of religious belief, the Communist Party still regarded religions as competitors for the minds of the next generation, and therefore the government tended to prevent minors below eighteen years old from participating in religious activities. In fact, in the early years after churches reopened, Sunday school in Xiamen was strictly prohibited. Even so, Trinity Church took the lead in reinstituting a children's Sunday school and a youth fellowship.

The church choir frequently made trips to visit churches in Southeast Asian areas, including Singapore, the Philippines, and Malaysia, as well as Hong Kong and Macao. Members of Trinity Church who had fled abroad before October 1949 created a bridge with overseas Chinese Christian communities and contributed enormous amounts to the Xiamen church during those financially difficult times. For instance, when the New District Gospel Church was built in Xiamen in the mid-1990s, 87.5 percent of the cost was borne by Chinese Christian communities in Southeast Asia.[22] Religious affairs authorities strictly prohibited religious organizations from accepting foreign funds, but under the pastoral leadership of Wen Yihan, Trinity Church was able to make it possible.

Trinity Church reached its peak in the 1990s with over two thousand registered members, of which around one thousand regularly attended Sunday services. It has been deeply involved in social welfare projects and assisted other churches within and beyond Fujian, part of the burgeoning trend of Christian philanthropy. The Lily Garden Retirement Home, financed and managed by a church member and located in the island's old Gospel Church building, was once selected as a national-level model unit. Trinity Church took swift action on the second day of the devastating

NEGOTIATING THE CHRISTIAN PAST IN CHINA

108

Sichuan earthquake in 2008 and participated in the reconstruction of local churches as well as training clergy in the region affected by the disaster. According to Reverend Wen, during the past three decades church-run charitable foundations have contributed more than one hundred million RMB to other churches nationwide.[23] Members of the church frequently go to remote regions to help their counterparts develop their ministries for the young and the elderly, as well as to train clergy.

In the aftermath of the Japanese invasion, civil war, and Communist political movements, Trinity Church's belfry and parsonage were not completed until 1948 and 1992, respectively. The main entrance was built in 2000, completing construction sixty-six years after the church was first established. In over eighty years the church has held only two anniversary celebrations, one in 2004 for its seventieth anniversary, and the most recent one, which I attended, in 2014. It is unquestionably one of the leading churches in Xiamen, perhaps even all of Southern Fujian.

To achieve a deeper understanding of the past glory the church members cherish, we now turn to the instrumental role of a key pastor, a bold and experienced church leader, Wen Yihan.

The Story of the Old Pastor

The struggles and successes of the church were evident in its eightieth anniversary celebration, in the memories of many of its followers and leading figures who were present that day, but nowhere are they better illustrated than in the figure of Pastor Wen Yihan, affectionately known by his flock as the "Old Pastor." In our first meeting, several days after the celebration, he spoke about what the church can look forward to, yet his own story, as I learned when I met him, was a complex litany of tribulations.

I had first met Pastor Wen on a hot, humid afternoon in early March 2014. He was sitting across the table from me and had made tea in a big plastic cup, which he then poured into two smaller cups, one for me and the other for Ma Zhenyu, a retired engineer who studies church history (described further in chapter 4). Ma opened the conversation by referring to my studies at Xiamen and Leiden universities, as well as the purpose of our visit. I smiled and nodded to show my agreement and appreciation, but meanwhile I was studying the man in front of me. I soon took my eyes off the Old Pastor to avoid seeming impolite.

The cup for tea-making was no longer transparent, stained from years of tea-making. I wondered if the stains could ever be washed away. Southern Fujian people are well known for their strong preference for tea—for example, Tieguanyin (Iron goddess of mercy), a premium variety of Chinese oolong tea—and the pleasure they derive from making it. They often have exquisite tea sets in their homes or places of work. It is the time-honored custom of the region to entertain guests with carefully prepared tea, so it is quite rare to see someone making tea like this in a plastic cup.

The Old Pastor is of unremarkable appearance and medium build. Although in his eighties, he was still in excellent health. He is so full of energy and speaks in such sonorous tones that he still impresses the congregation by delivering sermons without a microphone. In his deep voice, he calmly related his life history.

Pastor Wen's Early Years

Wen Yihan was born into a Christian family in Xiamen in 1930, four years before the founding of Trinity Church, where he has served for most of his life. His fate was destined to be intertwined with the momentous political and social changes that have affected China over his lifetime.

When the People's Republic was founded in distant Beijing, Wen was a nineteen-year-old apprentice in his uncle's dental clinic and an active volunteer in the Stream Church (Xiaoxi libaitang) in nearby Pinghe County, where he was placed in charge of the youth fellowship and choir. Pinghe, an early mission center, has achieved a prominent position in Fujian's Christian history. During the first few months after the People's Republic was founded, church members in Pinghe celebrated the long-awaited peace, unaware of the suffering that lay in wait for them.

There were no signs of any harassment against Christians until the sudden arrest of five church members late one night in 1950. Among the five, one was a pastor and school principal; the others were elders and deacons. The next morning, all of them were executed for "colluding with the enemy and countering the revolution" (*tongdi fan geming*). Subsequently, the Stream Church was raided by public security authorities and forced to close. The government would rehabilitate these five executed people several years later, and evidence proved that the pastor should actually have been commended, as he was reported to have had contact with the clandestine Communist organization and made a valuable contribution to the county's "peaceful liberation" (*heping jiefang*).

110

As the church was shut, Wen went into the countryside to lead house worship. He says he was so young and inexperienced that he did not even know how to preach to a congregation, so he confined his activities to teaching peasants to read the Bible and sing hymns. "Thanks to my inability to preach," Wen smiled and continued, "I was not arrested for 'counterrevolutionary activities,' although I was later told there were two plainclothes policemen following me."

In 1953, the Yanjing Union Theological Seminary and the Nanjing Union Theological Seminary held entrance examinations. Wen was eager to study at Yanjing, which he felt was more "spiritual" than Nanjing, as he put it, but he could not afford the transportation costs, tuition fees, and living expenses. In a stroke of luck, he met Zhang Hanqing, then head pastor of Trinity Church. Zhang took a liking to this young preacher who was serving in his hometown of Pinghe, especially appreciating his dedication to the church in such tough times. On Zhang's recommendation, the church committee agreed to sponsor Wen's theological education on the condition that he would serve Trinity after he graduated. Grateful for the sponsorship, Wen finished his studies at Yanjing and returned to Gulangyu in 1956.

That same year, Mao Zedong and the Communist Party launched the Hundred Flowers Campaign encouraging citizens to openly express their opinions on the new regime. Differing views and ideas for solutions to national policies were encouraged on the basis of Mao's famous expression: "Let a hundred flowers bloom and a hundred schools of thought contend" (*Baihua qifang, baijia zhengming*). The movement was designed to encourage the arts and stimulate the advancement of the natural sciences. In less than a year, in July 1957, this period of more liberal thought was abruptly terminated. The subsequent violent repression continued through the latter part of 1957, as the Anti-Rightist Movement was launched to root out those critical of the Party ideology and regime. Precisely at this politically charged time, Wen began his preaching mission in Trinity Church.

In the early years of Communist rule, the harassment of Christianity and Christians nationwide inspired a great deal of fear. Taking advantage of Mao's policy of airing their views, religious figures vented their anger and complaints. Wen says he protested at the time that the freedom of religious belief stipulated in the Chinese constitution was in fact nothing more than a useless flower vase on the table. He advocated that those who had been unlawfully killed should be immediately rehabilitated. He also wanted to do something about the present circumstances and future of the church youth.

The first hurdle to be overcome was that the youth were frequently mobilized to participate in agricultural production on Sundays, so they could not keep the Sabbath. The next problem was that the authorities encouraged young Christians who behaved extraordinarily well to join the Communist Youth League or the Party. This meant they were caught in a dilemma: those who refused the Party's offers were regarded as politically backward, while those who were recruited to political organizations were required to recant their Christian faith. The final stumbling block was that those who wanted to enter college needed to specify their religious background in political censorship procedures, and young Christians tended to be rejected.

Wen's complaints put him in a difficult situation. When the political tide suddenly shifted, he was denounced as a rightist. In the spring of 1958, the Xiamen TSPM spent approximately one month organizing Christian assemblies to specifically criticize Wen in the name of "consolidating a patriotic front," a typical mass movement under Maoism directed against those considered disobedient to the regime. On May 11, 1958, the *Xiamen Daily* (*Xiamen ribao*) published an article targeting Wen's "anti-Party fallacy," stating that Wen "is opposed to the religious sector's acceptance of the Party's leadership. He spread his fallacy that atheists cannot understand religion and will find it difficult to lead the religious sector."[24]

Wen was then sent to the countryside to undergo "reform through labor" (*laodong gaizao* or *laogai* for short). He was forced to participate in various infrastructural construction projects, building railroads, highways, saltworks, and a reservoir. On one occasion during the Cultural Revolution, Wen was paraded through the streets wearing a humiliating tall paper hat with a big wooden placard hung round his neck on a string, inscribed with the derogatory phrases "running dog of the American imperialists" and "ox ghost and snake spirit" (*niugui sheshen*), common slurs used against those who were targeted in the political campaigns of the time. Despite this public humiliation, he made no effort to give up his Christian activities: risking persecution, he safeguarded Bibles and circulated them among Christians, as well as organizing clandestine family gatherings at night.

The Old Pastor's Political Tactics

In the late 1970s, when Deng Xiaoping rose to power and effectively put an end to Maoism, the reopening of churches was put on the agenda. At the same time, those who had been wronged in Maoist political campaigns began to be granted redress. Wen resumed his service in the church. His twenty-two years of suffering political persecution had furnished him with extensive experience dealing with the authorities, a skill that would make him a resourceful representative of the Xiamen church. Telling me about his life experiences, Wen several times cited the Christian verse "As wise as serpents and as innocent as doves."[25] He insisted that church members need to master the tactics enabling them to deal with government officials; confrontation, he said, is not always the best option. Instead of avoiding contact with people from official backgrounds, as he had done in the Maoist era, Wen now takes pains to maintain a good relationship with the government. Nevertheless, this does not mean that he strictly observes religious regulations requiring him to report his activities to the authorities.

Wen outlined his tactics. One is to present officials with a fait accompli without any consultation or report beforehand (*xianzhan houzou*). For instance, in the early 2000s, Trinity Church began to establish branches on Xiamen Island and set its sights on Banyan Village (Rongcun),[26] a fishing village near the renowned Xiamen University. The authorities keep a sharp eye on church construction, and under current regulations it is not an easy undertaking. Before ground can be broken on the construction of a new church, believers need to obtain official approval of a venue for religious activity (*zongjiao huodong changsuo*) at the prefectural level, and thereafter consent from provincial Lianghui and religious affairs authorities.

To make the process easier, the church group decided to first establish a congregation rather than a registered church. Old Pastor Wen consulted with the director of the Xiamen RAB in private. Instead of giving a straightforward, unequivocal response, the religious affairs official told him this story: "There was a person who found rat holes in his house. It happened that his neighbor was constructing a new house. He asked a mason working at his neighbor's house for some cement to plug the rat holes. His direct request put the worker in an awkward position. The mason said, 'How am I supposed to answer you? You should have just taken some without letting me know it. Once you ask me for the cement, I have to ask my boss for permission.'" With this allegory, the Communist cadre was implicitly indicating that Wen could carry out his plans without a prior report. "It was an inspiration," Wen said to me. He realized that local officials would prefer to turn a blind eye to church activities and will avoid confrontation with the churches on the condition that ecclesiastical activities do not damage their political future. Therefore, in the absence of a written report, they can pretend they don't know what's going on.

Several years later, Banyan Village had built up a congregation of over two hundred young people. Wen then approached the official again and said, "Cooked rice cannot be uncooked" (*shengmi zhu cheng shufan*)—"What's done cannot be undone." The official was delighted to consent to their proposal for the construction of a church. When the city's Construction Bureau intervened in the plan, the religious affairs authorities even helped Pastor Wen with the approval procedures (for example, obtaining the state-owned land-use certificate). He found that in many cases individual officials were on his side. Unlike most church members, whether clergy or lay believers, who had poor views of religious affairs officials, the Old Pastor praised them highly, giving them the thumbs-up when he spoke to me.[27]

The Old Pastor is also proud of providing support to allow dedicated young people to study theology in seminaries in China or abroad. While there are many new converts, few of them have the opportunity to become officially recognized pastors, an imbalance found all over China.[28] There is a clash of authority between the Communist Party and Christian organizations about how seminaries should be run and what they should teach, offering an interesting insight into the Party's determination to keep the reins of institutional and ideological control firmly in its own hands. As Carsten Vala notes, political hurdles limit the expansion of Lianghui church leadership, "reflect[ing] both the Party's unease about Christianity's revival and its attempts to shape the future of that revival."[29]

To register at any state-sanctioned seminary in Communist-ruled China, an applicant must be affiliated with a registered church and supported by the church organizations. He or she has to be equipped with an official letter of introduction bearing the official seals of his or her affiliated church and local Lianghui. By screening religious motivation among candidates, the state strives to assure that only those with the appropriate outlook (i.e., political loyalty) are admitted to seminary training.[30]

This is the fly in the ointment, because it is precisely the insufficiency of educational opportunities in seminaries and the strict political screening that are opening the door to underground theological education and various types of foreign investment in training Chinese church leaders. Overseas seminary professors have certainly taught in China.[31] Over the past three decades, Trinity Church has supported six pastors and five preachers through this officially sanctioned channel, two of whom have obtained master's degrees in theology. Beyond the official (or "legal") channels, Trinity Church, in collaboration with overseas seminaries (mainly in the Philippines), has trained dozens of church workers.

Preacher Yu, who gave a sermon at Trinity Church's eightieth anniversary celebration, was educated in a Chinese-Philippine Bible seminary and has been awarded his bachelor's and master's degrees in theology. He is now registered in a doctoral program at a Chinese seminary in the United States. Yu has enjoyed plenty of recognition as an extraordinary evangelist and as the successor to Old Pastor Wen. However, his theological education in foreign institutions, rather than in an officially sanctioned seminary in mainland China, disqualified him from being a full-fledged minister of religion. The Xiamen Lianghui leaders, who had all received a "legitimate" theological education, refused to endorse his promotion, citing the official ordination rules. Undaunted, Pastor Wen negotiated with the religious affairs authorities. A cadre advised Wen to send Preacher Yu to register in a correspondence course at the Nanjing Union Theological Seminary, and consequently Yu was able to qualify for ordination after his certificate had been conferred. Wen's handling of the religious management cadres is by no means a unique case: in his ethnographic research on an urban church, Mark McLeister has found that church leaders' judicious handling of personal relationships with local officials paves the way for local-level religious policy implementation to be flexible, and consequently routine church activities are conducted beyond the remit of religious policy.[32]

As Pastor Wen told me, the Christian faith teaches its followers not only to be wise serpents and innocent doves but also to "be strong and courageous."[33] Though Pastor Wen is generally cautious and politic in his dealings with authorities, on one occasion he risked attracting the ire of municipal leaders to mobilize Christians in a public protest against plans to redevelop a Christian site.

In August 1992, an announcement giving notice of the expropriation of part of a Christian cemetery on Gulangyu was published twice in the *Xiamen Daily*. The land was scheduled to be taken over to form part of the Xiamen Overseas Chinese Subtropical Plant Introduction Garden. Relatives of the deceased buried there were required to claim their ancestors' remains within fifteen days. Those graves that were not claimed would be dealt with as if they had no owners.

The cemetery, which has around four hundred graves of pastors and lay believers, is immensely important to the Christian community. Some of those buried in the cemetery have been influential in local Christian history. Ye Hanzhang, one of the first two Chinese pastors ordained in the Xiamen area,[34] and Lu Gangzhang (1854–1928), who pioneered a romanized writing system for Chinese,[35] are both buried there. Many of the descendants of people buried in the cemetery have emigrated abroad but still maintain connections with the Xiamen church. Pastor Wen, on behalf of the Xiamen Lianghui, petitioned the Xiamen Municipal Government and the CPPCC Xiamen Committee and even went as high as the State Council of the PRC. Remarkably, the protest worked, and plans to take over the land were temporarily put on hold.

It is difficult to say why the government changed its plans. Perhaps their foremost concern was media coverage organized by overseas Chinese. Ye Zhiming, a grandson of Ye Hanzhang, published a critical comment in a Chinese-language newspaper in the Philippines. Because Xiamen was a significant *qiaoxiang* and an early Special Economic Zone, the local government was hoping to attract investments from overseas Chinese; consequently, its global image was of great concern.

Unexpectedly, however, the notice of expropriation appeared again in the *Xiamen Daily* on January 15, 1993. Besides officially petitioning the municipal leaders, this time Pastor Wen mobilized the Trinity Church congregation to stand guard over the cemetery to defend it against sudden demolition. Wen had informed the religious affairs authorities beforehand that he would take action to protect the church property. He asked church members to carry banners that read "Xiamen Christian Cemetery" and arranged for the church kitchen to prepare food for the guardians.

The collective Christian protest was reported to the mayor as a revolt against the Communist Party. When the municipal government contacted the RAB, the director was scared of being punished and blamed Wen for stirring up trouble. The irate mayor interrogated Wen harshly in a face-to-face encounter, asking him why he was opposing the Party and the government. Wen answered that what he was opposing was the expropriation of church property for the expansion of the Subtropical Plant Introduction Garden, not rebelling against the Party and the government. He reminded the mayor that the plan would greatly upset a large number of overseas Chinese and would certainly damage the international image of Xiamen; it might even threaten the political future of the mayor himself. Finally, after land deeds proving the church's ownership of the land were located, the municipal government compromised, agreeing not to requisition it.

The Old Pastor's tough stance in this event added to his formidable reputation. The challenge for religious leaders who interact with the Chinese state bureaucracy is balancing both vertical and horizontal ties. If the vertical connections, with government officials, are perceived as too dependent, the horizontal ties—that is, their rapport with lay believers—will suffer.

By standing up to authorities to safeguard the Christian cemetery, the Old Pastor was strengthening his horizontal connections at the risk of his vertical ties. Within the church, Old Pastor's actions enhanced his spiritual repute, demonstrating his belief that Christ, rather than the state, is the head of the church.

In fact, Wen has never wanted to stir up tension between the church or himself personally and the government. He attributes the hostility some officials display toward Christianity to their ignorance. Not one to point out a problem without offering a solution, he insisted that the government officials needed to be educated. Whenever he has visited churches in Southeast Asia, Europe, and Australia, he has invited one or two provincial- or prefectural-level religious affairs cadres to accompany the delegation and ensured that their expenses were covered by the foreign churches. The officials who benefited from free foreign travel appreciated Wen's invitations. In the early reform years, opportunities to see the outside world were few and far between, and although various authorities did organize tours for officials to participate in investigations abroad, opportunities of this kind often seemed to bypass officials in religious affairs, who actually have a rather limited status in the bureaucratic pantheon.

Wen's long-term strategy proved effective. Government officials who have been exposed to Christianity are friendlier to the faith and also realize that Christianity could be effective in maintaining ties between overseas Chinese and their ancestral lands. The current deputy head of the Xiamen RAB recalled a pleasant trip to Southeast Asia with the Trinity Church choir in 1995. At one point, the bus transporting the group had a flat tire and everyone was stuck by the roadside. The choir decided to hold an impromptu concert for some villagers as they waited for the tire to be repaired. Many choir members also saw this as an opportunity to evangelize the Communist Party member. The official asked some of the choir members if the tire trouble was part of God's plan, and they held a discussion with him about divine will, suggesting that the misfortune had actually created a pleasant memory. The official agreed.

Pastor Wen is undoubtedly a resourceful member of the religious elite, endowed with the talent to play a leading role in church affairs. He seems to possess a great inner power that allows him to exert an influence over the Christian community. His cultural advantage derives from his theological education at the Yanjing Union Theological Seminary, a widely accepted "spiritual" institution, considered to be streets ahead of the Nanjing Union Theological Seminary, which is regarded as too intimately connected to the authorities. In the wake of the decades-long interruption of theological education and pastoral training, the Xiamen Christian community, as elsewhere in China, suffered a shortage of trained clergy. After 1979, Wen's orthodox education imbued him with a sense of responsibility to revive not just Trinity Church but also Christian churches throughout Xiamen.

His social relationships with the government and other church communities within and outside of China have also been apparent in the past decades. Wen first took the position of secretary-general of the Xiamen TSPM in 1988 and was promoted to vice-chairman of the Xiamen TSPM and vice-president of the Xiamen Christian Council in 1993. He later held leading positions in Lianghui organizations on both provincial and prefectural levels. All of these posts have enabled him to participate much more widely in Christianity-related affairs. In the 1990s, he was even put on the standing committee of the CPPCC Xiamen Committee and selected as a deputy of the People's Congress of Gulangyu District.

As Wen said, he received "orientation trainings" before he was appointed to the Lianghui leadership. For instance, he attended three months of courses at the CCP's Central Socialism College in Beijing and visited Communist revolutionary bases such as Ruijin, Jinggangshan, and Gutian. Wen's influence was perceived and respected within the social structure in which multiple actors were involved. Within the Xiamen church community, he is usually referred to as the "Old Pastor" out of respect not only for his advanced age but also because of his prestige. A greater and greater number of churches and pastors both at home and abroad come to seek his protection. For instance, a Chinese American evangelist sought Wen's assistance when he was under police investigation in an inland province. Wen repeatedly emphasized his protective role as a kind of umbrella for clergy who are in trouble.

Wen's status and reputation peaked around the beginning of the new century. His influence over the Xiamen Christian community originated partly from his two decades of suffering, a common theme in many studies of China's Protestant and Catholic communities. In their studies of Catholics in North China, both the sociologist Richard Madsen and the historian Henrietta Harrison point out the centrality of the virtue of loyalty to the faith in the moral imagination of Catholics, and that those who uncompromisingly opposed the political regime in harsh political circumstances naturally claim moral superiority.[36] On the Protestant side, Alan Hunter and Kim-Kwong Chan show similar findings, stating that some Christians believe they have received more blessings from the Holy Spirit than other

Christians in China because they suffered more. Imbued with a strong sense of spiritual superiority, this notion has emboldened some of them to break

government regulations.[37]

One of Wen's contemporaries, Yang Enli (1928–2011), a female church worker who was condemned to imprisonment and "reform through labor" for sixteen years, strongly opposed the state and the official TSPM and built a noted house church after the Cultural Revolution (see chapter 4). During her lifetime, she despised Wen for serving a TSPM church and cooperating with the government. Yet in contrast to the church leaders in the studies mentioned above, Wen's suffering did not push him to oppose the secular regime; on the contrary, he has actively engaged with government officials and by so doing sought to expand the church's scope for action. His perseverance and faith during the Maoist era, which even the state recognizes as overly harsh, has garnered respect from local cadres as well as Christians.

However, the Old Pastor's interactions with the state have not been universally successful. At the turn of the century, in collaboration with Pastor Wen, a Chinese Christian community based in the United States organized church leadership training in Singapore and Hawaii. Wen was responsible for recruiting potential trainees and taking care of the domestic organizational work. Xiamen religious affairs officials were well aware of the plan but turned a blind eye until a third training session was reported to the SARA. When the SARA instructed the provincial religious affairs authorities to investigate, its Xiamen subordinates claimed they had not known anything about the transnational training. Although the American organizer had already reserved flights and hotel rooms for the trainees, officials strictly vetoed the training project, and Wen was given a stern warning.

Combined with Wen's successful interactions with local officials, it is evident that the way resourceful church elites deal with authorities through personal relationships can only be realized at local social levels. As soon as a higher state agency intervenes, the tacit agreement breaks down and, out of self-protection, local officials forsake their church contacts. Nevertheless, this instance reveals the differentiation between the central and local levels of government who regulate religion. In their interactions with the Xiamen Christian community, local government officials tend to function as members of local society rather than agents of state authority. In this sense, there is not such a clear ontological divide between the state and the Christian church. The study of the relationships between the state and church must take these concrete social realities into account.

Glory No More

"The Church Is Going Downhill"

The changes in any religion cannot be disembedded from the specific frames of time and space. To understand the changes in Christianity in general and Trinity Church in particular, we must refer to the role of the local changes on Gulangyu that touch upon how Christian practices are structured. Its economic exploitation has meant that Gulangyu has been losing its young, educated, and wealthy residents. Those who remain are disproportionately the aged, poor, and uneducated natives of the island. In the process of this social shift, thousands of street vendors and laborers have become "new islanders."

Although Trinity Church has done some work among the new residents (for instance, holding Bible classes), church members do not actually seem very interested in preaching the word of God to migrant laborers from poor inland provinces. Gulangyu (and Xiamen) natives generally view "new islanders" as being opposed to the "high quality" of native residents, and individual church members who are also members of the island community do not bother to conceal their disgust.

Looking at Christianity elsewhere in China, in Wenzhou, it is evident that "social differentiation is embodied in the practice of Christian space."[38] The emerging discourse of *suzhi* among Gulangyu Christians articulates a sense of urban elite subjectivity underpinning the development of Christianity there in the context of a highly commercialized economy. Present-day Christians seem to have forgotten the composition of the early converts who were drawn from underprivileged peasants and laborers. The past is selectively forgotten.

The upshot of the economic exploitation of Gulangyu is that Christianity in general and Trinity Church in particular are being confronted with an unprecedented crisis. Before the twentieth century, the ferry fare was RMB1, but later it was increased to RMB8. In fact, the increased fare was hardly a factor of significance to the island's church community. Every churchgoer might find it a headache to have to squeeze through the crowded alleys. In the 1990s, the church used to have a registered congregation totaling around two thousand people, of whom one thousand regularly attended Sunday services. In recent years, however, the number of registered members has decreased markedly to one thousand, of whom fewer than five hundred now regularly attend Sunday services.

As we were sitting in the pastors' office, Head Pastor Han was quite surprised when I repeated what she said at the ceremony: "The elderly [members] have moved to Heaven and the young [members] have moved to Xiamen [Island]." She smiled and turned the conversation to how she came to serve Trinity Church.

> The Old Pastor gave me a phone call and invited me. . . . When I decided to join Trinity Church in 2009, my fellow church workers advised me not to come as this church was going downhill. It was a pitiful sight! Only the choir and the children's Sunday school performed on stage at Christmas. The elderly members asked me where the young and middle-aged believers were, and why there were only two programs. They had no idea what was happening, but they knew there should be many acts in the Christmas show. Yes, I knew where they were; they had all left. . . . The youth fellowship had almost ceased to function. The young believers used to come to Gulangyu every Saturday evening around eight and had to return to Xiamen [Island] an hour later. It was almost midnight when they got back home. There are fewer than twenty members in the youth choir now. The aging problem is dangerous to our church. It is a crisis of some importance.

Early in this century the church committee became aware of the rapid drain of the congregation and set up three gathering points to retain adherents living on the main island of Xiamen. Despite the steps they have taken, the situation cannot be easily remedied. The first gathering point is situated in Banyan Village near Xiamen University and has developed into an independent church. The other two points are still nominally branches of Trinity Church but are essentially fully functional and able to operate independently. Even more importantly, their new followers are not aware of or interested in the connections with Trinity Church, their mother church. The branches on Xiamen Island have not maintained the members' affiliation and sense of belonging to Trinity Church effectively; instead, to some extent setting up the branches has widened the disconnection between the believers and their mother church.

The outflow of members definitely affected the anniversary celebration. The plan for the event was initially proposed in 2011, and the church members spent the subsequent three years working on the preparations. I received a formal invitation in May 2014 when I was staying in Xiamen.

The program attached to the letter of invitation revealed the forthcoming event would begin on the evening of October 24 and end on the morning of October 26. However, the program was later condensed into one day. The church committee rescheduled the event for fear of not being able to receive guests with all due ceremony. Subsequently, the event was reduced to an internal celebration and very few guests from outside the church were invited. The rescheduling affected my research plan. Considering Trinity Church a transnational community, with members scattered throughout Southeast Asia and North America, I had initially planned to investigate its transnational connections by interviewing the overseas Chinese Christians who are connected to the church.[39] The change in plan to hold a smaller ceremony and not extend many invitations meant that very few of the transnational members of the church attended or even knew about the celebration and, consequently, I was not able to talk to these members.

The impact of state on religions has attracted extensive academic interest. Of the five officially sanctioned religions, Buddhism and Daoism (its popular offshoots included) tend to draw the most attention, mainly in the light of the exploitation of religious venues in terms of tourism. Religions have indeed become a highly profitable business, and sometimes the stakes are very high. As religion-related activities help to strengthen and improve the local economy, local governments tend to lend a willing ear to and encourage religious revivals. By converting temples into tourist attractions, market-oriented tourism authorities interpose themselves in the planning and organization of temple activities. Relevant studies reveal that the government's overuse of religious sites for economic or personal purposes has intensified all sorts of contradictions. Although some temples have managed to avoid such state attempts at cooptation, others have reluctantly adapted, and some have been completely taken over.[40] Yet the state's economic exploitation of Christian sites is fairly rare compared to its exploitation of the sites of other religions, basically attributable to the fact that Christian sites do not generally attract non-Christian tourists. Instead, local governments often appropriate church structures in the name of protecting cultural heritage and developing international connections.[41]

Since government-initiated projects affect the state of Christianity on the island only indirectly, rather than directly targeting Christianity or any particular church, Trinity Church does not have a chance to prevent this and does not even know where it could complain or appeal. It has no choice but to comply with state projects, whose declared intention is to boost the local economy and thereby benefit the people of Xiamen. On account of this state intervention, Christianity on Gulangyu has been deprived of an equal opportunity to compete with the other churches on Xiamen Island.

The Reconfiguration of the Power Structure

The Old Pastor was one of the most influential pastors in Xiamen during the reform era. Under his care, Trinity Church became a leading church in the region. However, shrinking congregation numbers inevitably resulted in a reconfiguration of the power structure in the Xiamen church. Although the celebration was an internal event, the whole Christian community was well aware of it and those from other Xiamen churches or from abroad would have been welcome if they had come. In fact, the church committee did anticipate the arrival of other church representatives. As a deaconess said to me, "It would be inappropriate (*shili*) for other pastors not to appear." However, they did not make an appearance. Some were leading the Xiamen YMCA on a visit to Jinmen and hence were unable to be present, but other church leaders who were in Xiamen could surely have attended but chose not to.

After churches reopened from 1979 onward, Pastor Zhang Hanqing held the posts of vice-chairman of the Xiamen TSPM and vice-president of the Xiamen Christian Council. Pastor Wen then succeeded Zhang. As the representative of Trinity Church, he assumed leading positions in the Lianghui, CPPCC, and People's Congress systems. However, none of his successors at Trinity Church have ever been as influential. Head Pastor Han is certainly symbolically positioned in the leadership of the Xiamen TSPM as general vice-secretary, a largely honorific post with little real influence. No other member of Trinity Church holds any position in the Christian organizations. Contrary to the decline of Trinity Church, the Bamboo Church, and the New Street Church, two major churches on Xiamen Island, have been growing rapidly. Their congregations number more than five thousand and four thousand, respectively.[42] Now the leaders of these churches and the New District Gospel Church have taken over the leading positions in the Xiamen Lianghui organs. Trinity Church has gradually been marginalized in the local field of church politics.

This reconfiguration of the power structure within the Xiamen Christian community has also been promoted by the local authorities. As mentioned previously, the appearance of a religious affairs official at the anniversary event made some members uncomfortable, and the church committee was unwilling to report to the authorities that it was planning an event. Certainly the elderly and experienced Pastor Wen gained the respect of the cadres who often consulted him about how to tackle religious affairs. However, since Pastor Han has taken over the head pastoral role, the situation has begun to change. Han is very cautious when it comes to religious regulations and likes to report to authorities before activities are held; her approach is quite different from the way the Old Pastor worked previously.

Han made two decisions that aroused widespread discontent among members of the church committee. The roof of the main church building leaked when it rained. Old Pastor would have simply asked for the approval of the church committee, then directly asked roofers to make the repairs. However, because the church building had been classified as a cultural relic, Pastor Han's first step was to report the problem to the Gulangyu Management Council. Once government officials had been apprised of the situation, the church committee could not carry out the repair work before receiving official approval. When the 2014 anniversary was held, the church still had not been granted permission to make the repairs, even though it had been nearly two years since the application for renovation had been submitted. Since the church compound was recognized as national-level key cultural heritage site by the State Council in 2006, state power has penetrated church management in the guise of cultural heritage management. In 2015, three years after the repair plan was first submitted to them, the authorities did finally approve it and promised to cover the costs amounting to millions of RMB in the name of conserving cultural heritage. Han's formal report to the government saved Trinity Church a huge sum and helped assuage church members' discontent about her submission to the government. Nevertheless, it did not show that Han was more adept at managing church affairs or dealing with the officials than the Old Pastor was. Instead, it proved another example of the fact that providing funds was an easy way for the government to penetrate church affairs and influence church politics.

The postsocialist state resorts to well-constructed, rational bureaucratic structures and dispersive functional organs to guarantee that its authority is implemented. As Frank Pieke points out, "social management" in recent government rhetoric and action allows a considerable degree of pluralism while strengthening the leading social role of the Communist Party; in fact, the Chinese state is "both more powerful and resourceful and less direct and invasive."[43] Zhu Yujing's research on Christianity in Wenzhou demonstrates how state power penetrates the church by means of the public administration (for example, the registration system for land and property).[44] Contrary to its past dealings with the religious affairs authorities and city- or district-level governments, Trinity Church now has to interact with a range of different administrative departments: land resources, estate management, construction, city planning, tourism, and now even cultural heritage management and the like. The originally centralized state power has been dispersed, but church leadership is struggling to cope with interventions from every corner of the bureaucracy.[45]

Another decision made by Pastor Han was to extend an invitation to the religious affairs official, a step that was also in conflict with the church's long-standing tradition. Prior to joining Trinity Church, Han had served in the New District Gospel Church, whose leader is now the chairwoman of the Xiamen Christian Council. In that church, pastors do maintain contacts with government officials. When Han continued to work the same way as she had in her former pastoral service, members of the Trinity Church committee were dissatisfied. Some church members publicly blamed her: "Are you a government official or a pastor?" Pastor Han felt deeply wronged. During my talk with her, she suddenly asked me, "Do you think what I did was improper?" I was at a loss and did not know how to answer. Fortunately, she kept on: "The Old Pastor is so old that we have to respect him even though he does some things wrongly. He suffered from 'reform through labor.' He is capable of being in control of a situation. . . . However, I am not like him. Times have changed. We run the church in different ways."

As the Old Pastor gradually withdraws from the church community, Trinity Church is increasingly marginalized. For any one of Wen's successors, it will be a formidable task to regain the influence it once had, in particular for Head Pastor Han, who has modest qualifications. In our conversation, Han expressed her envy of the deaconess who translated the RCA representative's English address into Chinese, as well as of her fellow pastors and preachers who have bachelor's or master's degrees. She feels that she is at a disadvantage, having only studied in a two-year program in a provincial theological seminary and being unable to understand any foreign language. Moreover, in contrast to the Old Pastor, she lacks the skills to effectively make use of her vertical and horizontal relationships with both officials and church members and has become isolated and powerless. She has also been accused of incompetent leadership, sending her into a severe depression. I could imagine the complicated feeling she must have felt when the Old Pastor highly commended Preacher Yu's sermon from the stage on the occasion of the church's anniversary.

Han's respect for religious affairs authorities is completely understandable. Nowadays, agents of Christian churches are no longer passively subject to state dominance but actively take advantage of state power to gain social space and opportunities for development. It is in fact quite common to have government officials present at celebratory events in Xiamen church communities. Just weeks prior to the Trinity Church event, the same official had been invited to address a celebration held by the New Street Church. Although Reverend Han has failed to attract the support of her church, she has earned the trust of the state as an obedient "patriotic religious personnel" (*aiguo zongjiao renshi*). Paradoxically, it is her obedience and the consequent legitimacy conferred on her by the state that decreases her prestige among her fellow church workers and congregation members. Trinity Church now faces a transformation of legitimacy, as the retirement of the Old Pastor has opened up new paths for negotiation with the authorities.

Conclusion

The 2014 anniversary celebration was an opportunity for members of Trinity Church to review its glory over the course of its eighty years of existence and grieve about what they see as its dismal future. As I describe at greater length in chapter 4, they have put considerable effort into revisiting and inscribing the church's past by writing its history, yet the increasingly gloomy prospects for Christianity and for Trinity Church in Gulangyu seem irreversible to them. Church members might be unwilling to admit it, but they must know in their hearts of hearts that its former glory is a thing of the past. Yet however disheartening its prospects might be, Trinity Church is not passively accepting its glum future. The church committee has been working hard to retrieve its past glory by building branches on Xiamen Island and seeking the assistance of international Christian agencies, as I discuss in chapter 5.

Church members had prepared to commemorate the church's eightieth anniversary in full splendor for the previous three years, but eventually they held only an abbreviated ceremony that, although successful, was nothing out of the ordinary. For those who attended, it was no different from a typical church celebration held at Christmas or Easter. Therefore, I doubt that the celebration could propel participants into the particular historical time and space they so desired, not to mention making them become more engaged in the church's mission. However, if the members absorb the text, the writing of church history, as a form of inscribing practices in Paul Connerton's sense,[46] could contribute to memorializing the glorious past to a limited degree. Overall, a single celebration is insufficient to inscribe the past on people's memories, particularly in the rapidly developing modern world teeming with changes, making forgetting a characteristic of contemporary society.[47] In other words, Trinity Church might be successful in converting individual memories into a system of memory materials by collecting fragmented oral histories and making a book-length historical text; however, it is far less likely to be able to reconvert such a text into personal memories.

My postulation is that this anniversary commemoration will not help either to stem the irreversibility of Trinity Church's fate or to promote the closer integration of the congregation. The generational effects on collective memory must also be taken into consideration.[48] Just as I observed at the celebration, youth comprised a small proportion of the audience. As the elderly Trinity Church members gradually pass away, it is highly likely that collective memory will wither with them. If those who are alive fail to transfer their memories to the youth, the past of Trinity Church will soon be confined to the history books.

Chapter 4

WRITING AND CONTESTING
CHRISTIAN HISTORY

In Xiamen, in recent years, diverse interest groups have all shown a notable enthusiasm for producing historical texts linked to Christianity. While in past decades, writing about Christian history was within the purview of Marxist theorists or well-trained historians, it is now increasingly open to diverse players. This chapter examines the efforts of three distinct categories of actors engaged in writing Christian history: the government, churches, and amateur historians. A detailed analysis of how Christian history is produced in Xiamen reveals that state politics, historical agencies, and individual subjectivity (especially the psychodynamic dimensions of nostalgic sentiment) intersect in their official and unofficial efforts to create historical texts. It provides a basis from which to understand the state project of representing the past, where the mobilization of personal memories for historical reconstruction has paved the way for conditions under which competing versions can be expressed. To a certain extent, the emergence of unofficial or private narratives (for example, oral history) is challenging the grand master narratives of the state. Nevertheless, it is not my intention to put popular efforts in opposition to official accounts. In fact, the purpose is to show that the official production of history texts and unofficial efforts often mingle and cross-pollinate.

Shades of "Cultural Aggression"

128   Since it was founded, Christianity has been an evangelical religion, spreading and growing roots around the world. In some receiving countries or regions, the introduction of Christianity inevitably resulted in conflicts with existing traditions and, in some instances, upset the political and cultural status quo. Unquestionably, the spread of Christianity around the world in modern times was supported by the rise and rapid expansion of Western capitalism. The people in areas receiving Christian evangelism encountered not only the gospel but also the guns and privileges that came with it.

In China, an agricultural nation dominated by Confucianism, Christianity was treated as a "foreign religion" (*yangjiao*) that tested native sovereignty and the stability of its social structure. Christianity's encounter with the Chinese empire was intertwined with the relentless advance of Western imperialist powers in their nineteenth-century heyday. After the Opium War, the unequal treaties that were imposed on a defeated Qing China granted privileges to missionaries, giving them the freedom to preach and build churches in designated areas. In the Chinese view of history, these treaties became Christianity's "original sin." The stain of Christianity's association with oppression and imperialism could not be washed away. A consequence of this was the persistent criticism of "cultural aggression" leveled at Christian missionaries, which first gained ground as early as the 1920s, after the May Fourth Movement, and remains pervasive in official discourse even today.[1]

When the Korean War broke out in 1950, after the founding of the People's Republic, the image of Christianity worsened, and missionaries were categorized as enemy aliens. Research on missions in China was therefore made a restricted field, open only to officially appointed Marxist theorists for the purpose of constructing Communist ideology.

The year 1978 marked a new era not only for the economy of PRC and its foreign policy but also for the historical study of Christianity. Since then, constraints imposed from the top on research in the humanities and social sciences have been relaxed, and accordingly the study of Christian history has acquired its own space for development. Nevertheless, despite this relaxation, in the 1980s it still remained difficult to find a publisher for research that was not wholly critical of Christianity.

Change crept in in the 1990s, and a small number of well-received works of research written from the perspective of cultural exchange, education, modernization, and globalization were made available.[2] Since the turn of the twenty-first century, dozens of books have been published on mission-ary contributions to the modernization of China.

Since Xi Jinping and his administration rose to power, political constraints on social scientific studies of religion, especially those related to Christianity, have been reinforced. While empirical research on contem-porary issues faces more restrictions, space for Christian history is more available. Yet the restrictions are incomparable with those during the PRC's early decades.

Though some scholars of Christianity have attempted to depoliticize the discourse on Christianity, the complete elimination of political influence on either academic research or citizens' minds still does not seem feasible in the foreseeable future. The discourse of "cultural aggression" continues to prevail and is widely accepted in China even today. Although the govern-ment has permitted some publications, it has never made any considerable adjustments to its stance on foreign missions.

The Official Production of Christian History

When the Communist regime took over mainland China, it immediately initiated a national project to produce histories of the late Qing and Repub-lican eras. Although this endeavor was interrupted by the constant upheaval of political campaigns under Maoism, the official project fully resumed in the 1980s and led to the construction of a comprehensive set of grand historical narratives.

CPPCC Historical Projects

Zhou Enlai, then premier and chairman of the CPPCC National Commit-tee in the PRC, instigated the founding of the Historical Materials Research Committee (HMRC) in 1959 (eventually shortened to the Historical Mate-rials Committee, or HMC, in 1988). Shortly afterward, the government required provincial-, prefectural-, and county-level CPPCC organs to estab-lish HMRCs. The system, which featured "political consultation" and "unity of peoples," officially aimed to "reposition history" (*cunshi*), "benefit the government" (*zizheng*), "unite all walks of life" (*tuanjie*), and "educate the people" (*yuren*). Under the CPPCC system, senior deputies were invited to contribute firsthand retrospective accounts of their lives that were published sporadically in historical volumes. Though the subjects were drawn from all walks of life, many were chosen for being well-known figures who had "personally experienced (*qinli*), seen (*qinjian*) and heard (*qinwen*)" significant historical events in late Qing and Republican China.[3]

This campaign of historical production was unquestionably shaped by the ideological landscape of early Communism. The majority of the contributors were former Qing or Republican government officials, intellectuals, and officers of the defeated Nationalist Party army who had lost their influence under the new regime. Subsequently, such figures became the targets of the Anti-Rightist Movement and the political campaigns that followed in its wake. Without a doubt, their historical writings were strictly supervised and were used to achieve particular political purposes. Produced under the discipline of the new regime, their historical accounts were usually reconstructed in such a way as to support the party-state's vision of history as well as to avoid stirring up any political trouble.[4]

The work of the CPPCC has been the most influential project to construct authoritative historical accounts and thus official memories of the past. The incomplete statistics available indicate that from 1960 to 1990, including the interruption of the Cultural Revolution, HMRCs on and above county level (known as HMCs since 1988) produced approximately 2,300 series of historical publications: specifically 13,000 volumes, consisting of 300,000 essays and totaling 200 million Chinese characters.[5] Although Zhou Enlai declared that "all things from the most backward to the most advanced should be recorded," the main purpose of the project was to expose the negative sides of the "old society" (*jiu shehui*), creating a perfect foil for the "New China."[6] Generally, the CPPCC framing of pre-1979 historical accounts emphasized the reactionary elements of the past, and its post-Mao historical work was required to "hold high the banner of patriotism."[7]

Under the aegis of the 1959 national history project, the CPPCC Xiamen Committee established its HMRC and in 1963 published two volumes of *Xiamen Historical Materials*. In these works, Christianity was criticized as an aggressive entity rather than as a tool of imperialist aggression. The second volume was a special issue covering the process by which Gulangyu was forcibly occupied and transformed into an international settlement. In this monograph, Gulangyu was denounced as a "vampire camp" from which the Three Missions based there "made massive incursions into the hinterland of Fujian Province."[8] Besides the vehement accusations of "cultural aggression" and "interference in China's sovereignty," moral discourses were often brought into play to censure missionaries or their mission work. John Otte, among others, was denounced as an "imperialist rogue" and a "hypocrite with an extremely ugly soul." To further blacken his name, he was also accused of indecent assaults on women, a sinful charge calculated to erode his identity as a morally upstanding missionary (see chapter 2).[9] The Xiamen historical accounts of Christianity were framed strictly within a logical and explanatory structure consistent with an overall state-sanctioned framework of national history whose purpose was to reaffirm the Party's uninterrupted historical continuity as a national liberator.

After only two volumes, the CPPCC Xiamen Committee's historical work was interrupted by the Cultural Revolution, during which hundreds of unpublished manuscripts totaling two million characters were destroyed.[10] Not until 1979 was the initiative resumed and those cultural workers denounced as rightists reinstated in their positions. Over the course of the ensuing two decades, twenty-one volumes of *Xiamen Historical Materials* were published. One 1980 publication again brought up the position of Gulangyu as an international settlement and particularly the dishonorable roles of church-run hospitals and schools in propagating "mental anesthesia."[11]

A noticeable trend began to emerge in some articles whereby anti-imperialist patriotic movements within mission schools were highlighted and in fact exaggerated. One example repeatedly cited to illustrate the existence of an anti-imperialist movement was an incident that occurred in the church-run Anglo-Chinese College one day in February 1914, when three students decided to teach a lesson to an Indian policeman who had been hired by the Kulangsu Municipal Council, forcing him to drink seawater.[12] It would be impossible to authenticate the incident as all the witnesses have passed away. It might possibly have been true if we take into account the widespread antipathy engendered by the privileges and arrogance of the foreigners, though the incident occurred in February 1914, much earlier than the well-known May Fourth Movement of 1919, which did so much to arouse anti-imperialist sentiments in China. Nevertheless, true or not, this sole incident could hardly be characterized as an anti-imperialist campaign or struggle; rather, it reveals how stories involving Christianity could be molded into patriotic narratives.

The seventh volume of 1984 contains two essays written by Christians introducing the New Street Church and Trinity Church. Though both articles opened with a criticism of the unequal treaties that missionaries and their cultural aggression relied upon, the descriptions that followed took a positive tone.[13] The following eight volumes published in the mid- and late-1980s benefited from a much more relaxed atmosphere in which historical accounts of Christianity could be produced. The 1987 volume focused on the fiftieth anniversary of the outbreak of the Second Sino-Japanese War. Two articles outlined the contributions made by church schools to the war effort, for instance their reception and care of war refugees.[14] Subsequently, official narratives of Christianity in Xiamen began to purposefully refer to Christianity's association with anti-Japanese efforts, with the aim of constructing a positive image for Christians as part of China's united front against Japanese invasion.

The two volumes of 1988 contained two articles describing Christian histories authored by the late Wu Bingyao, an influential church leader. In the first, he praises the efficient missionary work of the Three Missions.[15] In the second, he attempts to defend the position that Christianity had been mistaken for a tool for imperialist aggression, and it was not the missionaries' intention to become entangled with foreign imperialism. He tries to excuse the role of Christianity in imperialism by using rhetorical turns of phrase such as "directly or indirectly, consciously or unconsciously."[16] Superficially at least, the state requires its citizens to comply with official narratives, but it is also clear that it is possible to produce and publish alternative histories by making compromises, employing state discourse to admit Christianity's disgrace.

In the late 1980s, partly because of the events in Tiananmen Square in June 1989, the state introduced tighter ideological control. Against this backdrop, *Xiamen Historical Materials* released a special issue in 1990 (volume 16) criticizing the Gulangyu International Settlement where they launched a fierce attack on Christianity and mission hospitals and schools.

Yet in spite of this, the increasingly relaxed atmosphere for historical work has not been fundamentally reversed. The volume published the following year, the eightieth anniversary of the 1911 Revolution, focused on how Qing rule in Xiamen was overthrown, during which "many patriotic pastors and Christians were revolutionary activists" and Xu Chuncao, an influential Christian who claimed to have "only accepted Christ but not submitted to foreign command," often confronted foreign missionaries.[17] In another essay, the *Egret River News* (*Lujiang bao*), founded by a British missionary, was praised for "raising awareness of anti-imperialism and anti-feudalism" and consequently promoting the "bourgeois democratic revolutionary movement."[18] Since then, further volumes in the same series have applied a revolutionary discourse intended to buttress the legitimacy of the Communist regime.

Over the next few years, essays about Christianity assumed a much more positive tone, introducing numerous celebrities who were raised as

Christians or educated in church schools (see chapter 1). Political issues were avoided. The last volume, which came out in 2002, marked the end of the 1959 historical project. According to the former editor-in-chief, the major reason for the termination of the series was a shortage of manuscripts and a decline in readership.

Like the CPPCC National Committee's historical project, the Xiamen historical work relied on contributors who were typically part of the regime's united front work, including Republican government officials, intellectuals, and members of the religious elite who had experienced significant events firsthand. While they contributed valuable historical accounts, they were subject to the constraints of the particular political conditions of the time and had to cater to the mainstream ideology in their descriptions of the past, meaning that censored personal accounts were presented as legitimate historical work.

In the mid-1990s, another round of the national historical project was initiated. It was launched just at the point when Xiamen's economic prosperity was stirring up a passionate interest in the city's past and the government-led historical team proudly traced the origins of Xiamen City back to 1394.[19] The project resulted in the second extensive production of Xiamen history in the new century. Between 2007 and 2013, the CPPCC Xiamen Committee HMC published twenty-four monographs covering a comprehensive range of subjects including (but not limited to) religion, music, physical education, films, newspapers, and the women's movement. It was an official task and it was unquestionably finished in a hurry. The production's enormous scale turned history into an industrial product. From commissioning to publication, a particular book might be completed in the space of a few short months, leaving little time for research and writing.[20] The authors or editors were local experts and ordinary cultural workers, typically laypeople in their fields who lacked any kind of historical training and created "history" on the basis of hearsay. Professional historians and university academics kept their distance. The books that were churned out could hardly be regarded as serious works of historiography. Not to put too fine a point on it, they were hotchpotches essentially devoid of originality and academic rigor.

Using government funding, authorities produced a large number of copies and distributed them to citizens free of charge. In a nutshell, the government produced the city's history and managed to popularize it with adequate funding. To some extent, this gesture catered to citizens with feelings of nostalgia, especially those who lamented Gulangyu's excessive commercialization. As Le Goff argues, "[The quest for collective memory] amounts to a conversion that is shared by the public at large, which is obsessed by the fear of losing its memory in a kind of collective amnesia—a fear that is awkwardly expressed in the taste for the fashions of earlier times and shamelessly exploited by nostalgia-merchants; memory has thus become a best-seller in a consumer society."[21]

In historical production, nostalgic memory is often used to piece together the history of a locality, and this process accelerates the commercialization and rapid consumption of the local history. This is amply illustrated in the way Christianity has been commended as the most significant promoter of Xiamen's modernization, to the detriment of the people of Xiamen, whose contributions were underestimated or even ignored in historical works.

Nowadays it has become the custom to link Christianity closely to themes like schools and celebrities. A book on *Noted Musicians of Xiamen* lists twenty-one famous musicians, of whom seven were Christians and benefited from what the church had to offer, for instance through musical training. The book argues that the musical legacy of Gulangyu, which nurtured many great musicians, originated in Christianity. However, the volume makes a notable omission in its treatment of renowned soprano Yan Baoling (1924–1966), who committed suicide because of her unbearable humiliation during the Cultural Revolution. A history in a 2012 church publication, documented below, describes the way political persecution drove Yan to suicide:

> Because she was a sociable person, the Red Guards slandered her as a courtesan and hung a pair of worn shoes (*poxie*) around her neck as she was made to stand in front of the crowd.[22] One day, a group of fierce Red Guards came to the headquarters of the Young Women's Christian Association (YWCA) and confiscated all Bibles and faith-related books. They threw printed matter on the ground and burned it as the [YWCA] staff members knelt around the fire. Yan Baoling was the director-general and was therefore ordered to kneel at the very front. Her legs were burned. But this was not the end of [her] nightmare. A couple of days afterward she was ordered to accompany the Red Guards when they raided her house in Gulangyu. I did not dare to speak to her and could only watch silently. A few days later Yan jumped from the third story of the YWCA building.[23]

Yan's contributions to the music scene in Gulangyu made her a local celebrity, yet *Noted Musicians of Xiamen* only mentions her in passing, in a couple of sentences in a chapter devoted to her son, a fact that provoked widespread discontent.[24] The author intentionally ignores both her significance to the music scene and the growing sadness about her fate. Apparently, Yan's suffering and the political causes behind her suicide were not supposed to be mentioned in the historical work.

Since the Xiamen government decided to move forward with its application to be listed as a UNESCO World Heritage Site in 2009, the Gulangyu Management Committee has organized intensive historiographic production that has led to the publication of dozens of monographs. This has been an exercise in quantity, not quality, and the project has been almost totally devoid of any creativity or originality. The organizers did not cast a wide net; they invited almost exactly the same editors or authors as the previous works and used the same materials without looking for new evidence. At the time, the books were still intended for a lay readership, but the project as a whole was supported by public funds. Tens of thousands of printed copies were widely circulated free of charge. In the application for WHS, over ten of the fifty-three core heritage sites of Gulangyu were related to Christianity, including the Christian cemetery, church buildings, and church-run hospital and schools.[25] The authorities had not paid much attention to Christian sites before planning the WHS application, but after the decision to go ahead with it, the religious issue—Gulangyu's connection to Christianity—could no longer be overlooked. Though Christianity played an undeniable role in the modernization of Gulangyu, generally speaking the historical evaluation in the official document fails to acknowledge this.

In spite of the publication of so many works related to Christianity, so far there has been no official reevaluation of the religion. Kong Qinmai, the former editor-in-chief of *Xiamen Historical Materials* and a delegate to the CPPCC Xiamen Committee, told me in an interview that although the religious policy was now less constraining, the government has never made any considerable changes to the official discourse on Christianity. He remarked that at CPPCC conferences, Christianity is often raised in conjunction with the names of patriotic religious figures and patriotic activities, yet it is important to note that the government has never slackened in its efforts to train patriotic socialists who are actively opposed to Christianity. For example, in 1999, Gulangyu's Next Generation Working Committee edited a textbook to promote the cultivation of youth patriotism where the editors collect abundant evidence of imperialist guilt in Gulangyu and

Christianity's inglorious past. With the exception of some of the Western-style buildings built by missions, the textbook does not acknowledge any useful contributions from Christianity or Christian missionaries. The only positive note is the grudging admission that missionaries chose scenic locations for their buildings.[26] While the editors do their best to encourage young people to love their scenic island, they do their utmost to dissuade them from loving the religion that was so intertwined with its cultural and economic development.

The Special Gazetteer of Christianity in Xiamen: Three Decades of Failed Efforts

China has a rich tradition of local history writing. *Difangzhi* (*fangzhi* or *zhi* for short), often translated as "local gazetteers" or "local histories," have existed in China since ancient times.[27] The rise in the production of local gazetteers can be traced back to the Song and Yuan periods.[28] A complete catalog, including Taiwan, lists over eighty-two hundred extant editions of gazetteers that appeared before 1949.[29] There are long-standing debates over whether local gazetteers belong to the disciplines of history or geography.[30] When referring to the production of Christian history, Xiamen government officials and church leaders refer to a text of this kind as *zhi* (gazetteer), distinct from *shi* (history), as its purpose is to chronicle without commenting. However, they have never intended it to be considered a geographical document, and *zhi* essentially refers to a concise history. This section, therefore, outlines the special *zhi* project as a historiographic endeavor.

In early imperial history, a local gazetteer was compiled and published for three basic purposes: namely, to draw attention to a particular place, glorify the emperor, and express local pride. James M. Hargett states that by the Song Dynasty, which saw the production of many more gazetteers on both the local and the national levels than any previous era, the general trend was to adapt these publications more than ever before to serve political, administrative, and military ends.[31] Using gazetteers, ruling groups could educate themselves about the geography and customs of different regions or the histories of particular periods. More often than not, the dynastic states played an active role in the creation and production of local gazetteers, usually relying on the local gentry to compile and print these works.

Traditionally, the compilation of local gazetteers was decreed by central authorities and implemented by government officials in the localities. The most celebrated local literati and official scholars assumed responsibility for their compilation, while the government was supposed to be financially responsible for the process as a whole. Nowadays, in contrast, the government is the sole authority responsible for compiling and publishing local gazetteers. A constant theme running through contemporary gazetteers is the emphasis on the need to present first and foremost a correct ideological picture and positive evaluation of both the CCP in particular and the government record in general, simultaneously extolling China's great economic and social achievements. In compiling gazetteers, through routinized historiography, the Party imposes its will on official history and reinforces the legitimacy of its rule.

To guarantee the political correctness of a gazetteer, the compilation is required to abide by state regulations. In 1963, the Publicity Department of the CCP Central Committee, which is responsible for ideology-related work, issued a circular entitled "Various Opinions about the Compilation of Local Gazetteers," proposing a system of censorship to control the publication and distribution of such works. This guideline document prescribes that a draft of a local gazetteer shall not be published until it has been reviewed and found unproblematic both politically and in terms of the protection of national secrecy.[32] The purpose of the "Provisional Guidelines on the New Compilation of Local Gazetteers," issued in 1985, was to institutionalize and standardize the boom in the compilation and production of local gazetteers. This document was finalized in 1997 and released in 1998 as the official "Guidelines on Compiling Local Gazetteers." The provisions of the "Guidelines" stipulated that Marxism-Leninism, the thoughts of Mao Zedong, and the theory of Deng Xiaoping must be the guiding principles of any such work, and the administrative and editorial activities must be "guided by the CCP and undertaken by the government." "Political quality" was to be the principal feature in the gazetteer project. The regulation declared that compilers need to "pay special attention to the political quality of the gazetteers. Local gazetteers are not personal works, but 'political books' (*zhengshu*) or 'official books' (*guanshu*) of a highly political nature. . . . The view that gazetteers ought to be distanced from politics is wrong."[33]

Under Mao, the compilation of gazetteers was revived in 1956, but few works were published because of the continuous political disruption of the ensuing decades. However, since the 1980s, when China embarked on a fast track of economic development, gazetteer compilation projects have returned to the political agenda. As the saying goes, "The compilation of history happens in prosperous times" (*shengshi xiushi*). Thus, it should come as no surprise that during the economic upswing of the 1980s, the

Chinese government decided that the time was ripe for the compilation of new local histories.

National institutions on different administrative levels were in a position to provide fairly adequate political, human, and financial resources for the compilation and publication of gazetteers. On the national level, the China Steering Group for Local Gazetteers oversees offices or departments in provinces, cities, and counties. The Local Gazetteer Office is a regular government unit, responsible for the compilation and publication of gazetteers on its local administrative level. The office is often headed by the top local government leader. In 1981, the Chinese Local Gazetteers Association was founded, leading to a high point in the compilation of local gazetteers. The first round of gazetteer work was completed in 1990, and more than nine thousand had been compiled by 1992.[34]

Before initiating the compilation of a comprehensive gazetteer for a particular place, the local official gazetteer office encouraged people from all walks of life to put together their own. The corresponding authorities (for example, of education, industry, commerce, transport, or religious affairs) were responsible for supervising those that fell within their remit. In the late 1980s, the Xiamen RAB was assigned the task of compiling a gazetteer of religion in Xiamen and apportioned the writing to different religious organizations. The Xiamen Lianghui accepted the assignment and swiftly set to work. The project was largely managed by the Lianghui and supervised by RAB officials.

Old Pastor Wen, then the leader of the Lianghui, entrusted the project to Guo Qinghuai, a retired seminary teacher and who was still active in the Christian community, notably as a volunteer pastor at Trinity Church. In order to make up for deficiencies in historical sources, Guo Qinghuai visited libraries and archives in Fuzhou, Nanjing, and Shanghai. He also consulted references in missionary memoirs and sources such as the *Chinese Recorder* and the *Christian Occupation of China*. In the early 1990s, ideological restrictions in China were still strictly in place, and Guo's writing was required to follow the Marxist-Leninist view of history. During the writing process, he traveled to America to visit his children and decided to settle there, giving up the gazetteer project.

Guo's writing duties were later transferred to Luo Anping, an editor at the Anxi County Gazetteer Office and a close relative of the Old Pastor. In view of Luo's government work experience and the pastor's personal recommendation, Luo was considered politically reliable and transferred to Xiamen to undertake the assignment. He finished the gazetteer in 1993, but both the Lianghui and the RAB were dissatisfied with the manuscript. Luo, not being originally from Xiamen, was not very conversant with the Christian history of the area. As he was engaged in a government-sponsored project, Luo had been permitted to access archives, so he listed many events that had taken place during the various political movements of the Maoist era.[35] His description of the state oppression of Christianity and the role of the TSPM put both the RAB officials and Lianghui leaders in an embarrassing situation, since allowing the manuscript to be published would put them at risk of political repercussions.

After much toing and froing, the manuscript was finally rejected. Besides its many palpable mistakes, the principal objection to the manuscript was that it was excessively politicized. The church saw it as lacking spiritual content, while the government was stumped by the detailed descriptions of the repression of the Christian community, precisely what it was doing its best to erase from the collective memory. The project was shelved until the 2010s, and to this date it has still not been completed.

Though Luo's manuscript was not approved, part of it was adapted for a twenty-five-page concise history in the *Xiamen City Gazetteer* that omits the charge of "cultural aggression" and avoids pointing to Christianity's role in Western imperialism. This is not to say that the narrative is free of any political tone. The only official intervention mentioned is the Cultural Revolution, and it is referred to several times as the reason why churches were shut. However, no details are given about the political campaign, and the Cultural Revolution is used to cover all repression of Christianity. Blame is shifted away from the Party to the ultra-leftism associated with the Gang of Four.[36]

After three decades of attempts, the government has failed to compile a systematic, detailed history of Christianity in Xiamen. The vacuum of officially approved texts has unintentionally resulted in a negotiable field for alternative narratives. Nevertheless, official censorship procedures and strict government control of publications on Christianity conspire to create a difficult environment for these unofficial narratives.

Individual Efforts at Making Alternative Narratives

To commemorate the 150th anniversary of the RCA mission to China, a history book entitled *The Reformed Church in China, 1842–1951* was published in 1992. It provided a detailed description of Xiamen's historical landscape. When three printed copies were brought to Xiamen, the book aroused great interest among local history experts.

In 2000, Yao Deming, a retired engineer, voluntarily assumed responsibility for the book's translation and publication. This proved to be extremely challenging for Yao, who never completed middle school and does not understand English. He finally turned to a university lecturer in English-Chinese translation for help and devoted himself to collecting old photographs and identifying proper nouns (that is, names of people and places). The journey was a long one, and the translation was not completed until 2010, when, financed by private donations and a major church, Yao was ready to have the Chinese version published. However, this in itself was a problematic undertaking.

At present, the legal publication of Christian works is possible in China but it is still subject to strict constraints.[37] For a book to be legal, it must secure an officially issued International Standard Book Number, which can only be obtained from licensed publishing houses operating under close official supervision. Christianity-related books published in Taiwan, Hong Kong, or anywhere except mainland China cannot be legally sold in bookstores nor in any of the mainland's several bookselling internet sites without being subject to strict and cumbersome import procedures.

Yao consulted an editorial director of a university press, who read the manuscript and explicitly pointed out that because the last chapter dealt with post-1949 political issues, any efforts to publish it in mainland China would be in vain. Yao also approached Kong Qinmai (mentioned above), who had served on the editorial team of *Xiamen Historical Materials* for many years and was highly aware of the political issues involved. The final chapter about the forced termination of the RCA mission between 1949 and 1951 presented the biggest problem. Kong explained:

> I have acted as a censor for the publishing authorities, so I know the hoops [that publishers and authors have to jump through]. By and large, the book is alright. But the last chapter, in particular the part on RCA missionary Henry Poppen's deportation and the details about those who were expelled under escort rudely, brutally, even savagely, is [politically] sensitive. This meant that the manuscript would not be acceptable to the authorities. Yao Deming came and sought my help. As an editor, I am practiced in the tactics of neutral description. I suggested they did not use any sensitive phraseology. The upshot is that we are not supposed to remain [literally] faithful

to the original texts, but we should nevertheless convey the intent of the original book. We should not publish it illegally and should abide by the Party's publishing and religious policies.

Our dilemma is that we must not deviate from the original book. In the last chapter, for instance, the words "struggle assembly" (*douzheng dahui*) should be replaced by the far more neutral "holding a meeting" (*kaihui*) and "struggle" substituted by "arguing about the issue" (*shuoli*). Speaking of Poppen's deportation, the description should be rephrased along these lines: he was told to leave the country after the meeting held to argue about the issue.

When I asked if he had received any instructions from his superiors about how to review books of this kind, Kong shook his head and continued, "When I was the editor-in-chief of *Xiamen Historical Materials*, I was never given any particular instructions from the top on what kind of topics could or could not be published. We understood what the government wanted. That is tacit knowledge. Whenever we referred to the politically sensitive past [connected to Mao's political movements], we said 'as we all know the reason that,' just a couple of words instead of a fuller description."

In fact, not all books about Christianity are difficult to publish. As Kong stated:

> I have examined many books about Xiamen, some of them about religion [i.e., Christianity]. The books dealing with incidents related to Christianity and the intervention of foreign consuls did not receive approval. Their topics fell outside the mainstream. Our favorites have to do with cross-cultural exchanges between China and the West, and modern Western medicine and the like. Some of these topics could and should be learned about. The most important guiding principle in examining manuscripts is that they should belong to mainstream themes such as cultural exchanges, integration, development and other positive issues. I know how to deal with the government and make use of policies to the utmost extent.

In spite of his former official posts, the good reputation he enjoys, and the influence he could exert on government officials, Kong has personally experienced failure when trying to publish sensitive material. In about 1999, a fine arts publishing house in Beijing organized a series of photographic books devoted to fifty cities and regions to commemorate the fiftieth anniversary of the "New China." At the publisher's request, Kong edited a volume entitled *Old Photographs of Tibet*. However, nobody was willing to review the manuscript. Under China's current publishing regulations, manuscripts cannot be given the go-ahead for publication without first being examined by the authorities. If a published book can be shown to violate laws and regulations, the authors or editors and the authorities responsible for them will face punishment. Therefore, censors may be unwilling to review or approve a "sensitive" work because their own career is on the line if they approve something that later attracts the negative attention of higher authorities. The process dragged on for five years, but the volume was never published. As Kong said:

> The fine arts publishing house wanted to publish the manuscript. However, no-one was willing to examine it, because no-one was willing to take the risk. It took five years but the project was finally abandoned. The publisher sent the manuscript to the State Ethnic Affairs Commission (SEAC), but they said the subject [of the book] was religion and therefore it should be reviewed by the SARA. Later the SARA rejected it, offering the explanation that the manuscript was about ethnic affairs. The manuscript was like a ball that the two authorities kept kicking back and forth. Eventually it was sent to the United Front Work Department [of the CCP Central Committee] that supervises both the SEAC and SARA. A deputy director read the manuscript but did not dare [to approve it] either. One of his concerns was that it might contain some "imperialist elements" (*diguozhuyi fenzi*) in the photos. We could neither verify nor refute this point because most of the people in the pictures have already passed away.

The Chinese version of RCA history faced a similar problem. The sensitive elements of the manuscript meant that it could not be published in mainland China; Yao and Kong were at an impasse. The only other possibility was to find a publisher in Hong Kong or Taiwan. This might have solved the publishing problem but still left the matter of its distribution: all printed matter produced outside mainland China must comply with formal censorship and import procedures before being allowed in, let alone being distributed and sold within the PRC.

Kong cast around, mobilized his resources, and finally introduced Yao Deming to the C&M Company, a firm focusing on cultural products. This company has quite a complex background, functioning as a multifaceted set of enterprises that can work around official constraints by exploiting regulatory loopholes without attracting official ire.

143

Understanding the nature of C&M is impossible without some idea of the economic context in post-1979 China. Early in the reform era, the government launched tax incentives to attract foreign investments. Undoubtedly this policy has contributed to the vast influx of investment and rapid development of China's economy, but it has also inevitably created a situation in which many Chinese enterprises or investors establish overseas corporations, then return to the mainland as foreign investors with access to preferential treatment. The manager of C&M explained:

> Our company is itself a concoction. It is not wholly state-owned, but state-owned assets preponderate. This firm is deemed an independent company that is fully foreign owned, nevertheless the major shareholder is the state. The firm's idiosyncratic identities make it easier for us to do business. The procedure is simple. Whenever we need to, we choose one of the particular identities. The Taiwanese publishing house is also under our control. It is a complicated set-up. The most important objective is not to violate policy. Hence, in this instance, the manuscript was published under the imprint of a Taiwanese publishing house, a choice that meant it was exempt from scrutiny by the RAB and the publishing authorities in mainland China. Instead, the company itself was responsible for its review. And we actually own and run the Taiwanese publisher. The whole process was legal. Public distribution through bookstores requires the intervention of an import company.

Under the imprint of a Taiwanese publisher, the Chinese version of the book was printed in Xiamen, and copies were disseminated organically through the community. Under official publishing policy, the printed copies should have been packed and delivered to Taiwan and should not have been circulated before being censored and permitted to enter the mainland. As it stands, the copies cannot be sold in bookstores and can only be distributed through personal channels.

Crucially, the fact that C&M has the privilege of avoiding official oversight of the manuscript does not mean there are no political risks for the firm and its manager. As the manager said:

We are the publisher and bear the main responsibility. If the authorities at the top blame us, I will be penalized and removed from my position and the firm will be ordered to shut down for two or three years. The company could be finished even within a year [not to mention two or three years]. The state's attitude toward religious culture has unquestionably changed. Books on Buddhism used to be difficult to publish. But in recent years the restrictions have been relaxed as Buddhism is considered an ameliorating factor in maintaining social stability and educating the people. [Taiwanese Buddhist] Master Hsing Yun's books have been published in the mainland, as his books have been acknowledged to be expressions of the Buddhist spirit. Nevertheless, books about Catholicism, Protestantism and Islam are still difficult to publish. Only if they deal with historical topics might it be possible to have them published. All books on religions are required to be subjected to RAB inspection and many of them are published by designated presses. Despite this change in attitude, most publishers are unwilling to touch them. To do publishing business in China, it is essential to learn how to work around the edges of policy. We are not supposed to violate policy or publicize the book's release. Never ever look for trouble!

Though C&M agreed to publish the book, the translators and editors were still cautious about the wording used. They deliberately omitted some details about how missionaries were insulted and mistreated when they were being deported. For instance, a description of local militiamen humiliating two women missionaries, Ruth Broekema and Jean Nienhuis, leaves out these details: "To show their disdain for the women, one of the young men spit on his hands and wiped them on Nienhuis's face. When she took a handkerchief to wipe her mouth, he grabbed it, threw it on the floor, and stamped on it."[38] The translated section on Henry Poppen's public trial omits the fact that he was "considered a common criminal" when he was deported and, "with his hands tied behind him, was separated from the others and placed in jail."[39] The translation makes no reference to a telling detail of Poppen's public accusation trial, attended by over ten thousand people, when the government employed a ruse to silence his testimony: he "was allowed to speak briefly in his own defense, although the loudspeakers were turned off."[40] In the Chinese version, it says that during that part of the trial, the sound quality of the speakers was so poor that Poppen's voice could not be clearly heard. Words in the original texts like "occupation" or

"Communist takeover" were translated as "liberation," a term uniformly used in official narratives to describe the just Communist revolution that "liberated" the Chinese people from the oppression of the "three big mountains" (*sanzuo dashan*, namely: imperialism, feudalism, and bureaucrat capitalism). True to the spirit of the original, the Chinese version remains critical of the Communist Party but nevertheless strikes out particulars about the persecution of missionaries. This trend signifies that, as far as Chinese politics are concerned, detailed description is more powerful than sharp criticism, and therefore such telling details are censored or omitted even if a work retains broad or general critiques of the party-state.

Rather than being sold in bookstores, copies of the Chinese version of the book have been widely circulated through unofficial channels among the Xiamen Christian community but also through government agencies. At one point Gulangyu officials were actually intending to sponsor the publication of the book. They finally gave up on the idea, precisely because they were so aware of the political sensitivity of post-1949 politics. Once copies of the Chinese version started circulating, the Gulangyu authorities took a pragmatic view, adding the book to their historical materials project to help boost their WHS application. Apparently the officials shelved their concern about sensitive matters, although they were still mindful of publishing regulations. Their rationale seemed to be that it was the responsibility of the publishing and religious affairs authorities to supervise the publication of historical texts relating to Christianity, while supervisory duties do not fall within the remit of officials of the Gulangyu government, which is a bureaucratic unit. Later, I realized that even the RAB officials knew about the book's release and had turned a blind eye to it. By and large, local cadres are not particularly motivated to carry out ideological controls of Christianity and tend to acquiesce in whatever civilians do.

The book, a significant source for Xiamen history, has elicited an enthusiastic response both within and outside of the Christian community. Two months after its publication, the *Xiamen Evening News* (*Xiamen wanbao*) carried a review of the book.[41] Reporter Sun Xiaowei did not avoid using words like "Christianity" or "missionary," but used cautious language. Rather than describing it as a religious undertaking, Sun treated the missions as a cultural phenomenon, looking at it from the perspectives of cultural exchange and integration (the "mainstream," as Kong said). Over the past several years, the newspaper has carried several reports related to Christianity's contributions to Xiamen society. In 2015, the *Xiamen Evening News* published two features about the development of culture and education in late Qing and Republican-era Xiamen, in which the missions played a key role.[42] By contrast, Sun told me in an interview, when he moved to Xiamen in 2003, nary a word was heard in public in praise of the missionaries. Each time he mentioned the Christian past, he had to quote the CPPCC's historical accounts and criticize the missionaries. The political atmosphere is now more relaxed, but the story of post-1949 Christianity might easily invite trouble, and as far as Sun is concerned, it is still forbidden territory.

In contrast, as an official organ of the Party (being part of the CCP Xiamen Committee), the *Xiamen Daily* strictly adheres to the CCP guidelines and seldom reports on Christianity. The *Xiamen Daily* was in fact the only legal newspaper in Xiamen during the momentous political movements of the Mao era and therefore actively propagated Party policy toward Christianity, putting itself at the forefront of attacks on missionaries and promoting the Three-Self Patriotic Movement. Since the beginning of the reform era, it has seldom made any references to Christianity, whether positive or negative. This is very different from the newspaper's policy toward Buddhism and popular religion, in particular when discussing the religious exchanges between Xiamen and Taiwan.

The *Xiamen Daily* and the *Xiamen Evening News* are both supervised by the Publicity Department of the CCP Xiamen Committee and are both subject to various restrictions concerning the kind of content they can publish. Nevertheless, there are noteworthy differences between them. The *Xiamen Evening News* is a semiofficial newspaper that cannot rely on steady revenue either from work unit subscriptions or from state subsidies; to survive financially, it must attract a wide readership within Xiamen. Unsurprisingly, in the past, special features on Christianity and Xiamen have proven to be of interest to its local audience. Conversely, as a Party newspaper, the *Xiamen Daily* is financed by subscriptions from work units and state subsidies and does not have any such concerns about its market.[43] Therefore, there is no incentive for it to take the political risk of touching on issues related to Christianity, which administrative organs have declared forbidden territory.

Apart from the translation of the RCA book, a number of other original works of local Christian history have also found an audience. Zhu Zixian, a preacher of the Museum Church,[44] an unregistered church in the Xiamen area, authored a manuscript called "Following the Footprint of Love," focusing on missionaries and influential church members, which was sponsored by a Christian bookstore owner.[45] It is not a work of academic historiography; the author has never had any historical training, and the narrative is intended as light reading for laypeople. The overwhelming majority of the content covers common-knowledge topics like mission schools and hospitals, which can easily be found in the official *Xiamen Historical Materials* of the 1990s. However, in spite of its lightweight content, the manuscript faced numerous challenges.

The first problem stemmed from the position of the Museum Church in the early days of the People's Republic. As a preacher of the church, Zhu is a faithful follower of its founder, the late Yang Enli (mentioned in the previous chapter), who refused to join the TSPM in the 1950s and insisted on holding gatherings in her private home. She was sent to prison and labor camps for sixteen years to undergo "reform through labor."[46] Her younger brother was also sentenced to six years of "reform." After she was released in the late 1970s, Yang Enli continued to lead her house gathering, and it became a leading church in Fujian's house church community. Yang gained a reputation as a spiritual leader at home and abroad, particularly after being featured in the widely circulated documentary film *The Cross: Jesus in China*.[47] Yang Enli had a profound effect on Zhu and his fellow workers, and Zhu devoted a very detailed chapter to the church he serves and the suffering of his spiritual mentor. Apparently, authorities have considered the Museum Church a thorn in their side since it was founded, and it remains active today, undeterred by occasional official interventions. Under religious regulations, it exists in a gray zone because it is not registered with the official Lianghui organizations. This is not an exceptional situation. House churches exist throughout the country, but the government views them as illegitimate and occasionally takes repressive action against them. Therefore, details about the Museum Church prevented Zhu's manuscript from passing official censorship.

Another sensitive issue has to do with the suffering of Shen Shengyu (1894–1969), the principal of the Anglo-Chinese College, and his wife Shao Youwen (1903–1982), the principal of the Lok Tek Girls' School. They were local celebrities who educated a number of students who later became influential in Xiamen society. After 1949, they became political pariahs and their children were deprived of access to higher education. Both were accused of ideological crimes and imprisoned in Longyan, a remote region of Western Fujian. The fact that Shen died in prison became a source of embarrassment for the government, particularly when he was posthumously declared innocent. After her release, his wife Shao refused to join the TSPM organization and worked as an independent preacher until her death. Recently, their students have commemorated them on various occasions.

Zhu's manuscript contains passages about the couple, notably describing Shen Shengyu as a martyr to his faith. This put the government in an awkward position. Certainly authorities declared Shen and Shao innocent as early as the 1980s, but they never apologized for the couple's suffering. The same could be said of a vast number of political victims. These two episodes have prevented the manuscript from passing censorship for the past five years. Even so, Zhu has steadfastly refused to strike out the sensitive content.

Recording the Suffering of the Church

At the beginning of the new century, churches in Xiamen began the work of collecting retrospective accounts and have recently started to publish occasional booklets on church history. The most important of these are Trinity Church's *Good News* (*Jiayin*), the Bamboo Church's *The Vineyard* (*Putao yuan*), and the New Street Church's *The Tree of Life* (*Shengming shu*). The booklets usually contain the personal testimonies of members of the congregation.

The most remarkable example of recent church history is the book-length history of Trinity Church. When churches in Xiamen publish special memorial volumes, these typically focus on congratulations from Lianghui leaders and government officials rather than on historical matters. As Ma Zhenyu said, Trinity Church was determined to produce a different kind of volume "emphasizing Christian history, theology and God's leadership so as to educate the younger generation, show the glory of God and afford people hope and faith." *Trinity Church 1934–2014*, released at the church's eightieth anniversary celebration, contains over 150,000 characters and hundreds of old photographs.

The editors of *Good News* collected as many personal testimonies as possible to create the book. Since 2011, issues of *Good News* have contained more items on church history, including essays on missionaries and mission schools and hospitals. The pieces that attracted the most attention from church members were an oral history series in 2012 on Shen Shengyu and Shao Youwen. In the three essays of the series, their daughter recollects the couple's suffering:

They were both arrested and imprisoned in 1951, in 1956 and again in 1966. The TSPM organization ejected them, so they were no longer able to serve. In the decades that followed, their children were implicated and hence became nonpersons. They were repudiated by universities and sent to remote mountainous regions to do manual labor. Misled by the pressure exerted in that era, we were disobedient [to our parents]. When our parents were released and returned home, their beloved daughters did not give them any welcome, but only criticism of themselves and their faith. . . . They were arrested three times. In 1966, the year the Cultural Revolution broke out, big-character posters (*dazibao*) encircled our small rented room. We had to bend forward to enter. One day, my parents were taken to be paraded [through the streets]. It was said that they were forced to kneel in the street with their hands tied behind their backs. Shortly afterward, they were put in jail. While my father died in prison in 1966 [NB: this should be 1969], my mother was jailed for six years and not released until 1972.[48]

Another popular oral history published in 2012 was about Yan Baoling, the Christian soprano who committed suicide during the Cultural Revolution (mentioned above). Yan's story was told in testimony by her neighbor.

A female elder of Trinity Church says that, when the *Good News* published personal reminiscences of this kind, church members particularly welcomed their copies and it was easy to distribute them. Well-known figures in the Xiamen church who had made significant contributions to local society were rewarded with overwhelming attention. However, neither the official historical work of the CPPCC nor the efforts of individuals or churches to write Christian history gave voice to the ordinary people who make up the majority of Christians. Generally speaking, the production of Christian history in Xiamen has been a mission or passion confined to the cultural elite. The memories of uneducated and socially marginalized Christians, who make up the silent majority, have tended to be ignored.

Under the Anti-Rightist Movement, seven members of Trinity Church, including one preacher, two elders or deacons, and four lay Christians, were denounced as rightists and publicly accused. One of the laymen was called Huang Douya (literally meaning "soybean sprout"). Among poor rural families in China, parents sometimes give their children a humble or derogatory name (*jianming*) to avoid tempting fate, in the hope that this can help them survive the vulnerable years of early childhood and live a longer life. To Chinese speakers, Huang's name conjures an image of someone who was born and raised in a poor family. Although Ma Zhenyu mentioned Huang

Douya during our conversation, his name and suffering never appeared in the church's history book. He was an example of someone who was thought to be too ordinary or unimportant to be worth recording in the history books; someone who could not inspire respect or feelings of nostalgia.

Ma Zhenyu, a member of Trinity Church and a retired engineer with a college diploma, was entrusted with the task of writing the book about church history in May 2011. Though he never received any training in historiography, Ma has his own views about it. He disagrees with prevailing ideas about how historical periods should be divided. Many academic scholars as well as ordinary people tend to agree that 1949 spelled the beginning of political repression, but Ma insists that the political situation did not deteriorate until the Anti-Rightist Movement of 1957. During the very early stages of Communism, Trinity Church continued to prosper, as then incumbent Preacher Wen recorded in an essay in the TSPM journal *Heavenly Wind*.[49]

When I read *Trinity Church 1934–2014*, I was surprised to find so many paragraphs devoted to the political repression of Christianity in general and Trinity Church in particular. I asked Ma if mentioning these issues was not overly sensitive. He responded confidently:

> Politically sensitive? No. I am critical of the Communist Party and I slap their faces with their own hands [a Chinese phrase akin to "hoisting them with their own petard"]. But I have never fabricated the evidence. I consulted the archives and included the reference numbers as they appear in the book. If you [the authorities] arrest me, I'll show you the archives and inform you of the sources. I quoted Pastor Zhang Hanqing's comment: "Each time a campaign is launched, Christians will have to suffer." It's true. They [the Party cadres] themselves have spoken in this vein. Since 1957, it has been their religious policy to treat Christians as class enemies (*jieji diren*). I have cited a paragraph of the CCP Central Committee. We should speak with the facts and should not spout nonsense as the Communist Party does. I have written that Trinity Church hung out the national flag [of the PRC] in April 1952 in obedience to the official instructions to "love the country and love religion." I have a photo of that scene.
>
> I have concealed some hatred in the text, but have done it covertly. Those who lived through the political movements will understand my intention, but those who did not share these experiences will not be able to make head nor tail of it. Perhaps they might even consider

it nonsense. I do not intend to publicize it [the political repression]. I just underline the real history rather than whitewashing the government's actions by saying everything was fine and dandy. I admit I do dwell on the past and haven't written much about the present situation. Of course, the manuscript will not pass [official] censorship and I never dreamed of publishing it formally.

When I assumed responsibility for writing the history, I preferred the title *Sanyi fengyun* (The wind and clouds of Trinity Church). I like to talk about class struggle and how the Communist Party fooled the people. I am also keen to expose ugly realities in society, but these outrages are not pleasing in God's sight. The church committee suggested the current title.

Although Ma Zhenyu concedes it was unpleasing in the sight of God to reveal so many ugly facts and conceal hatred in the texts, he was still willing to play the "cat and mouse game" with the authorities, which seems to offer him a sense of accomplishment.

In his talks with me, Ma also referred to the weakness of the clergy during the turbulent times of Maoist political campaigns, although, in contrast with its overt criticism of the CCP, his book omits any negative remarks about religious leaders. Instead, he writes that "Trinity Church members have witnessed the Sino-Japanese War and the Cultural Revolution, to say nothing of a series of political struggles and persecutions. However, as the servants of God, they have endured this hardship as it was imposed on them and none of them has betrayed the Lord in exchange for wealth and status or forsaken their missions halfway."[50]

The book turned out to be a great success, highly praised by both the clergy and members of the congregation. It covered a great deal of the history of Trinity Church but also the broader history of Christianity in Xiamen. Thousands of copies were distributed, not only to local members of the church community but to overseas Chinese Christians as well.

Conclusion

The production of Christian history in Xiamen occupies a zone of intense cultural and ideological work, where official history and unofficial narratives collide and sometimes combine. This makes Christian history a particularly significant site through which to articulate the confluence of Communist ideology about imperialism and sovereignty, grassroots efforts, and popular nostalgia. The regional and historical particularities of Xiamen throw these issues into sharp relief.

In the second half of the twentieth century, the CPPCC's collection and publication of personal testimonies produced a unified, coherent narrative whose purpose was to affirm the Party's legitimacy and its role as the liberator of the Chinese nation, which had formerly been mired in misery. Christianity, denounced for its seemingly inextricable links with imperialism, was the frequent target of ideological attacks in official historical works. The framework set up by the CPPCC project squeezed and colonized the space of private memory. Today, whenever the people of Xiamen look to reconstruct the region's Christian history, what they find are excessively homogeneous accounts and dwindling living memories. Decades of extensive ideological indoctrination shaped people's way of thinking, something that was made clear during my talks with Xiamen residents who tended to admit Christianity's dishonor in modern history before answering my queries. This particularly frames how citizens write Christian history: even though they intend to depart from the official narrative, this proves difficult to elide. The state has successfully imposed a stereotyped rhetoric on its citizens. When ordinary people talk about Christian history, they tend to use political clichés and monotonous vocabulary, in what seemed to me a striking echo of the fictional authoritarian universe of George Orwell's *Nineteen Eighty-Four*, where Newspeak is radically reduced as the ruling group controls the fluency of expression of those they rule.[51]

Compared to central authorities, officials in Xiamen show a greater tolerance for the publication of narratives about Christianity before 1949. However, for stories relating to the turbulent political movements that reveal the fault lines in the Communist regime—they have placed extremely strict restrictions on any alternative narratives of the Maoist era. Consequently, the production of Christian history is easier if political events are omitted. When it alludes to its political mistakes, the government typically blames the Cultural Revolution in general without allowing details to be publicized. The government closes archives and forces publishers to delete any detailed repression of Christianity, since it is well aware that details of the Party's mistakes will damage its legitimacy. The Cultural Revolution is used as a vehicle to give vent to public grievances while shielding the Party from blame.

In the representation of their city's glorious past, Xiamen authorities have positively represented Christian elites. An unexpected consequence is that elite Christians now have a more positive image and are playing an important role in depoliticizing Christianity, incorporating it into the city's proud cultural and historical legacy.

However, in recent years, Xiamen government efforts to commission new written histories, such as for the UNESCO World Heritage application, have produced conditions in which individuals have been able to articulate new narratives that frame Christianity in a more positive light. These cannot be defined simply as acts of resistance or indeed complicity with the hegemony of the state, nor can they be regarded as voices that have been silenced and need to be freed from official hegemony. Instead, it is precisely the state's systematic infiltration of historical narratives and attempts to dominate them that unintentionally paved the way for the emergence of alternative voices and perspectives, offering ways to navigate the fissures in post-Mao ideology and inscribe a very different set of meanings to historical events. The twenty-four monographs published by the CPPCC Xiamen Committee since the beginning of the new millennium indicate that the state does not dominate every aspect even of government-sponsored historiography.

After three decades of effort, the Xiamen RAB and the Lianghui have not yet published a complete official history of Christianity. From the perspective of ordinary people in Xiamen, the vacuum created by the lack of an official history has given them an opportunity to reconstruct the Christian past without being hamstrung by any obligatory points of reference. As the official restrictions on social memory have been watered down, civilians can find different channels through which to release what they want to say.

This does not mean the government is prepared to accept unofficial histories in lieu of their official counterparts. In fact, the three-decade-long special gazetteer project detailing the history of Christianity in Xiamen was never abandoned. At the end of 2015, a manuscript was finally finished by the fourth writer to attempt the project. This manuscript was eventually reviewed by the authorities and the Xiamen Lianghui. An officially recognized systematic history of Christianity is beginning to take shape.

Although the history of Christianity in China during the Cultural Revolution is still "a black hole,"[52] locals are dedicated to piecing together fragmented memories of the time. Collective memories of the era of early Communism still to some extent impede relations between the church and the state. The state never apologized for the suffering inflicted on churches or individual Christians, nor has it compensated them for their losses. To the Christian community, the Party has never been willing to accept its responsibility. Party leaders are conscious that the handling of this historical issue should not go any further, lest historical facts damage the Party's legitimacy. Apparently the painful past remains obstinately planted at the heart of present-day politics.

From a local point of view, the people of Xiamen no longer need to obey the Party's political logic and are showing great enthusiasm for reconstructing the region's Christian history. They feel a particular interest in unearthing almost forgotten stories and bringing them to light. There is a general consensus among the Christian community and cultural workers that the Cultural Revolution is largely to blame for the dearth of historical materials. Almost without exception, the fire set by the Red Guards at the YWCA is brought up in conversation but, apart from this, they can cite no other instances. Until recently, since they reopened, most churches had not yet taken the trouble to set up any sort of system to restore their historical materials. Their lack of enthusiasm for preserving historical materials does not really have much to do with the Cultural Revolution. Instead, it sheds light on the fact that the government, churches, and individuals are all disposed to use the Cultural Revolution pragmatically to explain interruptions in memory or historical lacunae.

The enterprise of history writing in Xiamen has not attracted much attention from well-trained historians. University scholars tend not to get involved. A few of the university professors I interviewed look down on the "low quality" of the local history experts and certainly had no interest in these projects. On the other hand, as far as government officials are concerned, academics are not welcome in the government-sponsored history projects, as they are difficult to discipline and are not particularly obedient in following the government guidelines.

Chapter 5

GLOBAL MISSIONS MEET LOCAL POLITICS

Around the year 2000, Christian churches in Gulangyu began to be affected by the problem of dwindling congregations. Trinity Church was particularly hard hit. Old Pastor Wen (see chapter 3), then Trinity's head pastor, worked hard to reverse the trend by establishing gathering points on the more populous main island of Xiamen and developing new approaches to attract young converts.

At this critical point in time, an American Christian agency entered the scene and initiated missionary activities directed at young adults. The two communities inevitably encountered one other, and they decided to establish cooperative efforts. Elsewhere as well, the ambitious American church has been attempting to play a greater role in the global missionary enterprise.[1] This chapter sheds light on the rarely studied interplay between this international Christian presence and the local sociopolitical context in China, an encounter that has profound implications for the study of Chinese Christianity and broader developments in Christianity worldwide.[2]

The tremendous economic development that China has been experiencing since the 1980s has stimulated massive population flows. Just in the past few years, international immigration to China has swelled and diversified to a far greater extent than ever before.[3] Many of these international migrants are devoted to the Christian mission. As discussed in chapter 1, foreign missions to China are not a new phenomenon; their history can be traced back more than a millennium, though there was a sharp break in the influx and activities of Christian evangelists in China after the founding of the People's Republic, when foreign missionaries were expelled and the links between the Chinese church and the international Christian church were severed.

Under the terms of the government's current religious policy, foreigners are still prohibited from establishing any organizations or sites for missionary purposes. Furthermore, they are not allowed to solicit followers among Chinese citizens, nor are they permitted to appoint any religious staff.[4] Foreign involvement, even if only perceived, greatly increases the likelihood that restrictions will be imposed on the organization. If any international funds or staff were discovered, this would arouse the suspicion of the Chinese government that such activities were being engineered from abroad, perhaps for political purposes such as "peaceful evolution" (*heping yanbian*, referring to Western efforts to gradually subvert and break down the system of CCP rule). And if this transgression were confirmed, Chinese Christian groups would face the serious charges of receiving foreign funding or allowing foreigners to preach.

Yet in spite of these restrictions, foreign Christian groups have long found ways to participate in the development of Chinese Christianity, as several researchers have pointed out. Daniel Bays and Ryan Dunch both note the presence of English teachers in missions, without providing any detailed descriptions.[5] Hunter and Chan refer to financial and training support received from Hong Kong, Taiwan, and a variety of international sources.[6] Nanlai Cao mentions Chinese American Christian entrepreneurs who visit and preach in the Wenzhou church; he notes that their "high morals," "politeness," and "humble manners" deeply impressed local believers.[7] A few scholars refer to the active participation of the South Korean Protestant community in training clergy in China.[8] In contrast to these very brief references unsupported by detailed evidence, Lyu Yunfang's study has been very clear about the missionary connections of foreign teachers (*waijiao*) in Xiamen today.[9] Miwa Hirono's research in ethnic minority areas of western China reveals the ways in which international Christian nongovernmental organizations have adapted to the current political situation and propagate their religious values through their promotion and support of development projects.[10]

So far there has been very limited empirical scholarly work on the presence of international Christian agencies in present-day China, particularly the unofficial channels that enable connections between the Chinese church and its foreign counterparts.[11] As Dunch points out, it is unclear how many Christians (Protestants) are associated with missionary organizations and movements based in the West and what kind of relationship they have with Chinese Christianity more broadly.[12] To the Chinese state, any growth in such efforts, however limited, triggers political sensitivities, increasing its wariness toward transnational Christianity. Aware of the high risk of expulsion they face if detected, most foreign missionaries keep their activities clandestine, haphazard, informal, and consequently lacking in consistency. Under present circumstances, it is not easy for foreign evangelists to maintain any long-term relationship with prospective converts or to continue to remain in contact with and encourage any new converts they might have made. Apparently, neither the Christian church nor lay Christians are willing to make their involvement known. Therefore, given the circumstances, any thorough investigation of this sort of international Christian agency would seem unlikely to be successful. However, I had the good fortune to be granted access to an international missionary organization whose activities are much more structured, visible, and long-term than is typically the case. The organization is run by an American couple, Larry and Anna,[13] who have developed strategies to attract potential converts through English teaching and a longing for cosmopolitan experiences rooted in the context of present-day Chinese society.

Rainbow: An American Mission in Contemporary Xiamen

Sitting in a café, Larry told me about his early life, a story of conversion and dedication. Larry's parents were both born and raised in Wenzhou, Zhejiang Province. To escape from the Great Famine (1959–61) during Maoism, they fled to Hong Kong, then a British colony. Larry was born there in 1965 and migrated to France with his family a few years later. Like many overseas Chinese, Larry's parents opened a restaurant where he often worked as a waiter.

Despite being raised in a Christian family, Larry did not really accept the faith. He moved to the United States for his studies at age seventeen, and it was there that he officially accepted the religion. Over the next few years, Larry completed his education, obtained a master's degree in engineering, and went to work as an engineer. He met and fell in love with Anna, who had migrated to the United States from Taiwan with her Christian family and was working as a prosecutor after obtaining her law degree. The couple got married and had three daughters. They took out bank loans so they could buy a house and a car.

When speaking to his audience, Larry often compares the two lives he has led in different countries, developed and developing, to explain why he and Anna decided to give up their fortunate life in America to spread the gospel in China. Larry says they were unable to stop thinking about the meaning of life until Anna's father, Reverend Zhang, convinced them it was the right thing to do. Zhang, a retired pastor of a Chinese church in the United States who once actively ministered in China, happened to be in Xiamen at the time. On his recommendation, Larry and Anna finally decided to settle in this coastal city and establish a ministry organization.

Speaking of why he chose to be an evangelist, Larry said, "We once lived the American dream. However, engineering was not a passion of mine but a means to make a living. It is theology that really interests me. After working as an engineer for four years, I decided to do a master's degree in theology. . . . It usually takes three years to finish the theological training. Nevertheless, it took me seven years because I had to take care of my family and young children, and I also served in the Chinese American church. During that period, I learned Greek and Hebrew."

In our conversation, Larry cited a memorable anecdote to illustrate the social status they left behind in America: "My wife worked as a prosecutor. Once, while driving, we were stopped by a policeman, but we were let go as soon as Anna showed her prosecutor's credentials." I heard this story retold several times by young people who admire the couple for sacrificing their comfortable way of life in America to devote themselves to the Christian mission. One college student commented, "Their dedication is extraordinary. Not everyone can achieve this. It really touched me." The couple also emphasized that they were motivated by what was happening in Chinese society; as Anna said, "The youth here lack faith and spiritual pursuits. So I decided to stay and guide them to know of the Lord."

They sold their house and car and paid off all their bank loans. In 2003, they began their big adventure as missionaries. Before long, they rented a private property in Banyan Village, a fishing village near Xiamen University. They started a discreet evangelical ministry directed toward young people and named it Rainbow. Because of its arch-like shape, a rainbow is usually associated metaphorically with a bridge, and indeed Rainbow's stated purpose is to "bridge the young Chinese people to the Lord," and, my observations suggest, to American society and culture.

Early on, the Saturday gathering drew only eight or so people, but this soon grew to over two hundred. Hence, Larry and Anna had to switch to renting a bigger private property. On special occasions, they had to put some of the people attending in another hall where they could follow the service via cable television. Unsurprisingly, these large gatherings attracted the attention of the police. Anxious about their precarious situation, the couple's first priority was to find a way to forestall trouble. Pastor Zhang, Anna's father, had close links with Chinese church communities and sought the help of the resourceful Pastor Wen. Wen and the church committee were glad to help, as Trinity Church urgently needed to foster the development of a younger congregation on the main island of Xiamen. In his own words, Pastor Wen's role was to "cover" (*zhegai*) Rainbow's preaching activities. Nominally Rainbow became a youth fellowship of Trinity Church and hence officially operated as the church's gathering point for young believers. To ensure that there was an official link between Rainbow and Trinity Church, Trinity sent its incumbent preacher, Mo Liwen, to take charge. After her appointment, Preacher Mo was responsible for dealing with the authorities. Trinity also supplied Rainbow with a piano, dozens of plastic chairs, and monthly rental subsidies to cover its rising expenditures.

To maintain good relations and secure a steady stream of financial support, Larry and Anna make occasional visits to American churches. Thanks to their efforts, American churches have sponsored Rainbow for the past decade. Once Rainbow was up and running smoothly, encouraged by its rapid growth, Larry and Anna established another gathering point called Kindness Family, focusing on "improving the quality of marriage and children's education." Members organize activities similar to those I have observed at Rainbow. Participants are mainly young and middle-aged couples with children. They bring their offspring to Kindness Family and the Rainbow members babysit for them, leaving couples free to focus on the activities. As in Rainbow, there are bilingual talks and discussions.

In 2007, the Banyan Village Christian gathering point was granted legal status as a venue for religious activity, and the following year what had been a deserted church was "(re)built" in the church compound. Three years later it was promoted to the status of a formal "church" (*jiaotang*) with the joint approval of the provincial Lianghui organizations and religious affairs authorities. Preacher Mo was assigned by the Xiamen Lianghui to take charge of the Banyan Village Church and ordained as a pastor in November 2012. After it was granted legitimate status as a *jiaotang*, the church also assumed responsibility for covering Rainbow, which was affiliated with it as an English corner (*Yingyu jiao*), part of the youth ministry, until the summer of 2015.[14]

Under existing government regulations on religion, a baptism service can be held only in officially registered churches. Some followers of Rainbow

160

were publicly baptized in the Banyan Village Church, which issued them with baptismal certificates. Some others received private baptism from members of Rainbow. In contrast to the standard certificate bearing the official seal of a particular church, the Rainbow equivalent is simply a card made of a thick paper bearing the words "Baptism witness card: we bear witness that you have been baptized a Christian," with signatures by Anna and other key members. All of those involved sign their English (therefore not legally binding) names. In 2008, Rainbow baptized more than one hundred people in a single year, more than half the number achieved by the Bamboo Church (195 baptized in 2008), which is one of the three biggest registered churches on Xiamen Island.

At the time, the English corner offering the opportunity to talk to native speakers was something of a novelty, and it was a source of fascination for a considerable number of young students and professionals. Another great advantage was that the mission gave young people the chance to be directly exposed to American culture, otherwise inaccessible to them in their everyday lives. Rainbow has created a lively and relaxed atmosphere where they can practice their English, one that compares very favorably to the rigid teaching methods used in schools, and early on it had already made a name for itself as an authentic English corner.

Running the Mission and the Company

The Company: A Cloak for the International Christian Agency

I came across the Brand-New Company completely by chance. Although I had frequently heard of it in conversations with Rainbow members whom I knew well, whenever I inquired about the company, they were reluctant to divulge any details. My curiosity was very much aroused. In August 2011, when I enrolled in the free English practice service at Rainbow, a junior member e-mailed me the details of an American contact. His e-mail address appeared to be linked to a particular organization, which I then searched for online. When I clicked through to the associated Web address, a business company Web site appeared on my computer screen. Surprisingly, I noticed several familiar faces, some of whom I had often seen at Rainbow's Saturday gathering. In fact, the Brand-New Company's core leadership consists of Larry (president), Anna (chairwoman of the board), Jacob (general manager), Kara (marketing director), plus a few other people from the organization. Jacob and Kara are both Caucasian American citizens.

The Company claims to be focused on consultancy. Below is the introduction on its Web site (as translated from the original Chinese):

> The Brand-New Company is an American-owned enterprise with a team of experts from around the world. By means of its worldwide network of resources, the company aims at designing series of training courses for individuals and enterprises at different stages of development. We believe that true excellence derives from the renewal of understanding, thinking and healthy characters. With global resources, we pave the way for your integration into a new world filled with vitality, inspiration and renewal; for a new journey to explore and grow in your life. Our team would like to accompany your life journey, no matter what challenges you are facing concerning business development, interpersonal relationships, marriage and children's education.

The company claims to assist in developing children's character, improving parent-child relationships, and enhancing the lives of white-collar professionals. It also offers management consultancy. These first two are services that Rainbow provides free of charge. The third closely resembles Rainbow's bilingual preaching. As for the last service listed, management consultancy, most of the expert consultants listed on the company's Web site had served or were still serving Rainbow as "English teachers." Later I was able to confirm that the principal aim of the company is to serve the missions rather than to make a profit. Besides training young ministry workers, its true role is to connect American churches and receive missionaries from outside mainland China. More importantly, it conceals transnational religious activities under the guise of "lawful" business. The company assists the couple and other missionaries in obtaining long-term work visas.

This covert agenda explains why the Web site has never been upgraded: it serves no real purpose except as a cover.

Given the strict regulation of religion in China today, especially the law that absolutely prohibits foreigners from preaching without the approval of authorities, the Brand-New Company's way of operating is an effective strategy to ensure the survival and development of the Rainbow missionary organization. This is particularly the case because the current government attaches great importance to local economic development, allowing Western missionaries to justify their presence and activities in the name of foreign investment.

Name-Tag Groups and Organizational Structure

At each Saturday gathering, people wear different-colored name badges that indicate their status in the organization. The groups are usually named after their tags:

White-tags are first-time visitors, whether Christian or not, to a Rainbow Saturday gathering.

Blue-tags are non-Christians who have come to the Saturday gathering at least twice. The organization pays close attention to these potential converts.

Green-tags are Christians who have attended the Saturday gathering at least twice.

Any blue- or white-tags who want to be baptized privately by Rainbow, or publicly by the Banyan Village Church on Rainbow's recommendation, must complete a course entitled "Exploring the Truth" given by senior members of the group. The course, consisting of eight one-and-a-half-hour sessions every Saturday afternoon, is designed to assist non-Christians to "reflect on atheism and realize the existence of God." After completing the eight-week course, applicants are interviewed by senior members of the group or by Larry and Anna personally to determine whether they are ready to be baptized.

Red-tags are part-time volunteers who are junior members of the ministry. Christians who actively attend Rainbow (usually green-tags) cannot qualify as red-tags until they have completed a series of courses on themes such as "Spiritual Discipline." The courses run for over half a year and are designed as a test of perseverance. Green-tags who lack the necessary steadfastness will either give up of their own accord or be excluded by the leadership. Red-tags are not required to work for the company unless they decide to dedicate themselves entirely to the gospel enterprise. After completing the compulsory courses, they are interviewed by key members or on some occasions the founding couple to ensure that they will be able to help others. Generally speaking, there are around fifty red-tags, but their numbers usually fluctuate. Each year some leave for different reasons; they might graduate from university or move to another city. Replacements are continuously being trained and selected to succeed members who have left. No matter how long a person has served as a red-tag, he or she would be considered a lifetime member.

Purple-tags are those who have completed Rainbow's formal theological training program and are now supported as full-time ministry workers. There are around fifteen purple-tags in the organization. To become a purple-tag, red-tags are required to take a complete series of courses and training, including Bible study, church history, organizational skills, and the like. Those who are currently receiving training are referred to as "trainees" within the missionary group and are not eligible to be selected as purple-tags unless they have passed the final assessment. Almost all purple-tags and trainees simultaneously work for the Brand-New Company while receiving systematic training courses.

In the early years of Rainbow, Larry and Anna set up a two-year program and trained a dozen full-time ministry workers who became central members of the establishment. Later the program was extended to six years, consisting of three years' training and another three years of mission service. Under the terms of their "contracts" with Rainbow, an agreement in the name of the Brand-New Company that studiously avoids any mention of missionary activities, purple-tag trainees must work for Rainbow (also in the name of the company) for at least three years upon completion of the training program. Their salary varies according to their status either as trainees or as qualified workers. However, in both cases their earnings are considerably below the average income in the Xiamen area.

Samuel, a key ministry worker who received his bachelor's degree in economics from an elite university and has been a purple-tag for several years, once compared his salary with those of his classmates. In 2013, he earned no more than RMB1,600 (USD260) every month of the year. He and his wife, who also served the mission full-time, had a combined monthly income of around RMB3,000 (USD488). They are not wholly dependent on their salaries, as the mission also provides them with housing and a general cost of living allowance, as well as covering his paralyzed father's living expenses, but Samuel's work for the organization certainly creates challenges for the young couple. When I asked whether they were going to have a baby, he sighed and answered, "It's hard to raise a child now." He mentioned the example of Donald, one of the first trained purple-tag workers, who resigned full-time service and found a new job under increasing pressure shortly after he had a baby.

To ensure their young workers' devotion to the evangelical enterprise, leaders offer single young people accommodation with full board, ensuring they can serve the mission at all times. Their commitment is reinforced by the six-year program and often by marrying within the group. Harry, a red-tag, explained the situation as follows:

> Trainees who graduated from college (usually around the age of twenty-three) will be nearly thirty by the time they finish the six-year program. Their future life will be somewhat fixed. If they decide to devote themselves [to the mission] full-time, their marital relationship will not survive if their spouses do not support it. Therefore it is better to find a mate within Rainbow. Both Anna and Larry hope for internal pairings, as this sort of marriage will be stabler. Biblical teaching requires Christians to marry people of the same faith. You might think that Rainbow is like a big family.

Indeed, Rainbow is buttressed by family relationships and contributes to the formation of new ones. For instance, one woman who was a purple-tag had a younger brother who was a trainee; her mother is a cook for members of the organization. Later, the woman married another trainee, meaning that four members of her family are now serving the mission. In recent years, over a dozen internally paired couples have formed. Their babies are called "Rainbow kids." Extended kinship and family-like relationships, as well as their multiple years of training together, create strong bonds between full-time members of the group.

Subculture theory tells us that groups of like-minded people may establish their own distinctive ways of thinking and behaving. If most members of a group with close ties to one another hold the same views about a particular significant issue, those who initially do not agree with the majority way of thinking will soon come round to the same view. As people interact with each other, they are constantly passing on all kinds of information, thoughts, and feelings as well as rewarding similar opinions and behaviors. Disagreements within the group might arise; nevertheless, powerful forces press members into greater similarity.[15] Full-time members of Rainbow interact with each other through strong ties. On consideration it would seem fair to say that the rather "authoritarian" couple dominate the organization and hence play an important role in shaping the members' religious faith and practice, perhaps even their personalities.

Rather than focusing on more old-fashioned methods of preaching and conversion, the mission is dedicated to "equipping those who are capable of equipping others." Besides accepting the tenets of faith, a person who aspires to become a red- or purple-tag is also required to become a member of the organization. Rainbow is a relatively closed group: it is quite distinct and separate from outside society. Members pay a social and material cost to belong to the group, sacrificing time spent with people outside it, higher salaries, perhaps even the opportunity to start a family. In return they receive strong emotional support, close ties with other group members, and other nonmaterial rewards that they highly value, including their spiritual gains. Finally, the tension generated by the group's separation from the rest of society encourages members, who may feel somewhat lost, to commit themselves to the mission even more.[16]

Members who are accepted as red-tags are invited to an annual ceremony, a "rite of passage" where they receive uniform T-shirts as well as Bibles.[17] Through a total of six years of courses and training, these young workers establish a close relationship with Larry and Anna that is very like the discipleship in traditional priestly training. However, the young workers are instructed with a degree of religious commitment that contrasts with the level of engagement usually found in official, state-approved seminaries. The strictly established selection and training mechanisms ensure that Rainbow is strongly integrated both to reduce free-riding and to lead to the exclusion of those without a great commitment to the mission.[18]

Finally, orange-tags are non-PRC citizens, the majority from the United States, who serve Rainbow on a temporary basis and who are referred to as "English teachers." On a typical Saturday gathering, there are several Americans present, sometimes even dozens. The orange-tag group is rather miscellaneous and can be divided into five main categories.

The first is composed of full-time missionaries sent by American churches. They hold nominal posts in foreign companies or teach in schools based in China, but their real duty is to give instruction in Christian activities and train Chinese evangelists. They are paid by the American churches that sent them rather than by Rainbow.

The second category includes missionaries sent by American churches to serve Rainbow on a short-term basis; they are often tasked with introducing or trying out new types of ministerial activities. When it is felt that Rainbow has properly adopted these new activities, the American church will send experienced missionaries to offer more comprehensive guidance.

The third group is made up of American citizens whom Larry and Anna have specifically invited to teach foreign languages or give lectures on particular themes. The guests themselves bear all their costs, including travel and accommodations. Recently, a growing number of groups of American college students have come to hold music concerts or outdoor sports events, or simply to communicate with their Chinese counterparts. These young American students have attracted a large number of young Chinese people to Rainbow.

The fourth category is drawn from a miscellaneous group of Westerners working in Xiamen who are invited to participate in the Saturday gatherings. Due to the increasing need for the service of foreign Christians in worship, in 2005 the city's religious affairs authorities approved the establishment of the Xiamen International Christian Fellowship (XICF).[19] This group is open to non-PRC citizens, including people from Taiwan, Hong Kong, and Macao. Anyone who wants to attend the fellowship is required to show their passport. Larry and Anna are members of the XICF, and from time to time, they invite other Western members to Rainbow, particularly when the number of language teachers present on Saturdays is too low.

I never saw Larry and Anna wearing name badges, but they do not really need them. As the founding leaders of the organization, they are well known to all but the newest attendees, and they appear to have absolute authority over Rainbow.

English Teaching and Evangelism

A Cosmopolitan Language to Transmit a Christian Message

When they think of missionary work, Christians in Xiamen are likely to think of the evangelists or medical personnel reminiscent of the pre-1950 Christian mission, or even people working in the social services, much more so than English teachers. Yet almost from the start, English teachers have had an important part to play in the mission work of churches whose roots are in the English-speaking world, and Xiamen is no exception. Since Christianity was introduced in the 1840s, missions have established dozens of educational institutions on different levels where it was a requirement to know English (see chapter 1). Today, by teaching English (and rarely, other foreign languages) to young Chinese people, foreign teachers constitute a unique group that influences young people's faith.[20]

As Donald Snow points out, English teaching is regarded as "a useful mission vehicle in part because Christian English teachers have the opportunity to live and work in countries which for religious, political, or cultural reasons do not accept missionaries who openly work as evangelists, pastors, or in other church-related capacities."[21] This is particularly true in Muslim and communist countries.

Unquestionably, English teaching is also a useful approach to everyday mission, since English proficiency is a valuable commodity, and the opportunity to learn from native speakers, particularly in a more relaxed and friendly setting than formal Chinese education, invariably attracts an audience. In modern urban Xiamen and elsewhere, those who would never choose to attend an evangelical meeting in either Mandarin or vernacular Fujian Chinese will tolerate the gospel when it is presented in English, simply because it gives them a chance to improve their English skills and meet Westerners, and many of my informants honestly admitted to these "utilitarian motivations."

The dominant role played by English as the world's international language of diplomacy, business, and scholarship has created an enormous demand for English teachers worldwide. English is a compulsory subject in the Chinese school education system, and the reform era has seen a mushrooming market in private schools and training agencies catering to the need to acquire English skills to improve professional, educational, or social prospects. In both state-run and private educational institutions, native speakers of English are highly valued not only for their linguistic and cultural background but also because their very presence makes studying English seem much more real and exciting to students and does a huge amount to raise their interest and motivation. This guarantees regular employment for a large number of Western English teachers throughout China.

Nevertheless, it is often made explicitly clear by China's educational authorities or by employing institutions that English teachers are expected to behave as secular workers rather than missionaries. To ensure that this stipulation is observed, restrictions are often placed on any religious activities they might have been contemplating. Accordingly, those language teachers are often very discreet about their mission activities and tend to preach outside the classroom.[22]

As Baugus argues, one consequence of this sort of practice for the missions to China is a "foreign Christian presence dominated by young, adventurous, short-term workers with little to no training in church development or pastoral experience and no access to the Christian church."[23]

It has to be said that this criticism does not apply to Rainbow, run by a Chinese American couple with Christian roots. It is a rare example of a foreign evangelical enterprise in China that is highly organized, operating through open and above-board English teaching. A typical Saturday gathering, described directly from my fieldwork notes, shows how this works.

A Typical Saturday Afternoon at Rainbow

On June 18, 2011, around 2:30 in the afternoon, I arrived at Banyan Village, half an hour before the Saturday gathering was scheduled to begin. There was no one at the entrance of the church. After I pushed open the front door and entered the church hall, I saw a group of people sitting in rows of armless chairs arranged in pew-like fashion at the front. They were speaking to one another in low voices, with their heads bent down, holding each other's hands. I heard "I hope all the brothers and sisters who are coming today. . . . Amen." They were praying.

Around ten minutes later, as soon as the group prayer had finished, preparatory work began. Two young ladies sang hymns and at the same time reminded their colleagues to get rid of echoes and adjust the pitch on the audio equipment. Another young woman was carrying a stainless-steel rack with a number of name badges hanging on it to the church entrance. Beside the rack, a square red cloth organizer with dozens of pockets on it was hanging on the iron church gate. An English letter was inscribed on each pocket. The name tags of people who have not shown up recently were placed in these pockets, placed according to the first initial of their personal (usually English) names. The badges of those who often attended were hung on the rack. This arrangement allows them to easily distinguish participants who are active from those who are not. Several young people were arranging indoor seats into six circles, three on the left half of the church hall and three on the right. A sign placed outside the front door said "Intermediate," another saying "Elementary" was outside the annex, and an "Advanced" sign was placed upstairs, directing participants to the English conversation groups that suited their language proficiency.

While they were busy, more and more people arrived. Each of them was led to the reception desk and asked if they had come for the first time. If so, they were requested to register with their names (in both Chinese and English) and give contact information and the like. Once this had been recorded, they wrote their names on white badges. As far as I could observe, every newcomer was encouraged to use an English name. Anyone who did not yet already have an English name would be advised to take one, sometimes recommended by the receptionists. Most of the participants did use English names, but a few insisted on retaining their Chinese names. Participants joined different English conversation groups according to their self-evaluated level of English proficiency and members' advice. Each group consisted of six to eleven participants, under the guidance of one English native speaker. As is typically the case in China, the foreigners guiding the groups were respectfully called "teachers."

I joined an intermediate group. The teacher, Alex, was a young man of Asian appearance. He is second-generation Chinese from Houston, Texas. At the time, he and his wife were working at his parents-in-law's garment factory in the neighboring city of Putian. He held a brief outline, printed on A4-size paper. During the conversation, he glanced down at the paper from time to time and tried to guide the talk back to the topic: How to be attractive. Participants were not very proactive in speaking, leaving Alex somewhat at a loss. Moreover, though he tried to ensure the conversation was Christianity-related, most of the participants were non-Christians and easily diverted from the main theme.

Suddenly, we heard music, signaling that the English corner was coming to a close. Someone stood on the front stage with a microphone announcing the end of the conversation groups. People began to replace all the chairs in rows, as they had been before the English corner. When this was finished, two women holding microphones stepped onto the stage and greeted the audience. One, a middle-aged woman, was Anna, the host. The younger woman was an interpreter who translated what Anna said into Chinese.

I glanced quickly around the church hall and estimated an attendance of around 150, most in their twenties or thirties.[24] Anna asked the white-tags to raise their hands and invited those who were sitting around them to greet them as a ritual welcome. I, a non-Christian green-tag, shook the hand of a woman sitting on my left. There were twenty or so people who had come for the first time. Once this was done, a short video entitled *Six Stages* played on a projector to acquaint the newcomers with Rainbow.

After the video, attendees proceeded to the section where English songs were practiced. Lyrics, both in English and Chinese, were projected onto two screens at the front. Anna led the audience in reading out the English lyrics. The songs were all Christian hymns, two of which were "The Lord Is My Light" and "Knowing You." As we were singing, Anna asked the audience to stand up and wave their arms in time with the melody. She also urged people to relax both physically and emotionally.

Around twenty minutes later, English language lessons began. An incomplete English sentence related to that day's English corner topic appeared on the front screens. Anna asked the audience to raise their hands and read out the whole sentence, filling in the blanks. Only a few people raised their hands. With Anna's permission, red-tag volunteers handed microphones to one man and one woman in the audience. They stood up and read out the sentence with the words filled in. Anna praised them and asked the audience to applaud, then encouraged everyone to repeat the sentence to the people around them. This lasted only about a minute.

After the English language lesson, Anna introduced foreign guests and invited an American couple, Jim and Lorrie, onto the stage. The couple had been married for twenty-eight years and had a son and a daughter. Jim was a certified public accountant and had run his own business focusing on accounting and tax services for eighteen years. Lorrie was a high school health teacher. Later Anna presented another couple from Guangzhou and asked them to stand up. The wife conveyed their greetings to everybody in less-than-fluent English. Anna was at pains to emphasize that the couple had come to Xiamen on this occasion solely because of Rainbow.

It was 4:30 and time for the Life Talk segment to begin. Larry, wearing glasses and a long-sleeved striped shirt, walked onto the stage, accompanied by a young lady as his interpreter. At the beginning, someone introduced her, saying that she was formerly a Rainbow interpreter but had since moved to Guangzhou. The topic was "Relationships 101: How to Be Attractive (Kind)," and the content was related to the theme of the English conversation. In his speech, Larry referred to his life experiences in France and America, as well as to biblical teaching.

Around an hour later, the Life Talk finished at the scheduled time. Several purple-tags took the stage and reported details of forthcoming activities, including times, places, people in charge, and how to register. Specifically, these activities were: first, a range of courses on "Exploring the Truth" to be given by purple-tags to blue-tags who wanted to learn more about Christian beliefs; second, a lecture entitled "Dating in Different Cultures" to be given by American guests especially for blue-tags; third, a lecture on "How to Plan Well" to be delivered by Jim, the American accountant; fourth, a lecture on "Healthy Diet" to be delivered by Lorrie; fifth, the Globe E-Friend program for blue-tags who had come to Rainbow at least three times and wanted to communicate with Americans online. Over the next few days, people would phone candidates and check whether their oral proficiency in English met the standard requirements. Interested parties could register with their details, including Chinese and English names, mobile phone number, English proficiency, affiliated institution, and so on. Finally, there was a call for volunteers to serve as tourist guides for the American guests, repeatedly emphasizing that all costs would be borne by these "teachers."

Once this business had been rounded off, the Candlelight Conversation began. Tables had been already prepared in the front yard, and six to ten plastic chairs were allocated to each. On each table stood a sign reading "Student," "Work," "Freedom," or "Marriage," indicating the respective themes. Rainbow members had also prepared candlesticks and snacks. As it was not at all dark, the candles were not lit. People who wanted to continue their English practice stayed and chose their favorite theme. The people who left were asked to remove their name badges and hang them on the rack. Rainbow members said warm good-byes. When I left before the Candlelight Conversation, there were still a couple of young adults registering for the forthcoming activities.

The Saturday gathering, which has been held for years, has made Rainbow well known among college students as a place to learn English. Many young people have been particularly attracted by the presence of American faces. By providing opportunities to practice English with native speakers, the missionary organization has also gained popularity among young Christians. Although it states that it provides foreign language practice as part of the English corner, the topic for each gathering invariably has a link to the Christian faith, closely linked to biblical teaching. Rather than preaching the gospel directly, the mission employs English teaching and American culture as the vehicles for its message. While young people are becoming acquainted with the Christian elements here, they are also fulfilling some of their yearning for opportunities to come into contact with America specifically or a global capitalist market in general.

Imagining America Through Rainbow

William Bainbridge once wrote that "religion offers a way to transcend and transvalue relative deprivation. In heaven, all will be equal and all will be fulfilled. Membership in the religion can be a private badge of status, compensating the individual for lack of status in secular society."[25] In the same vein as what might be called the deprivation explanation, some scholars espouse the idea that the growth of Christianity in China is most likely to occur in underdeveloped rural areas; many believers are female, elderly, and either illiterate or semi-illiterate. Recently, however, researchers have increasingly noted an upwardly mobile stratum (for example, Christian entrepreneurs and educated young people) attending urban churches in economically advanced regions, a trend that is gradually changing the composition of the modern Christian population.[26] As I have observed in Rainbow meetings, the vast majority of attendees are young college students or well-educated professionals.

Formerly, when sociologists of religion sought the motives behind religious conversion, two approaches tended to take center stage, the individualistic and the institutional. The individualistic approach emphasized the significance of such microlevel factors as individual crisis, personal bonds, and networks that might grow or, conversely, break down. The institutional approach shifted the focus to competition between religious organizations.[27] However, in looking for other reasons for the rise of Christianity in urban China, Fenggang Yang argues that besides these two approaches, the contextual aspects, above all the globalized market under political repression, should be examined as the primary influence.[28] In a joint piece, Yang and Abel alert us to the fact that the importance of global contexts is now crucial to understand Christian conversion.[29] From my observation of how matters are conducted in Rainbow, I am convinced that a yearning for the West, in particular for America, plays a major role. To young, urban Chinese people, Christianity, together with the English language and American faces, convey a modern, cosmopolitan image. The attraction of learning the English language and coming into contact with Americans is largely propelled by a sense of wanting to connect with the outside world. It reflects young people's desire to be in touch with the modern West, as well as to participate in global integration.

One key feature of Rainbow is the English corner. Another is the gatherings it holds every Saturday afternoon, like the one described above. Rainbow also holds a full range of activities, including lectures by American guests, retreats for young men and women, outdoor sports, mini English corners, plus the Global E-Friend platform for those who want to communicate with Americans. In contrast with local churches, Rainbow's target groups tend to be young college students, white-collar professionals, and businesspeople with a higher educational background. With this in mind, its mission activities take place in a relaxed and lively atmosphere that is attractive to young people who long to learn about American society and culture. Moreover, Rainbow emphasizes the sense of foreign experience by inviting Americans to each gathering and advising Chinese members to adopt an English name.

Anna uses at least three names or titles on different occasions: her 173 English name in the Saturday English corner, "Professor Zhang" in the Kindness Family counseling for marital relationships, and her Chinese name when she delivers sermons to local Christians at an officially registered church. She is very conscious of the fact that English or Chinese names and titles mean different things to different audiences. For the young people, her English name stands for her American identity and helps to create an informal atmosphere. Her self-proclaimed "professorship" at an elite university brings her respect among the young and middle-aged couples who attend Kindness counseling. The title of *Professor* is somewhat misleading, as her position was in fact a one-year job some time ago, and she was an ordinary foreign teacher without a professorial appointment.[30] Whenever she has been invited to give a sermon to local Christians, she uses her Chinese name instead of her English name, apparently to cater to the tastes of Chinese-speaking audiences and also to keep a low profile in a state-sanctioned church, where preaching as an American would be an evident violation of the law.

Larry, who apart from his native Cantonese is multilingual in Mandarin Chinese, French, and English, takes a rather different tack. He always prioritizes English at public events, although he grew up in France. For both Anna and Larry, their English fluency, their years of living in the United States, and their travels across the world are all indicators of their American identity and cosmopolitan qualities. A postgraduate student recollected that Larry was once invited to give a speech at his university, and he was fascinated by Larry's English fluency. However, his admiration for Larry's cosmopolitan experience evaporated as soon as he was given the opportunity to study in a French institution for a semester and travel across Europe.

However, unlike this particular student, many students who attend events and activities at Rainbow are often deeply impressed with the cosmopolitanism of the experience, which is instrumental in their conversion. One of these was Andrew, a student who was then pursuing his master's degree in engineering management. Sitting in a coffee shop, Andrew told me his story. He began to acquaint himself with Christianity at college but did not accept Christ until he was introduced to Rainbow. He attributed the gap to the fact that

> local churches are usually filled with elderly Christians. My younger
> sister once attended some churches in Zhejiang Province where [the

congregation] was completely [made up of] elderly ladies. The young people her age no longer wanted to go there. They had even got the impression that Christianity is a faith for the old or those who have nothing to do after filling their stomachs. These churches are very unlike Rainbow where you can find a group of really outstanding young people and white-collar professionals like Larry and Anna.... It offers many different interest groups that other churches do not have. Some people do come here because of these interest groups rather than the gospel, and subsequently acquire an interest in Christianity. Rainbow supplies various and abundant packages, so you can at least try some. People are very enthusiastic and hospitable. In contrast, other churches are dull, stuck-in-the-mud and lack vitality.

Jordan, another student, went to the Saturday gathering for the first time in 2006 and immediately favored the way the gospel was preached. As he said, "Most importantly, these topics are awesome. They do not dogmatically talk about beliefs; instead, they refer to those that are significantly connected to our own lives, values, and worldviews, subjects that we can't learn about at school. These open discussions let you reflect on the sorts of things you don't think about outside that particular atmosphere. Another plus point is that their English songs are great, especially when they are led by Anna. Third, I do like the contents of Larry's talks, as well as his humility and good manners."

These testimonies bear witness to how Rainbow awakened their interest in Christianity, but in many cases, the people who attend events and activities there seem to be much more motivated by their affection for America, a country virtually none of them has visited. Mary, a fashionable girl who recently graduated from college, is an example of this. Her parents are both government officials and "loyal" (in her words) to the Communist Party. Yet she is grievously disappointed in China and constantly complains about the numerous social problems there. The country's one-party rule is what causes her the greatest discontent: "I think faith has nothing to do with political parties. I trust you, therefore I shall join your Party, but I can have my own faith. The two are not contradictory. Nevertheless, the CCP is afraid because it is well aware that it is not perfect. Hence, it adopts many tools to take control and ensure you have no other beliefs. I think this is wrong."

When she spoke of going abroad, I sensed the intensity of her desire to visit the United States. She admitted that her affection for the United States is rooted in her sense of discontent and disillusionment with the social realities around her. "The word 'xenophilia' (*chongyang meiwai*) seems a bit negative to me. Since I have never been to America, I have no idea if I am right or wrong. But at least, [I know that] I do not like my own country." 175

Mary imagines America in extremely positive terms, as a society with a much higher degree of freedom than China. She insists that Christianity is what made American society better. "I do not believe that people will be granted God's grace as soon as they convert. When individual Americans convert to Christ, they change gradually but will experience a substantial transformation."

Though she might not think of herself as a feminist, Mary is also unhappy about traditional Chinese marital relationships, in particular men's lack of appreciation for their spouses. In contrast, she has a very positive view of American marital relationships, as she has witnessed them through events and activities at Rainbow.

> After coming into contact with foreigners, I have become even more xenophilic. I am not a traditional person, and I am concerned with men's responsibilities and experiences. A good man must be the soul of his family. Certainly, his wife can back him up, but this does not mean his spouse should be just a housewife, occupied with the laundry and the cooking. A housemaid can do it. They should be mutually supportive. I think American people do it well. In Chinese families, the most frequent things I have seen are quarrels, divorce and the other woman. Although I am not knowledgeable about America, from those [Americans] I've met I definitely have a sense of American men's love for and appreciation of their wives. How many Chinese men would say they appreciate their wives? They might say their ladies are good, kindhearted, honest and decent. But very few of them would say they appreciate their wives. American men do this very often.

For many attendees, Rainbow provides a pathway to understanding both the Christian faith and American society. Spurred on by their American dream, some are exploring a range of possibilities for migrating abroad. Among my respondents, Victoria shows the greatest desire to migrate to America. Born and raised in remote Xinjiang, she graduated from a local teachers' college; later, her career took her to a coastal province. She moved to Gulangyu for the sake of her only daughter's musical education and sent her to the noted Gulangyu Piano School, leaving her husband to look after their business in northern China.

176

I met Victoria for the first time in 2011, when a missionary couple had been invited to visit her home on Gulangyu Island, and a purple-tag asked me to act as a guide and interpreter for them. It was a cloudy and windy morning when the American couple and I landed on the island, where we were received by Victoria. Though she spoke barely any English, on a Rainbow member's recommendation she used her English name. Her apartment is only ten minutes' walk from the ferry terminal, but it took us more than an hour. She frequently stopped and asked me to take pictures of her with the two Americans. I do not have very pleasant memories of the meeting. Here's the thing: Victoria made it clear she had no interest in me, a mere Chinese postgraduate student from a local university. I was little more than an accessory to facilitate the meeting with the foreigners, whose presence carried with it the reflected thrill of America.

While we were speaking in the living room, her daughter Wendy came home from school. On her mother's instructions, Wendy performed on the cello and then the piano. I sensed her displeasure at her mother egging her on. Nevertheless, an obedient daughter, she played for the guests as requested without complaint. During the conversation, Victoria was mainly interested in finding out how she could send her daughter to an American school; she then wanted to know if the couple could help. She had heard that American schools were happy to accept students from Christian families recommended by an American church.

The following year, I left to pursue my doctorate in the Netherlands. This time, whenever I did field research in Xiamen, Victoria showed an interest in my European connections. She has kept in touch with me via social media and persistently inquires about the possibility of migrating to Western Europe. By going abroad, I became someone worth knowing, whereas before she showed no interest in me as a person.

Unquestionably, the revival of Confucianism and other native religions indicates that many people are still attracted to traditional religion and culture in China. However, for Chinese people who are more interested in the West, Christianity represents the antithesis of traditional, conservative, or restrictive Chinese culture, providing a vector for their yearning. In fact, Christianity is typically seen as a modern, cosmopolitan, universal faith, the diametrical opposite of more traditional beliefs.[31] The case studies of people who choose to attend Rainbow gatherings instead of native Chinese churches indicate that the involvement of Americans and American culture strengthen their perception of Christianity as a modern religion and a vehicle for modernity. Their American background in itself makes the international agency's proselytizing efforts more effective.

This success has not come easily, as Rainbow's mission faces numerous challenges. Besides political restrictions, the Chinese American organizers have always had to find sophisticated ways of coping with the Three-Self church structure; even so, they are inevitably dragged into church politics.

177

New Missionaries, American Ministry, and Church Politics

The indigenization of Christianity in China has attracted widespread attention among Chinese researchers. Undeniably, this scholarly interest has been driven at least in part by the expectations of the party-state. At a recent national religious work conference in April 2016, Xi Jinping emphasized that "in adapting religion to socialist society, one of the most important tasks is to adhere to the path of Sinicization (Zhongguohua)."[32]

Looked at historically, since the beginning of the twentieth century, the Chinese Christian elite has initiated a far-reaching reform of the "foreign religion." While this transformation has been underway, a vibrant and multi-faceted popular Christianity has also emerged.[33] In Xiamen, as early as the second half of the nineteenth century, the Three Missions based in this area had begun to empower the local church by deliberately granting it a certain degree of autonomy, a fact that the Christian community celebrates even today (see chapter 1). Thus, in contemporary Xiamen, Christianity is seldom associated with the label of "foreign religion."

Yet in stark contrast to the indigenous churches that have taken root and adapted to new social and cultural environments, Rainbow is at pains to retain its American characteristics, going to great lengths to distinguish itself from the Xiamen Christian community. Its history of conflict with an officially recognized church reveals some of the reasons behind this self-marginalization, and its somewhat ambiguous position in the local ecosystem of Christianity.

The Relationship Between the American Mission and the State-Sanctioned Church

For political reasons, Anna and Larry made the tactical decision to nominally affiliate Rainbow with Trinity Church. Pastor Wen describes Rainbow as one of Trinity's gathering points, and in fact he was once invited to teach theology at Rainbow's worker training sessions. Rainbow leaders do not deny the role of Wen's church in legitimizing their organization, but they tend to frame it as a reciprocal relationship rather than unidirectional support. For the first few years, their cooperation was mutually satisfactory. They were not in competition, and Rainbow in fact acted independently of Trinity. Pastor Wen did not impose any restrictions on it. Those who wanted to be baptized at Trinity Church were recommended by Rainbow.

The situation changed when approval was granted for a church compound to be "(re)built" in Banyan Village. When it was completed in 2008 the church was "(re)opened" after a lapse of half a century. Shortly afterward, on the grounds that it was a youth ministry, Rainbow was transferred from Trinity to the new minor church, which it was nominally affiliated with as an English corner. The Banyan Village Church took over the task of shielding the Rainbow missionary organization. To underline the link between them, Larry repeatedly emphasized that Rainbow had contributed enormously to "building" the church. As I have observed, both the founders and the members of Rainbow have actively taken part in the restoration and religious activities of Banyan Village Church.

Although Rainbow had to be affiliated with the church in order to obtain a legitimate status, in a pragmatic sense it was mostly independent. The relationship was mutually beneficial: the church gave Rainbow a legal status, and in return, Rainbow improved attendance and made the church more attractive, especially to young people. Moreover, Christians who converted because of Rainbow (baptized in Banyan Village) could be counted among the church's successes, contributing to its status vis-à-vis the Xiamen church. Even more importantly, thanks to Rainbow, the Banyan Village Church became the recipient of many more donations, divided in two according to their agreement: half for the church and half for Rainbow.

Despite their ostensible cooperation, a growing competitiveness set in. When Rainbow seemed to be enjoying a much better reputation, some church members were evidently dissatisfied.

Mo Liwen, then a young preacher at Trinity Church, was sent to be in charge of the Rainbow ministry, but Larry denied her any substantial role; he treated Pastor Wen as the person in charge. Even Mo's role as a messenger was not acknowledged. Larry told me, "Actually she seldom came [to see us]. We usually contacted the Old Pastor directly." Preacher Mo was in an awkward position because, in her own words, she was being bypassed. The Rainbow leaders made it clear that the Old Pastor was the real umbrella they needed, and they therefore tended to communicate with him in person rather than through Mo. When Mo was ordained and appointed head pastor at Banyan Village, her authority went unrecognized, exacerbating the conflict.

The honeymoon period seemed to be over before it had really begun. The status of each party was unclear and subject to a lengthy negotiation process. Rainbow was gradually marginalized and, to regain lost ground, Larry and Anna had no option but to give in gracefully, as they could not operate without the "umbrella" of Pastor Mo and her church. Rainbow's bargaining position was weak, and its situation became even worse when the leaders were warned that Mo was unwilling to shield their organization. Dissatisfied with the relationship, the Rainbow leaders sought other churches they might be able to cooperate with, but their attempts failed. I was told that the founding couple's strong personalities and the perception that they might try to dominate church affairs worried the leaders of other churches. More importantly, most were unwilling to take the risk of covering for a foreign mission led by influential pastors. Although Mo Liwen is not very influential in the church community, her husband is a resourceful figure in the official church organizations on prefectural and provincial levels, giving her valuable connections with local authorities.

The tension in the everyday relationship between Rainbow and Banyan Village Church was also reflected in their styles of worship. As an American youth ministry, Rainbow specializes in attracting young people. Mo, on the other hand, takes a traditionalist approach and even went as far as to strongly advise Rainbow to adopt the *Amoy Hymnal* widely used in the Southern Fujian region. Under Mo, the newly (re)formed church adopted a more traditional style of worship, prompting some young people in the Banyan Village congregation to stop attending the church. The distribution of financial resources was a further point of friction: at first, Banyan Village Church had been responsible for some of Rainbow's expenses incurred for printing and hospitality; as time went on, it was no longer willing to bear these costs.

"Building" or "Rebuilding": Controversy over the Birth of the Banyan Village Church

Rainbow members describe Rainbow as being established before its host organization. The narrative is "first Rainbow, then the Banyan Village Church." As Larry commented, "The request to build a church was initially objected to by the RAB on the grounds that there were not many Christians in the village and that Buddhism was actually the prevailing religion.

Only when the number of Christians exceeds two hundred can the application for a church be approved [by religious affair authorities]. In response to the criticism, the Old Pastor told the officials that there was in fact a gathering point, with two to three hundred in regular attendance. After his intervention, the Xiamen RAB finally authorized the building of the Banyan Village Church."

Mo Liwen disputes Rainbow's statement. From her point of view, the village church was established as early as 1926. Although the church building was heavily damaged in the Japanese bombing and finally destroyed in the 1950s during battles between Communist and Nationalist forces across the Taiwan Strait, the remains of the belfry still bore witness to its past existence. There is no question that before the construction of the new church building, part of the old belfry still existed. I saw the pictures during my field research. Members of Rainbow must have known about the old church, since the ruins were still there during their first five years in the village. As far as RAB officials were concerned, the construction of the new church building was a "reconstruction" of the old church. Pastor Mo emphasizes that the RAB approved the plan on two main grounds: first, the fact that the old church had once stood on the same site; second, on the basis of the post-1979 national religious policy on the restoration of religious sites.

Rainbow members dismiss Mo's account. They argue that the new church has nothing to do with the historical one; specifically, they say there was no continuity in worship, nor in the makeup of the church congregation. Furthermore, they added that the original site of the old church had become a rubbish dump. They say it was even the property of a local villager, rather than a church organization, until the new church was built.

Rainbow and the Banyan Village Church did not reach a consensus on the "building" versus "rebuilding" dispute until December 2012, when Mo was raising donations to erect a stele with an inscription created by the first preacher of the historical church in Banyan Village, Cai Zhenxun (1874–1968). Cai composed the text entitled "The Stele Epigraph for the Xiamen Banyan Village Church" in imitation of a widely read essay—"The Epigraph on My Humble House" (*Loushi ming*)—authored by Liu Yuxi (772–842), a prestigious scholar-official in the Tang Dynasty. The short text, made up of eighty-one characters, was originally published on April 2, 1931, in *Daonan*, an important Christian publication based in Xiamen that also covers the Three Missions and other churches throughout Southern Fujian. Cai's epigraph reads as follows:

A church need not be high;
It is holy as God is with us.
The teaching does not have to be abstruse;
So long as it is practiced and widespread.
The saints are those
Whose great virtue gives out the true fragrance.
Our sanctuary is where the light of God graciously shines;
Our hymns are written in elegant, ethereal rhyme.
Christ converts stones;
God calls good soldiers.
In this sanctuary we can play the organ and read the Bible.
No heresies intrude;
No obsession with fame and wealth.
The two stone tablets transmit the Ten Commandments;
The Cross celebrates redemption.
The Savior warned us to watch and pray.[34]

In the 1930s, the historical Banyan Village Church, situated in what was once a remote fishing village far from the urban periphery of Xiamen, had a fairly small congregation and stood on the outskirts of the city's Christian community. In his concise text, Preacher Cai Zhenxun draws an analogy between this church and Liu Yuxi's house—although it is a humble building, the host maintains a civilized demeanor.

Pastor Mo's husband found the text and informed the church. Subsequently, it initiated a series of historical writings and planned to install the stele. When the stele was erected, Mo invited Cai's grandsons to come see the "rebuilt" church compound and the stele that acknowledges their grandfather's contribution. Under the circumstances, Cai's descendants were effectively mobilized and one of them finished a biography of Cai, where he described his grandfather's life as revolving around the establishment and development of the historical Banyan Village Church.[35] Nowadays church flyers handed out to visitors and people attending Sunday service give a historical introduction to the church, and although it is very concise, it traces a continuity between the historical church and the present one.

When I asked Rainbow members about the stele and what they thought of it, they tended to make comments like "We just focus on preaching the gospel." Apparently, the erection of the stele was enough to supply convincing evidence of the historical continuity of the Banyan Village Church. Since

Fig. 11 Cai Zhenxun's grandsons having their picture taken in front of the stele. Courtesy of Lin Muli.

then, Rainbow members have not spontaneously brought up the disputed narrative.

Local Tradition and Power Structure

Pastor Zhang, Anna's father, has played a vital role in Rainbow ever since it was established. Whereas Larry and Anna are US citizens, Zhang is from Taiwan, which is extremely convenient from many points of view—linguistically, culturally, and historically—to help them communicate with the people of Southern Fujian.[36] Both Larry and Anna are familiar with the conditions in China and aware of how important it is to avoid conflict with local churches. Samuel, a key purple-tag of the missionary organization, once explained:

> There are many American people in Xiamen, but nobody else could carry it [the organizational missionary enterprise] off. Larry and Anna do not want to be dragged into church affairs. Most of the time they just plead ignorance. Of course, they are well aware of the rules. If they were not, how could they deal with them? They have an American network but use it only if and when the need arises.

Some foreigners might speak out against the inappropriate conduct of the local clergy, but that is not our way. We know the rules of the game. If we speak out, everything will be exposed. Other foreigners are not in the same situation. They are not in the same circle and have no conflicts of interest. You [foreigners] might speak your mind about [something], but we [local church members] will pay no attention to you. However, if anybody within the Xiamen church were to behave like this, they would find they had enemies to contend with. In this sort of environment, you can decide whether or not you want to get involved.

Referring to the Lianghui organizations, Samuel continued, "We need a subtle strategy. Specifically, we just [go ahead and] do it rather than say anything. It is better for us to stay in the gray area. Never try to clarify. Do not pay attention to the religious regulations. We are obedient to God. So far, there has been no intervention [by the government or the Lianghui]. Perhaps there is always someone in the audience [sent by authorities] who observes everything."

When a fellow researcher based in Xiamen asked a Xiamen RAB official about religious groups formed by non-PRC citizens, he swiftly responded, "Do you mean Rainbow?" Religious affairs officials are quite aware of Rainbow's activities, but they have never interfered. As a representative of the XICF, Larry has been invited to dinner several times by RAB officials, but the hosts never mentioned Rainbow to him. Larry, of course, is wise to the fact that the authorities know about his organization. As he said, "Everyone knows what we are doing here. We have no secrets." However, as long as Rainbow keeps a low profile, authorities can pretend it does not exist, even when they undoubtedly know what it does.

When I asked Larry if they had a long-term plan, he became melancholic. He shook his head and said:

> Since we came, we have realized we couldn't make many plans. The situation has changed rapidly. When we arrived, we expected to cultivate the youth and we succeeded. In the next decade, we shall continue to dedicate ourselves to the missions, God willing. In China, we cannot make plans because of our identities. These are very subtle things. The fact that we have been here for ten years is a miracle. Over the past two or three decades, a number of missionaries have come to this country under the cover of some other identity.

However, none of them has achieved anything like Rainbow. It is a miracle. As soon as they began their missions, they were taken away [by the authorities]. . . . So far, we have not had to deal with the RAB. We shall [certainly] be in trouble if we are caught. It is hard to say [what the prospects for the next ten years will be]. . . . As far as the government is concerned, it would be ridiculous for officials to make trouble for us because we convey positive information [about China today] abroad. Bad news will follow if we find ourselves in trouble. Rainbow makes a favorable impression on foreigners.

As the ongoing tension between Rainbow and the Banyan Village Church led their relationship to deteriorate, the former found the situation increasingly unfriendly and felt the risk of being reported to the authorities. Eventually, Rainbow leaders decided to part from the Banyan Village Church and the two organizations went their separate ways.

In search of a new umbrella, Rainbow sought a collaboration with the Bamboo Church. This new relationship is severely asymmetrical. Rainbow needs the cover of the Bamboo Church, but Bamboo does not need Rainbow to attract more members to the congregation. As one of the main churches under the leadership of the influential chairwoman of the Xiamen TSPM, Bamboo has over five thousand registered members and provides various ministries for different age groups. The most obvious manifestation of the inequality is that Rainbow is not allowed to use its name and logo; instead, it has to conduct its activities overtly in the name of the Bamboo English Corner. As a purple-tag explained:

The Bamboo Church is a major institution. There is no shortage of either money or workers. The English corner will have to content itself with enriching its youth ministry. We now duplicate our activities in the Banyan Village Church in the Bamboo Church and pool all our resources. Nowadays, all of the registered churches are doing this [English corners with foreigners involved]. The TSPM [leaders] are aware of it and acquiesce in it. The churches led by courageous pastors have all espoused this. However, none of the Bamboo pastors appears [at these gatherings]; only a lay church member who has been assigned to coordinate our work attends. . . . Once there were dissenting voices. The main issue is how to identify the converts who have been influenced by Rainbow. Are they with the Bamboo Church or with Rainbow? This has a direct bearing on financial donations.

Money! This is a sensitive issue. . . . The pastors all have families to raise and cannot survive without their followers' donations. . . . We are unwilling to discuss the matter with the Bamboo Church.   185

Conclusion

Contemporary Chinese Americans have now assumed the mission of building a bridge between young Chinese and the Lord. The English language, American faces, and Christianity are a potent cocktail to produce a cosmopolitan and global image. As the Communist government strictly prohibits traditional foreign missions, English teaching plays an important role in helping missionaries obtain long-term visas and attracting Western-oriented youth.

Rainbow is not the only foreign agency involved in the Xiamen church. Other Southeast Asian churches of Southern Fujian origin and seminaries have also established a close cooperation with churches to train clergy.[37] One of the reasons they have been welcomed is their forefathers' connections with the Xiamen church. The new-era American missionaries are reluctant to fully join the church community, since they are aware that maintaining a distance will keep them safer. Thus, although the American missionary organization in Xiamen has been successful in converting the youth, it is not in a position to be either localized in or assimilated with the indigenous Christian tradition. The prosperity and success of the mission enterprise in late nineteenth-century Xiamen is a sharp contrast to today's international Christian agencies and the dilemma they are caught in.

Religious affairs officials, who are well acquainted with Rainbow but pretend not to know it as long as it does not stir up any trouble, probably feel confident that the organization will not be able to develop into a big movement. Mired in church politics, the most immediate difficulty Rainbow has to deal with is the official churches. The controversy aroused by disagreement over the "building" versus "rebuilding" of Banyan Village Church reflects a tension between the contemporary missionary agency and the state-recognized church. It is worth noting that the dispute between them involved the reconstruction and contestation of historical narratives within the Christian community. The Banyan Village Church, which enjoys official recognition, easily prevailed. As a Lianghui leader told me, "They should obey the regulations, otherwise. . . ." He did not continue, but I could guess what he left unspoken from his tone. He even reminded me not to get involved.

On the opposite side of the fence from the young Christians who wish for fuller involvement in the global world, church workers in Xiamen do not show much interest in the present American mission. This situation is in sharp contrast with the historical tradition of Christianity in Xiamen, the result of American and European missions and the passion for reestablishing religious networks with Southeast Asia. The Xiamen Christian community is now proud of its global connections, mainly in historical terms. Through their yearning for the Christian past, Xiamen Christians have found a sense of belonging to global Christianity.

As it had to face up to the independence of the Banyan Village Church and the transfer of Rainbow to another leading church, Trinity Church's strategy of international cooperation was declared a failure. For the declining Trinity Church, the future seems even darker than it did before.

CONCLUSION

When scholars write about Christianity in China, they are often writing about Christian communities, churches, and individuals. Yet the different facets of Christianity I describe in the previous chapters reveal how Christianity is intimately embedded in the social, political, and cultural milieu of Xiamen. There, Christianity is not just a system of religious thought and practice; instead, it is woven into the social fabric and it matters to the whole of society.

As a source of local pride, Christianity lies at the center of reinterpretations and reconstructions of Xiamen's glorious past. Local government, churches, grassroots groups, and individuals attempt to construct or reconstruct narratives revolving around Christian history in dynamic and ongoing interactions. I hope to push studies of Christianity in the Chinese context beyond a Eurocentric approach to reflect on acculturation and the place of Chinese Christianity on the global stage.

Revisiting Church and State in Contemporary China

The Zhejiang demolition campaign and subsequent political movements directed at various religions were a watershed for religion-state relations in contemporary China. Having been predominantly perceived by the public and overseas observers as a campaign specifically against Christianity, they have had a profound effect on scholarly perspectives, leading back to the dichotomous paradigm of state domination and church resistance.[1] Yet the extensive ideological education movement launched by Xi Jinping and his administration, which is currently underway, suggests that these campaigns have more to do with center-periphery dynamics within the government. They appear to be intended to restructure the bureaucratic system as a whole and mobilize millions of government officials at various levels to ensure their political loyalty to the central leadership and the Communist Party.[2]

The Zhejiang campaign has challenged previous research on Wenzhou Christianity, in particular the overemphasis on the negotiating ability of elite Christians who, as Nanlai Cao says, have entered mainstream local society in the wake of their economic success.[3] The current situation indicates that the role of the state in interacting with Christianity is not going to be downplayed any time soon. Although the state has not significantly changed existing religious policy, any minor adjustments can still considerably reshape the landscape of Christianity. As long as the current political system remains in place, churches will struggle to obtain a more favorable position in their dealings with the state.

To advance our understanding of Chinese Christianity, we need new visions. Looking at various manifestations and forms of Christianity in different contexts can enrich our knowledge of how Christianity, a religion imported in the nineteenth century, has become integrated into Chinese society, impacting many aspects of society and public life.

Looking at Old Pastor Wen and his interactions with local officials, it becomes clear that much of the scholarly research on church-state relations in contemporary China fails to acknowledge the local and personal dimensions that often influence exchanges between church leaders and state bureaucrats. When religious policy implementation is not discussed at the local level, the tendency is to reify the state as an all-encompassing entity. In fact, actual policy implementations are much more flexible than what may appear from a distance. As Koesel's interest-based theory of religion-state interactions suggests, it is not uncommon for religious groups and authoritarian government to form a mutual alliance.[4] In the Chinese context, Adam Chau reminds us that "because of its nested interest in the locale, the local state necessarily behaves differently than the central state."[5] When we look at the complex linkages more closely, we may recognize greater flexibility and an array of options in church-state interactions.

Even so, in the era of governmentality, the shift in the governing tactics of the Chinese state does not necessarily mean its influence over society is waning. Instead, the authorities commit themselves to building a less direct but more resourceful social management system. The state still has a powerful but mostly imperceptible grip on the church. Although there have been no conflicts of any magnitude and church-state relations have been running smoothly since the 1980s (as Old Pastor Wen commented), the state's authority affects and constrains the Christian community in a variety of ways.

The Christian community in Xiamen and Gulangyu must now confront a number of challenges from within and outside the church. Its historical legacy has been recognized and appropriated by the government, and it is faced with new methods of governing, one of the chief ones being heritage management. Moreover, the policy of intensive tourism development on Gulangyu led to a trend of decreasing and aging congregations that is now irreversible. Under pressure to revive the local economy, the Xiamen government will certainly not cut back on its economic exploitation of Gulangyu in the interests of the church. Urban development planning will not take the future of Christianity into consideration. In the relentless onward march of government projects, the local church has no option but to concede and adapt.

When I discussed the Zhejiang campaign with the Old Pastor, he said it would never happen in Xiamen given the city's relatively relaxed political atmosphere and friendly religious affairs officials. Over three decades of experience in dealing with local government, he has gained great confidence. Local officials who are deeply embedded in local society tend to behave as social actors rather than agents of the state in their interactions with Christianity. As long as their political future is not in jeopardy, they will not refuse to cooperate with the church and will even help it to benefit from local politics.

When referring to good church-state relations, the Old Pastor apparently did not take into account the unregistered churches that have been disturbed by public security authorities from time to time. He also overlooked the fact that each time higher-level state agencies have intervened, local-level "friendly" officials immediately terminated their cooperation.

Some resourceful religious elites are adept in dealing with the local government and church politics. However, the advantage enjoyed by Christianity in dealing with the authorities or those of a particular church within the Christian community will disappear as soon as influential religious elites retire. The decline of Trinity Church is not just attributable to a shrinking elderly congregation; undeniably the Old Pastor's successors have been lacking in strong, charismatic personalities. This situation demonstrates that the capacity of negotiation with the state heavily relies on strong figures, revealing the fragility of Christianity in shifting political conditions.

Dynamics of Negotiating the Christian Past

The case studies in this book shed light on the continuities between the past and the present. As a direct consequence of China's defeat in the Opium War, hundreds of Western missionaries settled in the Xiamen region and launched widespread activities in education, medicine, newspapers, and other social enterprises, and in these endeavors they greatly contributed to shaping the landscape of the locale. These activities cast an aura of Westernization and modernity over the whole missionary enterprise in nineteenth- and early twentieth-century China. Although missionary activities were forcibly terminated and intentionally discredited by the ruling Communist Party, their far-reaching influence has never been eliminated. Certainly, colonial and missionary modernity left a profound imprint on the collective psyche of Xiamen society. Xiamen citizens' internalization of Western forms of modernity, seen in the Western-style architecture and heard in the collective enthusiasm for Western-style music, has certainly been shaped and maintained by the romantic temperament of the city. Thus, the successful construction of reform-era Xiamen's romantic image must in part be credited to its Christian legacy.

In modern China, Christianity has invariably and inextricably been associated with imperialism. The missionaries' privileges were the fruit of China's defeat by the major Western powers and its subsequent fall in a rapidly changing world order. The Chinese people's hatred of foreigners and the denunciation of Chinese Protestants and Catholics, who were condemned as traitors to their country, surged around 1900, eventually culminating in the massive Boxer Uprising. During the Republican period, the sentiment was taken on board by nationalists struggling to build an independent nation-state. The Communist Party inherited the prevailing public perception from peasant rebels and nationalists. After 1949, the CCP exploited the discourse around Christianity to proclaim its historical mission to put an end to China's long suffering and humiliation and liberate the people from imperialism.

Since the Communist Party rose to power in mainland China, the reconstruction of historical narratives has been a national project in which the Marxist social engineers continually strive to dictate what citizens remember and forget. The Christian past has been an inescapable part of the official memory project. During the 1950s, there was a series of nation-wide accusations whose principal target against the backdrop of the Korean War and the Cold War was American missionary activity. The Xiamen region was no exception to the general trend. Missionaries, once privileged and respected, became the targets of public humiliation.

Church-related schools, hospitals, and other carriers of memory ceased to function, some of them smashed or appropriated during the Communist era, some later transformed by government-led tourism projects. With these material reminders of the missionary past gone or absorbed into another system of meaning, the social frameworks on which collective memory was established and shared have eroded. This environment exacerbates the difficulties of retaining a complete picture of the past, since the concrete sites of memory have faded.[6] Fortunately, many Christianity-related buildings across the city—churches, mission schools, and hospitals—were not demolished during the extreme campaigns but expropriated for government or public use and preserved in relatively good condition. Other forms of carriers of historical memory like the foreigners' cemetery and the more ephemeral archives and the like were not as fortunate and were destroyed, partly because they were regarded as useless in the process of socialist construction.

Historical writing is among the most significant forms of official memory. The PRC government's collection and compilation of personal testimonies served as a way to demonstrate the new leadership's commitment to absorbing those experiences within a unified, coherent narrative that would simultaneously affirm the Party's legitimacy and the part it played in a continuous lineage, as a liberator of the miserable Chinese nation. Christianity, which had been denounced for its entanglement with imperialism, was targeted in official historical works. The framework set up by the CPPCC project (for example, the *Xiamen Historical Materials*) further squeezed and colonized the space allowed for private memory. Even after the launch of social reforms and the policy of opening up to the outside world, the government has not slackened in its efforts to dominate narratives that deal with the Christian past. The Xiamen authorities' as yet unsuccessful but still ongoing history writing project, initiated in the 1980s, reveals that a unified history for Christianity, like that for any other religion, is still an item on the agenda of the state.

The grassroots efforts to write history in Xiamen is not an isolated episode; rather, it is part of a nationwide oral history movement. Although ideological control lies at the center of the Party's rule, governments and officials on local levels are not particularly motivated to take a firm grip on ideology-related matters at all times. Consequently, ordinary citizens' historical reconstructions of less sensitive issues are achievable in some locales.

The central state has become aware of the booming civic movement and has given a proactive response. The label of "historical nihilism" (*lishi xuwuzhuyi*) is attached to those who "deny histories of the Party and the nation" and even "rewrite history." "Historical nihilism" has been under heated debate since 2013, when a few scholars with quasi-official backgrounds began to publish in the official media. Xi Jinping openly opposed "historical nihilism" and, on different occasions, has blamed it on "domestic and foreign hostile forces." In Xi's words, the primary hazard posed by "historical nihilism" is that it will "deny the guiding position of Marxism, the inevitability of China progressing to socialism, and the leadership of the Chinese Communist Party."[7] Following Xi's guidelines, some official theorists have advocated reconstructing grand narratives to combat this emerging "historical nihilism."

Like many other memory studies, this research shows that the official manipulation of social memory is no longer effective in China today. A number of history enthusiasts, Christians and non-Christians alike, within and outside of churches, are dedicated to reinterpreting the legacy of Christianity and, in the course of their work, publicly commemorate its connections to the past. This civic movement is not confined solely to Christian groups or individuals. The majority of the people who organized the commemoration of John Otte (described in chapter 2) were non-Christians, and their efforts were spurred by their affection for the city's past rather than any religious motivation. Missionaries in Xiamen presented themselves as leaders of modernization, establishing a variety of modern institutions, and few expressed their power by exploiting any connection to the imperialist forces behind them; they won the respect of the people of Xiamen. Virtually no stories about any kind of antimissionary struggle have been transmitted to the present generation.[8]

Churches or individuals have gained considerable space for publishing (albeit sometimes "illegally") about historical matters. They are now able to reconstruct the history that is premised on their own understanding. History matters considerably to them because the version made and endorsed by the state appears to conflict strongly with their own understanding of their shared past. However, the fact that people do not believe in the state narratives does not mean that the great master narratives disappear.

State discourse shapes or even manipulates people's ways of thinking and doing; authority has been incorporated into the structure of social memory. This was clear in the recurrent theme that emerged at the beginning of my interviews, when respondents invariably referred to Christianity's inglorious entanglement with imperialist aggression before going on to make other points.

Although the state is a shrewd and often relentless manipulator of society's memory, ironically, it is the local government's pragmatic purposes (for example, the World Heritage Site application, or the competition for an international award for livable communities) and tacit approval that make alternative historical discourses on Christianity possible. The source of the socialist regime's legitimacy has, to some extent, shifted from its historical discourse or political ideology to economic performance. The socialist ideology that Christianity is facing today is far different from what it was in 1949. As Frank Pieke has argued, "Socialist ideology is no longer the end served by Communist Party rule, but the mere means by which party rule is perpetuated. . . . The specific relevance of ideology in justifying the CCP's rule means that . . . ideology [is deployed] as part of the party-state's ongoing quest to reproduce and reinvent itself: ideology is treated not as the objective of rule but as an inseparable aspect of practical governance."[9]

In the study of contemporary Christianity, it will no longer be seen as a consistent victim of the atheistic or antireligious socialist ideology. The relationship between Christianity and state ideology is not fixed but fluid, a fact that is exemplified in official attitudes toward the production of Christian history. Despite authorities' greater tolerance for narratives about Christianity before 1949, the history of Christianity after 1949—particularly stories about political movements that highlight the errors of the Communist regime—is still subject to extremely stringent restrictions. The revolutionary Party now tends to dilute its revolutionary image; the Party agenda has shifted to harmony and social stability. Under the circumstances, the production of Christian history is getting easier, as long as no reference is made to Mao's political campaigns. When it speaks of the traumas it inflicted on ordinary people, by and large the Party usually blames the Cultural Revolution but balks at allowing details to be publicized. The authorities still close archives and force publishers to delete details about the repression of Christianity, since they are well aware that these would damage its hard-won legitimacy, sustained by thirty years of economic achievements. Hence, the Cultural Revolution has been used as a handy vehicle to vent public grievances.

The reconstruction of the Christian past is actually an ongoing and dynamic process of negotiations. It illustrates the limits to the power of different actors—the state, churches, grassroots groups, and individuals—to remake the past according to their present interests. It also demonstrates that official projects and unofficial attempts at history-making often intertwine and infiltrate one another's domains. Consequently, memory viewed from a dynamic perspective should not reduce remembering to either an instrument of official manipulation or a form of popular resistance. In the context of postsocialist China, social memory inhabits the space left over between the ideology enforced by the state, suggesting other potential ways of understanding the Christian past. This perspective acknowledges that various elements that make social memory constant are often at play together. It postulates a complex view of how the relationship between past and present forms social memory. Importantly, it treats social memory as an active process of sense-making that has been taking place over time.[10]

Though it is still under one-party rule, it is not easy for the state to continue to monopolize the social memory related to Christianity. However, the people's ability to challenge official ideology should not be overstated. Any attempt to probe the reconstruction of the Christian past should investigate the negotiating mechanisms that have spontaneously formed in the social fabric. These do not function in any united or fixed form; rather, they are everyday maneuvers located in a particular social and cultural context and should be treated as a process that incorporates conflict, contestation, controversy, and cooperation as the hallmarks of memory.[11]

The historical and social changes in the landscape of Gulangyu and the collective passion for history there did not originate directly from a denial of official narratives. Intriguingly, the changing trajectory of Gulangyu represents two diametrically opposed discourses. Following the logic of market economy, the local government maximizes the potential of the island for economic purposes. In contrast, citizens with a sense of nostalgia see what is happening there as a process of "deterioration" and are convinced that excessive tourism exploitation is the main culprit. Gulangyu Island was once the center of the historical Three Missions and witnessed the flourishing of missionary enterprises in the region. Today, its shrinking congregation numbers show it is doomed to decline. In recent years, the center of gravity of Christianity has shifted to the main island of Xiamen, which has experienced a surge in the number of its Christian population. The changes on Gulangyu and within the church community there have triggered a series of subsequent events in Xiamen, including a growing nostalgia for the past glory, church anniversaries, and a commemoration of the late missionaries. In making sense of the collective passion for reinventing the past, it is important to understand local pride and nostalgia as ways in which individuals and social groups resort to reconstruct the past to relieve their strong sense of regret about the present.

The citizens who are engaged in the civic movement to (re)write history do not intend to challenge state ideology, even though the challenge does arise as an unintended consequence. This explains why, in the early stages of the cultural reinvention movement, its members did not envision the prospect of a more civil society. It might also help elucidate why clergy and lay Christians in Xiamen have no interest in present-day American evangelists, however much they cherish mission history and endorse the missionaries' contribution to the prosperous history of the area. There is no clear boundary between Christianity and the state, between unofficial narrative and official discourse, to define the space of each. The production of history texts described in chapter 4, for example, shows that official projects and unofficial attempts often permeate each other's narratives; they do not represent two completely separate domains. And, as long as the movement continues, what it produces will gradually enter the public consciousness, particularly when official narratives are contradictory to public understandings of the city's past. In the long term, this process will contribute to the growth of alternate viewpoints on history and what might be called civil society.

In Xiamen today, the writing of Christian history remains largely a passion of the cultural elite. They have devoted significant attention to the respected Christians who made such a large contribution to the city's glorious past and thus its local pride. Yet in stark contrast, the voices of early converts who were frequently uneducated, economically deprived, and socially marginalized are still largely unheard.

There is also a gender imbalance in how Christian history is told. Compared to male converts in the late nineteenth and early twentieth century, the vast number of female converts in the Xiamen area, with the exception of a very few examples of outstanding women, are often left nameless. In Christian history, the pioneering Chinese women of the early missionary period have left very few personal records and were given scant coverage in missionary reports.[12] This situation is not confined to China; it can be found throughout most of the world. For example, in her study of Christianity in the Middle East, Heleen Murre-van den Berg points out that the most difficult question to answer is how the early missionary activities

196

informed women's daily lives (such as marriage and career) and stimulated women to rethink their roles in family and society.[13] Recently, this issue has begun to receive some attention, albeit very limited, in the historical study of Chinese Christianity.[14]

Finally, there is still relatively little research on how Christians or members of Christian-influenced communities understand their own past. My intention has been to record how such a group of people view and reconstruct the Christian history that has substantially shaped their sense of identity and local pride. The case of Xiamen shows that a civic movement to produce alternative narratives brings Christian history into the mainstream. Nevertheless, it does not mean the spiritual aspects of Christianity have entered the mainstream. Christianity remains a minority religion on the periphery of Xiamen society. Therefore, I am dubious about Nanlai Cao's argument that "the presence of a business community organized at the grassroots level can . . . move Christianity from the margin to the mainstream of Chinese society in everyday maneuvers."[15] I am convinced that we need to distinguish between the presence of the religion of Christ and Christianity-related issues.

Reestablishing Links to Global Christianity

Thirty years of isolation from the outside world in the Maoist era once estranged the Chinese Christian community from the Christian world. Since 1979, the Xiamen church has resumed connections with Chinese diaspora churches, most of them in Southeast Asia. Members of the Southern Fujian church who fled abroad prior to October 1949 created a bridge between the Xiamen church and overseas Chinese Christian communities, who contributed huge amounts to the Xiamen church during tough times. This sort of Christian network was stimulated by state-led economic reform and the opening-up policy. In the early reform era, the government indirectly encouraged the reestablishment of transnational religious connections in order to attract foreign investment and boost the economy. In the course of negotiations, both sides made compromises.[16] For example, in the mid-1990s a county-level government permitted overseas Chinese Christians to rebuild a church on the condition that the latter agreed to bear the construction costs of a public hospital for a local township.

Since the late 1990s, China's economy has continued to develop and Xiamen became one of China's most economically prosperous regions.

The China side is no longer as hungry as it once was for economic invest-ment or assistance from overseas Chinese; in fact, the latter have lost their economic superiority. This considerable change in their economic situations has substantially reshaped the network between Fujian and Southeast Asia. Another important point is that the restoration of transnational connec-tions originated from the long-term emigration tradition of Fujian. Since the turn of the century, transnational networks based on geographical and lineage origin have weakened as more and more elderly overseas Chinese Christians have died.

Nevertheless, the Southeast Asian churches are still very much pres-ent. Alongside the decline in their economic contributions, these churches have initiated other channels to engage in the Xiamen church. The foremost among these is the training of clergy and church workers for both registered and unregistered churches. Hence, instead of making economic contri-butions, Southeast Asia is now influencing the Xiamen church through theology and training. This connection has been stimulated by prestigious and influential evangelists from Chinese Christian communities such as Stephen Tong, an Indonesian Reformed pastor who was born in Xiamen. Tong's Reformed theology is attractive to many Xiamen Christians, and his promotion of this tradition is boosting its recovery in the mainstream church in Xiamen.[17]

Of the Three Missions, the RCA was the first to reconnect with the Xiamen church after 1979. In 1992, the RCA headquarters in the United States invited Zhu Siming (1923–2015), a respected Christian, to attend the 150th anniversary of its mission to China as a representative of the Xiamen church. At Trinity Church's eightieth anniversary in 2014, a representative of the RCA was sent to attend and give a public speech. The publication of a history book about the RCA in the Xiamen area has helped to expand the historical knowledge of the local Christians. All these events have contributed to the Christian community's emerging sense of adhering to the authentic RCA tradition. A deaconess of Trinity Church who was study-ing Reformed theology in a Southeast Asian seminary once told me that she was hoping the RCA would produce a detailed instruction manual on how to lead a church in the RCA tradition. It is clear that many Xiamen Chris-tians relate to the global church in two senses: first, relishing the heritage of the historical church as a part of nineteenth- and twentieth-century global-izing Christianity; second, wanting to strengthen the Reformed theology and church governance structure so as to make it conform more closely to their mother missions. Apart from these two aspects, they do not really have a sense of integrating into the world Christian community in other forms. The Xiamen church shows no desire to regain its former place in the global institution of Christianity.

In her study of a Shanxi Catholic village, Henrietta Harrison found that the new generation of priests have attempted to retrieve the faith community's connection with the global Roman Catholic Church by asking the Vatican for recognition and by "rejecting some of the community's traditional practices and imposing new practices that they defined as belonging to the global church."[18] In contrast to the Roman Catholic tradition that the Vatican exercises authority over faith communities across the world, there is no such institution that Protestant communities have to obey in terms of either theology or church structure. Although the Reformed tradition has had far-reaching effects on the Xiamen church, the latter does not necessarily have to conform to the institutions of its mother missions.

This institutional disconnect between the Xiamen church and historical Western missions is largely the result of the fact that early missionaries purposefully worked to establish a native church of China rather than a branch of foreign missions. As Mark Noll remarks, the missionaries' forced departure was "the birth of Christian China,"[19] prompting local communities to turn inward for spiritual sustenance. In the absence of Western missionaries, Christianity grew deep roots in Xiamen during the series of violent Maoist political campaigns. As soon as political space was opened to religious practices, Christianity reentered public life.

At the beginning of the century, as it faced the problem of a declining congregation, Trinity Church did seek cooperation with international Christian organizations. At present, the ambitious American church has been attempting to play a greater role in the global missionary enterprise, particularly in the Global South movement. As a consequence, the Xiamen church is once again encountering the American church. This time, both Xiamen society and the global missionary enterprise are very different from what they were in the era of imperialism. In China, the stigma once attached to membership in a foreign religion in the late nineteenth and early twentieth century has been transformed by the widespread yearning for all things Western, a desire especially apparent among young people. Unquestionably, its foreign background has been crucial to the success of the American Christian agency in converting a large number of college students and young professionals. In contrast to the negative connotations associated with nineteenth-century Western imperialist powers, in the current international environment Rainbow's American-ness contributes to its competitiveness in attracting young potential converts. The English language, American faces, and Christianity together construct a cosmo-politan, global image. Through contact with and acceptance of American Christianity, the young people expect a fuller involvement in the global world.

Despite the enthusiasm it generates, for political reasons Rainbow's American image hampers its acceptance by the local church. The success of the historical Three Missions and the indigenized church provides a good lesson for present missionary groups. They cannot truly survive and expand in contemporary Chinese society if they refuse to become rooted for a second time. The reencounter of Chinese Christianity with the global missions today is inevitable. The internet, tourism, migration, and many opportunities to study abroad allow Chinese people easier access to world Christianity. Whether or not the Chinese state allows it, Chinese Christians can now frequently interact with the world Christian community and will integrate more actively into the global missions (for example, the mission-oriented "Back to Jerusalem" movement).

As this research indicates, scholars of world Christianity should probe more deeply into the connections between Chinese Christianity and global Christianity today. As the Christian networks are contextual, fragile, and continually changing, the nature of Chinese Christianity and its place on the global stage should not be taken for granted. Some Chinese Christians might say "All believers under heaven are brothers and sisters," but they are saying this mainly in terms of faith. It is not an indication of any plans to integrate more deeply into the world community. Conversely, researchers should not see Chinese Christianity as being isolated from world Christianity. Scholars should attend to how local traditions and international Christian presences interact. Therefore, a perspective that combines globalization and local-ization, both in the past and in the present, can help us better understand Chinese Christianity in a local, national, and global context.

Notes

Introduction

1. The Chinese term for *Christianity* (*Jidujiao*) is almost always used as a synonym for *Protestantism* (*Xinjiao*). Throughout this research, unless noted, the term *Christianity* refers to Protestantism. When I refer to Catholic Christianity, the term *Catholicism* will be adopted. In reference to the entire Xiamen Christian community, the phrase "the Xiamen church" or "the local church" is used.

2. Berger, *Sacred Canopy*.

3. Berger, "Desecularization of the World." When referring to Berger's desecularization thesis, a fact easily overlooked is that, in the same text, he also points out that "in Western Europe, if nowhere else, the old secularization theory would seem to hold" (9). As Grace Davie has argued in the same volume, "In a world characterized by religious resurgence rather than increasing secularization, Western Europe bucks the trend." Davie, "Europe," 65.

4. Berger, Davie, and Fokas, *Religious America, Secular Europe?*

5. Stanley, *Christianity in the Twentieth Century*, 360.

6. Jenkins, *Next Christendom*; Jenkins, *New Faces of Christianity*; Sanneh, *Disciples of All Nations*; Sanneh and Carpenter, *Changing Face of Christianity*.

7. Bautista, "About Face," 201–2.

8. C. S. Park, *Protestantism and Politics in Korea*, 3.

9. Arrington, *Songs of the Lisu Hills*; Bays, "Chinese Protestant Christianity Today"; Cao, *Constructing China's Jerusalem*; A. Hunter and Chan, *Protestantism in Contemporary China*; J. Kang, *House Church Christianity in China*; X. Lian, *Redeemed by Fire*; Ma and Li, *Surviving the State, Remaking the Church*; Y. Sun, "Rise of Protestantism"; Vala, *Politics of Protestant Churches*; F. Yang, *Religion in China*; F. Yang, "Lost in the Market."

10. Bays, "Chinese Protestant Christianity Today," 488.

11. Bays, "Growth of Independent Christianity in China"; Cheung, *Christianity in Modern China*; Dunn, *Lightening from the East*; Inouye, *China and the True Jesus*; X. Lian, *Redeemed by Fire*; P. T. M. Ng, *Chinese Christianity*; X. Wang, *Maoism and Grassroots Religion*.

12. Jenkins, *Next Christendom*, 13–16.

13. Bautista and Lim, *Christianity and the State in Asia*.

14. Adogame and Shankar, *Religion on the Move!*; Jenkins, *Next Christendom*; Walls and Ross, *Mission in the 21st Century*.

15. Moon, "Missions from Korea, 2019," 188.

16. Kim, *Spirit Moves West*.

17. Hattaway et al., *Back to Jerusalem*.

18. In 2017, a Chinese woman and man in their mid-twenties who had served at a clandestine mission were murdered by the so-called Islamic State in Pakistan. See BBC News, "Risky Road."

19. Mullins, *Christianity Made in Japan*.

20. P. T. M. Ng, *Chinese Christianity*, 41.

21. Cao, *Constructing China's Jerusalem*; J. Huang, "Being Christians in Urbanizing China"; Wielander, *Christian Values in Communist China*; F. Yang, "Lost in the Market."

22. Van der Veer, *Conversion to Modernities*.

23. Paramore, *Ideology and Christianity in Japan*.

24. Vanderbilt, "Post-War Japanese Christian Historians."

25. Takayama, "Revitalization Movement."

26. For the Christian history and politics of Korea, see Buswell and Lee, *Christianity in Korea*; W. J. Kang, *Christ and Caesar in Modern Korea*; C. S. Park, *Protestantism and Politics in Korea*.

27. C. W. Park, "Christian Reactions to Government-Led Cremation."

28. Dunch, *Fuzhou Protestants*; White, *Sacred Webs*.

29. Sanneh, *Disciples of All Nations*, 243.

30. A. L. Park and Yoo, "Introduction," 6–7.

31. It is not uncommon for many unregistered churches to have hundreds or even thousands of members, and their activities are no longer confined to private housing but rather take place in hotels, abandoned factories, or rented office spaces. At present, the term *house church* is still often used in the Christian communities and in scholarship mainly because of the tradition inherited from the early house church movement.

32. Chao and Chong, *Dangdai Zhongguo Jidujiao fazhan shi*; Kindopp, "Politics of Protestantism in Contemporary China"; Kindopp and Hamrin, *God and Caesar in China*; R. Wang, *Resistance Under Communist China*; Wenger, "Official vs. Underground Protestant Churches in China."

33. Koesel, *Religion and Authoritarianism*, 45–47; F. Yang, *Religion in China*, 81–82. For a detailed analysis, see J. Liu and White, "Old Pastor and Local Bureaucrats."

34. F. Yang, *Religion in China*.

35. For a discussion, see P. C. C. Huang, "'Public Sphere' / 'Civil Society' in China?"

36. Cao, *Constructing China's Jerusalem*, 7–8.

37. Bays, "Tradition of State Dominance"; C. K. Yang, *Religion in Chinese Society*; A. C. Yu, *State and Religion in China*.

38. Koesel, *Religion and Authoritarianism*.

39. Cao, *Constructing China's Jerusalem*; K. H. Huang, "Dyadic Nexus Fighting Two-Front Battles"; J. Liu and White, "Old Pastor and Local Bureaucrats"; McLeister, "Three-Self Protestant Church"; Reny, *Authoritarian Containment*; Vala, *Politics of Protestant Churches*.

40. It is worth noting that Christie Chow once analyzed a church demolition event in rural Zhejiang in 2012. She has pointed out that "this incident seems to have set a precedent for a regional anti-Christian campaign in 2013–14, because it signified a qualitative shift in the Chinese state's anti-Christian discourse." See C. C. S. Chow, "Demolition and Defiance," 250.

41. Renmin wang, "Zhejiang Yongjia yifa chaichu Sanjiang weifa zongjiao jianzhu."

42. See, for example, Cao, *Constructing China's Jerusalem*.

43. For a detailed review and discussion of the Zhejiang campaign and its aftermath, see F. Yang, "Cross of Chinese Christians."

44. F. Yang, "Failure of the Campaign"; Ying, "Politics of Cross Demolition."

45. McLeister, "Chinese Protestant Reactions."

46. *Xinhua ribao*, "Mei le yanwu liaorao, duo le manmu xinlü."

47. McLeister, "Chinese Protestant Reactions"; Xie, "Religion and State in China."

48. Koesel, *Religion and Authoritarianism*.

49. Bays, *New History of Christianity in China*, 85–86.

50. Lutz, *China and the Christian Colleges*, 204–36; Yip, *Religion, Nationalism and Chinese Students*.

51. Callahan, *China*.

52. Bays, *New History of Christianity in China*, 47.

53. Fairbank, "Introduction," 2–3.

54. Bays, *New History of Christianity in China*, 47–48.

55. De Jong, *Reformed Church in China*, 13.

56. Mao, *Mao Zedong xuanji*, 2:629–30.

57. Ibid., 4:1505–6.

58. Ibid., 1491–98.

59. For example, in 1950 on several occasions Zhou Enlai (1898–1976), the first premier of the PRC, told representatives of the Protestant church that Christianity had obtained the missionary rights by threats with guns against the Qing government; therefore, he concluded, the major problem with Christianity was its relationship with imperialism. See Zhonggong zhongyang wenxian yanjiushi, *Jianguo yilai zhongyao wenxian xuanbian*, 1:220–27.

60. Ying, "Fandi aiguo yu zongjiao gexin."

61. C. Gu, *Chuanjiaoshi yu jindai Zhongguo*.

62. This change in view is mainly reflected in his autobiographical English book. See C. Gu, *Awaken*.

63. See, for example, G. Luo, *Qianshi bu wang houshi zhi shi*; Zhongguo Jidujiao sanzi aiguo yundong weiyuanhui and Zhongguo

Jidujiao xiehui, *Jidujiao aiguozhuyi jiaocheng (shiyong ben)*. For a detailed analysis of the Christian patriotic education campaign, see Kuo, "Chinese Religious Reform."

64. For a discussion, see J. Liu and White, "Consuming Missionary Legacies."

65. There are very few studies dedicated to historical accounts of Christianity during the Cultural Revolution. See, for example, Kao, "Cultural Revolution"; Kao, "Materiality"; X. Wang, *Maoism and Grassroots Religion*.

66. Cohen, "Remembering and Forgetting," 2.

67. Z. Wang, *Never Forget National Humiliation*, 9.

68. Zhonggong zhongyang wenxian yanjiushi zonghe yanjiuzu and Guowuyuan zongjiao shiwuju zhengce faguisi, *Xin shiqi zongjiao gongzuo wenxian xuanbian*, 177.

69. Madsen, "From Socialist Ideology to Cultural Heritage."

70. For a discussion, see X. Li, "Zongjiao shengtai haishi quanli shengtai."

71. Pieke, "Party Spirit," 709.

72. A. Sun, *Confucianism as a World Religion*, 174–75.

73. *Guardian*, "Chinese Cities Crack Down."

74. Cao, "Spatial Modernity, Party Building."

75. Harrison, *Missionary's Curse and Other Tales*; A. Hunter and Chan, *Protestantism in Contemporary China*; J. Liu and White, "Old Pastor and Local Bureaucrats"; Lozada, *God Aboveground*; Madsen, *China's Catholics*; F. Wu, *Maimang shang de shengyan*.

76. Cao, *Constructing China's Jerusalem*.

77. Ashiwa and Wank, *Making Religion, Making the State*; Cao, *Constructing China's Jerusalem*; Dunch, *Fuzhou Protestants*; White, *Sacred Webs*; M. M. H. Yang, *Chinese Religiosities*.

78. Ong, "Chinese Modernities."

79. Cao, *Constructing China's Jerusalem*.

80. F. Yang, "Chinese Conversion to Evangelical Christianity," 251.

81. Cao, *Constructing China's Jerusalem*; Wielander, *Christian Values in Communist China*.

82. Cao, *Constructing China's Jerusalem*, 164.

83. Ashiwa, "Positioning Religion in Modernity," 44.

84. Bays, "Chinese Protestant Christianity Today," 502.

85. Dunch, "Protestant Christianity in China Today," 212–13.

86. Madsen, *China's Catholics*.

87. Cao, *Constructing China's Jerusalem*, 166–67.

88. Harrison, *Missionary's Curse and Other Tales*; Lozada, *God Aboveground*; Madsen, *China's Catholics*; F. Wu, *Maimang shang de shengyan*.

89. J. Liu and White, "Consuming Missionary Legacies"; White, "History Lessons."

90. White, "Sacred Dwellings."

91. Nosco, *Remembering Paradise*, 4.

92. Q. Zhang and Weatherley, "Rise of 'Republican Fever.'"

93. Béja, "Forbidden Memory, Unwritten History"; Ci, *Dialectic of the Chinese Revolution*, chapter 2; Jing, *Temple of Memories*; Schwarcz, "Out of Historical Amnesia"; R. S. Watson, "Making Secret Histories"; H. Zhou, *Jiyi de zhengzhi*.

94. Jing, *Temple of Memories*, 18.

95. See Cubitt, *History and Memory*; Le Goff, *History and Memory*.

96. Halbwachs, *On Collective Memory*.

97. Mead, "Nature of the Past," 241.

98. I. M. L. Hunter, *Memory*, 203.

99. Connerton, *How Societies Remember*, 3.

100. Quoted in Megill, "Foucault," 500.

101. Hobsbawm, "Introduction," 1.

102. See, for example, Evans, *Politics of Ritual and Remembrance*; Lane, *Rites of Rulers*; Wertsch, *Voices of Collective Remembering*.

103. See, for example, Y. Chen, *Qing dai qianqi de zhengzhi rentong yu lishi shuxie*.

104. Dirlik, *Revolution and History*; Unger, *Using the Past*.

105. Goldman, *Literary Dissent in Communist China*.

106. Ci, *Dialectic of the Chinese Revolution*, 81.

107. Béja, "Forbidden Memory, Unwritten History."

108. R. S. Watson, "Introduction," 19.

109. Guo and Sun, "Suku"; H. Zhou, *Jiyi de zhengzhi*.

110. Ci, *Dialectic of the Chinese Revolution*, 82–83.

111. Confino, "Memory and Cultural History," 1395.

112. Schudson, "Lives, Laws, and Language," 5.

113. Ci, *Dialectic of the Chinese Revolution*, 75.

114. Jing, *Temple of Memories*, 171.

115. Foucault, *Language, Counter-Memory, Practice*, part 2.

116. Popular Memory Group, "Popular Memory."

117. Goldman, *Literary Dissent in Communist China*; Goldman, Cheek, and Hamrin, *China's Intellectuals and the State*; E. Gu and Goldman, *Chinese Intellectuals*; Mok, *Intellectuals and the State*; Unger, *Using the Past*.

118. Olick and Levy, "Collective Memory and Cultural Constraint," 922.

119. Misztal, *Theories of Social Remembering*, 127.

120. Schudson, *Watergate in American Memory*.

121. Misztal, *Theories of Social Remembering*, 73.

122. F. Wu, *Maimang shang de shengyan*, 31.

123. Zhongguo shehui kexueyuan shijie zongjiao yanjiusuo ketizu, "Zhongguo Jidujiao ruhu wenjuan diaocha baogao."

124. X. Liu, "Sino-Christian Theology."

Chapter 1

1. R. Chen and Li, *Xiamen fangyan*, 28–31.

2. Xiamen shi tongjiju, "Xiamen shi 2020 nian guomin jingji he shehui fazhan tongji gongbao."

3. Lehmann, *Transnational Lives in China*.

4. K. Zhou et al., *Xiamen zhi*, 1.

5. X. Lin et al., *Tong'an xian zhi*, 41.

6. K. Zhou et al., *Xiamen zhi*, 79.

7. Xue et al., *Lujiang zhi*. The page with the description of the walled city is unidentified.

8. For private sea trade ports in Fujian during the Ming and Qing dynasties, see R. Lin, *Ming mo Qing chu siren haishang maoyi*, chapter 4.

9. Antony, *Like Froth Floating on the Sea*.

10. Andrade, *Lost Colony*.

11. R. Lin, *Ming mo Qing chu siren haishang maoyi*, 117–26.

12. R. Lin, *Fujian duiwai maoyi yu haiguan shi*, 144–48.

13. Xue et al., *Lujiang zhi*. Page of preface by Liao Feipeng is unidentified.

14. R. Lin, *Fujian duiwai maoyi yu haiguan shi*, 164–68.

15. C. K. Ng, *Trade and Society*.

16. Catholic missionaries had been penetrating the area since the late Ming era. It is said that a Catholic church was built in Zengcuoan, a fishing village. However, this site has not been located and no remains have ever been found. See Gong, "Xiamen Tianzhu tang."

17. L. Lian, *Fujian mimi shehui*, 137–48.

18. Ching, "Guojia ruhe taoli."

19. Scott, *Art of Not Being Governed*.

20. Interviews with retired Communist Party cadres.

21. The Chinese state is functionally divided between the Communist Party, which provides ideological guidance, and the government, which handles the administration. Organs of both coexist at all levels of the state, with the Party having authority over the government at the same level. The Central Committee is the highest level of the Party, whereas the State Council is the highest level of the government. The overwhelming majority of officials are CCP members.

22. Howell, "Political Economy."

23. Dai, *Quyuxing jingji fazhan yu shehui bianqian*, 310–11.

24. Cook, "Bridges to Modernity"; Dai, *Quyuxing jingji fazhan yu shehui bianqian*; S. M. Li and Zhao, "Xiamen"; Y. Yu, "Remaking Xiamen."

25. Cook, "Reimaging China."

26. Tan, *Southern Fujian*.

27. Ashiwa and Wank, "Globalization of Chinese Buddhism"; Kuah-Pearce, *Rebuilding the Ancestral Village*; J. Liu, "From Vegetarian Hall to Revolutionary Relic"; J. Liu and White, "Old Pastor and Local Bureaucrats"; White and Liu, "Going Global and Back Again."

28. Kuah-Pearce, *Rebuilding the Ancestral Village*.

29. Pitcher, *In and About Amoy*, 16–17.

30. Bowra, "Amoy," 816.

31. As of 1926, the number of Chinese representatives was increased to three, and their foreign counterparts decreased to four.

Z. Zhang et al., "Gonggong zujie shiqi de Gulangyu," 27. For the organizational system, see appendix 2 in "Xiamen Zhengxie wenshi ziliao weiyuanhui," *Xiamen wenshi ziliao* 3 (1980).

32. See Giles, *Short History of Koolangsu*, 14–15.

33. See Xiamen shi zhi bianweihui and Xiamen haiguan zhi bianweihui, *Jindai Xiamen shehui jingji gaikuang*, 356.

34. See Gulangyu guanweihui, *Zhongguo shijie wenhua yichan yubei mingdan shenbao wenjian*, 2–81.

35. The 5A-class is at the highest level recognized by the China National Tourism Administration in its evaluation system for tourist attractions.

36. For the official planning of Gulangyu, see Xiamen shi difangzhi bianweihui, *Xiamen shi zhi*, 1:382–83.

37. Xiamen tongjiju and Guojia tongjiju Xiamen diaochadui, *Xiamen jingji tequ nianjian 2019*, 112.

38. Siming qu zhengfu, "2019 nian huji renkou ji qi biandong qingkuang."

39. References to *suzhi* are used to justify the formation of all manner of social and political hierarchies. People with "high" *suzhi* are seen as having a natural right to more income, power, and status than those people with "low" *suzhi*. See Kipnis, "Suzhi."

40. On Gulangyu any kind of motor vehicle is forbidden (police patrols and tourists use storage battery cars). The transport of goods relies on a large number of laborers, the majority from Anhui and Henan provinces.

41. Nosco, *Remembering Paradise*, 4.

42. Niu, "Gulangyu: siqu haishi huozhe?"

43. Bays, *New History of Christianity in China*, chapter 1.

44. Ibid., 21.

45. See, for example, Harrison, *Missionary's Curse and Other Tales*; X. Zhang, *Guanfu, zongzu yu Tianzhujiao*.

46. Daily, *Robert Morrison and the Protestant Plan*.

47. De Jong, *Reformed Church in China*, 13.

48. White, "Xinjie Church and Christianity."

49. See, for example, Sanyi tang, *Sanyi tang bashi nian*, 13.

50. Cheung, *Christianity in Modern China*, 13.

51. Quoted from De Jong, *Reformed Church in China*, 16.

52. White, *Sacred Webs*.

53. De Jong, *Reformed Church in China*, 30.

54. Dunch, *Fuzhou Protestants*, 32–47.

55. Y. Huang et al., "Xiaozhang yunji de Shao shi jiazu."

56. See, for example, White, "To Rescue the Wretched Ones."

57. See Fagg, *Forty Years in South China*, 106–7.

58. For a historical account, see Cheng, "Sing to the Lord a New Song."

59. Jenkins, *Next Christendom*, 140–43.

60. Fagg, *Forty Years in South China*, 192.

61. De Jong, *Reformed Church in China*, 76–77.

62. See Cheung, *Christianity in Modern China*, 288–93.

63. Fagg, *Forty Years in South China*, 192.

64. De Jong, *Reformed Church in China*, 62–63.

65. See, for example, Ding, *Ding Guangxun wenji*, 18.

66. A. Chow, "Calvinist Public Theology in Urban China"; Fällman, "Calvin, Culture and Christ?"

67. SARA was renamed the National Religious Affairs Administration (NRAA) in 2018, when it ceased to be affiliated with the State Council. However, I use the acronym SARA throughout this book on the grounds that the research was completed prior to the change; additionally, SARA is more commonly used in the literature.

68. The two organizations do not always have the same official views. In July 2015, for instance, the Zhejiang Christian Council publicly appealed to authorities to cease the removal of crosses, which damaged the relations between the Party and the masses, whereas its counterpart, Zhejiang TSPM, did not stage any public protest.

69. London Missionary Society, *Chronicle of the London Missionary Society*, 220.

70. This body held its first general conference in Shanghai in 1927 and the second in Guangzhou in 1930. The third general conference took place in Gulangyu in 1933.

71. Freedman, *Chinese Lineage and Society*; Y. H. Lin, *Golden Wing*; Szonyi, *Practicing Kinship*; Z. Zheng, *Family Lineage Organization*.

72. Menegon, *Ancestors, Virgins, and Friars*; X. Zhang, *Guanfu, zongzu yu Tianzhujiao*.

73. For example, Ashiwa and Wank, "Politics of a Reviving Buddhist Temple"; De Groot, *Religious System of China*; Dean, *Taoist Ritual and Popular Cults*; Dean, *Lord of the Three in One*; Dean and Zheng, *Ritual Alliances of the Putian Plain*; Feuchtwang and Wang, *Grassroots Charisma*; Kuah-Pearce, *Rebuilding the Ancestral Village*; J. L. Watson, "Standardizing the Gods."

74. White and Liu, "Going Global and Back Again."

75. Walls, *Missionary Movement in Christian History*.

76. Phan, *Christianities in Asia*, xv.

77. Cheung, *Christianity in Modern China*.

78. De Jong, *Reformed Church in China*.

79. White, *Sacred Webs*.

80. White, *Protestantism in Xiamen*.

81. Colijn, "One House, Two Paths."

Chapter 2

1. This account of the event is an ethnographic reconstruction based on documents and extensive interviews with direct participants.

2. Most of Otte's biography in this chapter is drawn from Warnshuis, *Brief Sketch*.

3. It was named after the Neerbosch Orphanage in the Netherlands, from which the first donation, a Dutch girl's pennies, was received.

4. Several years later, it was renamed the Wilhelmina Hospital in appreciation of the generous support from the then queen of the Netherlands, Queen Wilhelmina (r. 1890–1948), who gladly consented to being named the hospital's patron. Subsequently, the hospital as a whole was renamed the Hope and Wilhelmina Hospital, usually abbreviated to Hope Hospital in most sources.

5. In the RCA tradition, a classis is the equivalent of a presbytery.

6. See De Jong, *Reformed Church in China*, 326.

7. The number of foreign missionaries in China had started to decline even before the Communist victory, as many left the country due to concerns over the deteriorating domestic situation caused by the civil war. However, some missionaries still remained in the country after 1949.

8. X. Zheng and Huang, "Meiguo yisheng Yu Yuehan ruci ling ren," 64.

9. No living person knows where Otte's remains lie. After the reopening of China Rev. Walter de Velder (1907–2005), an RCA missionary who served on Gulangyu and married Otte's daughter Margaret, returned to Gulangyu at least four times to look for the graves of Otte and Margaret, but he failed to find them.

10. QQ is an instant messaging software offering a variety of services, such as private message, group chat, online games, music, shopping, and microblogging.

11. In Chinese history, the literary and political elites distinguished between civilized peoples and barbarians (*fan*). Westerners were formerly known under the umbrella term *fanzai*. Numerous texts from the first half of the nineteenth century refer to Westerners as "barbarian devils" (*fangui*; see Dikötter, *Discourse of Race in Modern China*). In my interviews, local history experts denied the derogatory sense of the ancient usage of *fanzai* and rephrased it more naturally: people who came from different cultures. However, the term's derogatory connotations were recorded by missionaries at the time. See, for example, Fagg, *Forty Years in South China*, 184; Macgowan, *Beside the Bamboo*, 179–80.

12. John's father, Walter de Velder, had been married to Otte's daughter Margaret. Margaret Otte died in childbirth and Walter de Velder later married Harriet Boot, John de Velder's mother. He lived in China for several years as a young boy while his parents were serving there as missionaries. He remembered leaving China with his mother and siblings in 1949, when the Communists took over; his father returned to the United States two years later when the situation grew even worse.

13. John de Velder, who was close to Otte's descendants, established relations with very

few church leaders and locals. Hence, the connection between Otte's family and Xiamen is limited to a very small circle.

14. De Jong, *Reformed Church in China*, 347–49.

15. Unger, *Using the Past*.

16. The conflict about land for church construction has been regarded as a major factor in the upsurge in anti-Christian cases (*jiaoan*) in late imperial China. For official narratives on missionaries occupying land to build churches and villas on Gulangyu, see Gulangyu guangongwei, *Gulangyu qu aiguozhuyi jiaoyu cailiao xuanbian*, 38–39.

17. Dean, *Lord of the Three in One*, 261–63.

18. Xiamen shi difangzhi bianweihui, *Xiamen shi zhi*, 5:3469.

19. Chau, *Miraculous Response*; Gao, "Yizuo bowuguan-miaoyu jianzhu de minzuzhi"; X. Wang, *Maoism and Grassroots Religion*, chapter 7; Yue, "Chuantong minjian wenhua yu xin nongcun jianshe."

20. Cao, *Constructing China's Jerusalem*.

21. R. S. Watson, "Making Secret Histories."

22. See Johnson, "Grieving," on a Hakka funeral in Hong Kong as a vehicle for protest.

23. The Anti-Rightist Movement launched by Chairman Mao was a reaction to the Hundred Flowers Campaign. It was a series of campaigns to purge alleged "rightists" that lasted from roughly 1957 to 1959. Who and what a "rightist" might be was not always clearly and consistently defined. The official use of this derogatory term was to identify and stigmatize intellectuals who appeared to favor capitalism and oppose collectivization, although it could even include critics to the left of the government. The campaign led to the persecution of half a million people.

24. World Heritage Centre, "Properties Inscribed on the World Heritage List" and "Sites on the Tentative List."

25. Oakes and Sutton, *Faiths on Display*.

26. For her book, see He, *Gonggong zujie Gulangyu yu jindai Xiamen de fazhan*.

27. It is worth mentioning that the only use of the term *imperialist aggression* in the application appears to describe the Japanese invasion in the 1940s. In the official documents for the WHS application, the Japanese occupation, a major catastrophe resulting in

casualties in the tens of millions, is blamed for the disruption to the plurality of cultures on the island. Although the application materials reinterpreted the imperialist history of Gulangyu, authorities were still unwilling to rewrite the history of Japanese imperialism, in keeping with the government's attitude toward the Second Sino-Japanese War.

28. World Heritage Centre, "Kulangsu."

29. Gulangyu guanweihui, *Zhongguo shijie wenhua yichan yubei mingdan shenbao wenjian*, 2–2.

30. Nora, "Between Memory and History."

31. J. Liu, "From Vegetarian Hall to Revolutionary Relic"; Matten, *Places of Memory in Modern China*.

32. Flath, "How the Chinese People Began Their Struggle," 167.

33. H. Lee, "Ruins of Yuanmingyuan."

34. Potter, "Belief in Control."

35. Gulangyu guanweihui, *Zhongguo shijie wenhua yichan yubei mingdan shenbao wenjian*, 2–2.

36. De Jong, *Reformed Church in China*, 167.

37. Xiamen Fojiao xiehui, "*Hong Yi Gulang xiejing* chongkan diancang yishi zai Gulangyu Riguangyan si longzhong juxing."

38. For an extensive discussion, see Xiang, *Transcending Boundaries*.

39. Pan and Xu, "China's Ideological Spectrum," 254.

40. *Xiamen ribao*, "Bu Xianli yi bei wo quzhu chujing."

41. De Jong, *Reformed Church in China*, 334.

42. Qihuang Shanren, "Fanzai mu kou de bianqian."

43. For the traumatic memory of destruction of ancestral graves, see Jing, *Temple of Memories*, chapter 4.

44. *Xiamen ribao*, "Ben shi Junguanhui xuanbu guanzhi Jiushi yiyuan chanye."

45. Xiamen archive (ref.: B36-1-33).

46. *Xiamen ribao*, "Ben shi Weishengju jieban Jiushi yiyuan ji fushe hushi xuexiao."

47. *Xiamen ribao*, "Ben shi Junguanhui xuanbu guanzhi Jiushi yiyuan chanye."

48. Unger, "Introduction," 1.

49. Eric Henry Liddell, a 1924 Olympic 400 m gold medalist, was born in Tianjin, Northern China, in 1902. After graduating from

208

Edinburgh University, he returned to China to serve as a missionary and schoolteacher until his death in a Japanese internment camp in Wei County (now Weifang City), Shandong Province, in 1945. For official commemorations of Liddell and government officials' exploration of Liddell's reputation to improve the city's fame, see J. Liu and White, "Consuming Missionary Legacies."

Chapter 3

An earlier version of chapter 3 has been adapted by permission of Springer Nature: Palgrave Macmillan, from *Protestantism in Xiamen: Then and Now*, edited by Chris White © 2019.

1. Red books are a tradition at important events in China. Visitors may sign their names or reception personnel may record their names and the amount of their donation or gifts in the book. Trinity only requested that guests of honor sign their names.

2. On April 17, 2014, I attended a church anniversary celebration in rural Pinghe County, a mission base dating back to nineteenth-century Southern Fujian. The names of all the donors and the amounts they had contributed were written down on big posters hanging on the walls. The background of the red poster was a traditional treasure bowl (*jubaopen*) with a boy and a girl of wealth standing in each corner at the bottom.

3. *Pastor* and *preacher* are two different levels in the church system. In a registered Three-Self church, young church workers who have graduated from officially sanctioned seminaries are eligible to preach. After several years of service, they can be recommended by their affiliated churches to be ordained as pastors with the official approval of the Lianghui organizations and religious affairs authorities, both at the provincial level.

4. This is a reference to the food God provided to the Israelites during their forty years in the wilderness. See Exodus 16:31.

5. Corinthians 14:40.

6. In the Chinese context, the use of words like *we* and *our* by the official was only a linguistic means to express his friendliness. He was not implying he was part of the Christian community.

7. Romans 12:17.

8. Job 12:12.

9. Jiantang chouweihui, *Wei jianzhu Gulangyu Sanyi tang mujuan qi*. In this section, the historical information comes mainly from Sanyi tang, *Sanyi tang bashi nian*.

10. In the church structure, each governing body affiliated with the LMS was independent. On the other hand, the RCA/PCE churches operated on a presbytery/synod system. Within a presbytery were many divisions. These churches were governed by elders and deacons, whereas LMS churches were not. In Huian County today, there are no elders but church directors (*tang zhuren*), since this area was traditionally influenced by the LMS. Members were acquainted or even simply related; in other words, they felt more comfortable with people from their own denomination. Christians on Gulangyu who were connected to RCA/PCE churches in Xiamen would feel a little uncomfortable at the Gospel Church in terms of social connections and habit, but theologically there is not much difference.

11. For details, see H. Zhu, "Ben hui zhi chengli yu jingguo."

12. Dr. John Sung, a famous Christian evangelist, was one of the most prominent figures in the Christian revival movement, not just among the Chinese in mainland China but also in Taiwan and Southeast Asia, in the second and third decades of the twentieth century. See Ireland, *John Song*.

13. Only one of the first members was still alive when the 2014 event took place.

14. Lu, "Rikou yu zhong qiunan ji."

15. Xiamen archive (ref. B058-001-0058).

16. Xiamen archive (ref. B058-001-0058).

17. Wen, "Xiamen shi Gulangyu Zhonghua jidu jiaohui Sanyi tang."

18. See *Xiamen ribao*, "Zhou Qingze shi zongjiaojie de youpai fenzi"; *Xiamen ribao*, "Zhou Qingze pizhe zongjiao waiyi fangdu fanghuo."

19. It is now a nursing home, privately run by a Christian entrepreneur, but the property belongs to the Xiamen Lianghui.

20. Stark, *Rise of Christianity*, chapter 1.

21. According to Fenggang Yang, the "red market" of religion refers to all legal (officially recognized) religious organizations, believers, and activities; the "black market" indicates all illegal (officially banned) religious organizations, believers, and activities; the "gray market" of religion consists of all religious and spiritual organizations, practitioners, and activities with an ambiguous legal status. Authorities see the "gray market" as an unmanageable state of religious affairs that could potentially provide fertile soil for new religious movements. See F. Yang, "Red, Black, and Gray Markets."

22. White and Liu, "Going Global and Back Again."

23. One of my informants questioned the amount that Trinity Church had contributed to its counterparts and implied that Wen had exaggerated his contribution.

24. *Xiamen ribao*, "Shi Jidu jiaotu gonggu aiguo zhenxian, bodao Wen Yihan Du Zunneng fan Dang miulun."

25. Matthew 10:16.

26. This is a pseudonym, chosen for the village's ubiquitous banyan trees.

27. This does not mean the Old Pastor (or other church members) believes that the CCP will really accept the "incompatibility" between the Christian faith and its political stance. He and other members mentioned several times the state's real attitude toward Christianity—namely, "utilization," "restriction," and "transformation."

28. Vala, "Pathways to the Pulpit," 97.

29. Ibid., 118.

30. In the training of the younger generation of religious personnel, the official guidelines are: "To provide talents for the mutual adaption of religions and the socialist society, we should support and help patriotic religious organizations to run various religious educational institutions to train a corps of young religious personnel who love the motherland; accept the leadership of the Party and the government; adhere to the socialist road; safeguard the dignity of law, the people's interests and the unity of the country and the Chinese nation; have fairly rich religious knowledge; maintain contacts with the religious masses." Guojia zongjiaoju zhengce

faguisi, *Zhongguo zongjiao fagui zhengce duben*, 101.

31. K. H. Huang, "Sect-to-Church Movement in Globalization"; A. Hunter and Chan, *Protestantism in Contemporary China*, 81; Vala, "Pathways to the Pulpit"; White and Liu, "Going Global and Back Again." A few scholars have noted the active participation of the Southern Korean Protestant community in the training of Chinese clergy. See, for example, Baugus and Park, "Brief History," 91–93; J. Kang, *House Church Christianity in China*, 33; McLeister, "Three-Self Protestant Church," 238.

32. McLeister, "Three-Self Protestant Church."

33. Joshua 1:6.

34. White, *Sacred Webs*, 128–31.

35. C. Qiu, "Zhongguo pinyin wenzi yundong de xianqu."

36. Harrison, *Missionary's Curse and Other Tales*, chapters 6 and 7; Madsen, *China's Catholics*, chapter 3.

37. A. Hunter and Chan, *Protestantism in Contemporary China*, 204.

38. Cao, *Constructing China's Jerusalem*, 162.

39. Very few academic studies have been done on the transnational Christian connections in contemporary Southern Fujian. See, for example, White and Liu, "Going Global and Back Again"; White, "Influence Across the South Sea."

40. Ashiwa and Wank, "Politics of a Reviving Buddhist Temple"; Chau, "Introduction," 8–11; Fisher, "In the Footsteps of the Tourists"; Ji, "Buddhism in the Reform Era"; J. Liu, "From Vegetarian Hall to Revolutionary Relic"; McCarthy, "Gods of Wealth, Temples of Prosperity"; F. Yang and Tamney, *State, Market, and Religions in Chinese Societies*.

41. J. Liu and White, "Consuming Missionary Legacies"; White, "Appropriating Christian History in Fujian"; White, "Xinjie Church and Christianity."

42. The once influential Xiamen Port Church was closed during the Cultural Revolution and has not been reestablished. Its church building was assigned to the True Jesus Church by the Xiamen Lianghui. The current Xiamen Port Church has nothing to do with the previous one. Descendants of

Yang Huaide (1866–1946), then head pastor of Xiamen Port Church, established the earliest house church in Xiamen, a group that has served as a leader of the unregistered churches around Fujian.

43. Pieke, "Communist Party and Social Management," 149.

44. Y. Zhu, "Guojia tongzhi, difang zhengzhi yu Wenzhou de Jidujiao."

45. For a detailed analysis of how a religious community strives to recover their Buddhist venue in a decades-long struggle with various departments of the intricate bureaucracy, see J. Liu, "From Vegetarian Hall to Revolutionary Relic."

46. Connerton, *How Societies Remember*, 73.

47. Connerton, *How Modernity Forgets*.

48. Schuman and Scott, "Generations and Collective Memories."

Chapter 4

1. Tao, "Wenhua qinlüe yuanliu kao."

2. For an overview of reform-era research on the history of Christianity, see Tao and Yang, "Gaige kaifang yilai de Zhongguo Jidujiao shi yanjiu."

3. M. L. Lin, "Zhonggong Zhengxie wenshi ziliao gongzuo de tuizhan," 149.

4. Ibid.

5. Y. Li, "*Qianyan*," 1.

6. E. Zhou, *Zhou Enlai xuanji*, 297.

7. S. Huang and Liu, *Wenshi ziliao gongzuo gaishu*, 8–12.

8. F. Yu, Zhang and Zeng, "Gulangyu lunwei gonggong zujie de jingguo," 78–83.

9. X. Zheng and Huang, "Meiguo yisheng Yu Yuehan ruci ling ren."

10. Xiamen Zhengxie wenshi ziliao weiyuanhui, "Kantouyu."

11. Z. Zhang et al., "Gonggong zujie shiqi de Gulangyu," 4.

12. Ibid., 79.

13. Y. Lin, "Zhonghua diyi shengtang Xiamen Xinjie libaitang"; H. Zhu, "Gulangyu Sanyi tang jianzhu shimo."

14. B. Chen, "Gulangyu nanmin jigou he Guoji jiujihui"; H. Zhu, "Xiamen lunxian hou Gulangyu Yude nanmin shourongsuo."

15. B. Wu, "Bainian lai de Minnan Jidu jiaohui."

16. B. Wu, "Jidujiao Minnan dahui de yici shenghui," 131.

17. S. Zhang, "Xiamen Xinhai geming de linzhao," 22.

18. Y. Qiu, "Xinhai geming qianhou de Xiamen baokan," 115.

19. Fang et al., *Xiamen cheng liubai nian*.

20. See, for example, Hong, "Houji," 205.

21. Le Goff, *History and Memory*, 95.

22. In China, this is an insulting reference to women who are alleged to have committed sexual misdemeanors and are accordingly disparaged as "worn shoes."

23. Hao, "Yeying zhi si: Ji Xiamen zhuming nü gechangjia Yan Baoling," 25–26.

24. Y. Peng, *Xiamen yinyue mingjia*, 222–26. Her son is a professor of music at an elite Chinese university. Although it is impossible to disguise Yan's identity, I avoid naming her son here due to privacy concerns.

25. Gulangyu guanweihui, *Zhongguo shijie wenhua yichan yubei mingdan shenbao wenjian*.

26. Gulangyu guangongwei, *Gulangyu qu aiguozhuyi jiaoyu cailiao xuanbian*, 38–39.

27. The history of the development of the local gazetteer in China from its embryonic form to its full maturity in the Ming and Qing periods is too long and complex to chronicle here in full. For details, see Lai, *Zhongguo difangzhi*; J. Peng, *Zhongguo fangzhi jianshi*.

28. Bol, "Rise of Local History."

29. See Zhongguo kexueyuan Beijing tianwentai, *Zhongguo difangzhi lianhe mulu*.

30. See Lai, *Zhongguo difangzhi*, 21–27; J. Peng, *Zhongguo fangzhi jianshi*, 4–8.

31. Hargett, "Song Dynasty Local Gazetteers."

32. Zhongguo difangzhi zhidao xiaozu bangongshi, *Difangzhi gongzuo wenxian xuanbian*.

33. Zhongguo difangzhi zhidao xiaozu bangongshi, "1990 nian quanguo difangzhi gongzuo huiyi jiyao," 4–5.

34. Quanguo difangzhi ziliao gongzuo xiezuozu, *Zhongguo xin fangzhi mulu*.

35. A. Luo, *Xiamen Jidujiao zhuanye zhi*, chapter 6.

36. Xiamen shi difangzhi bianweihui, *Xiamen shi zhi*, 5:3801–25.

37. Remmers, "Emergence of Legal Christian Publishing."

38. De Jong, *Reformed Church in China*, 337.

39. Ibid., 335.

40. Ibid., 334.

41. *Xiamen wanbao*, "Ya Bili jiqi houjizhe men."

42. See *Xiamen wanbao* of February 1, 2015, and November 1, 2015.

43. For types of newspapers in China, in particular their institutional affiliation and finances, see Stockmann, *Media Commercialization and Authoritarian Rule*, chapter 3.

44. The house church is adjacent to a museum and was therefore named after it by the church members.

45. See Z. Zhu, *Gensui ai de jiaozong*. I am grateful to Zhu Zixian who supplied me with a copy of his unpublished manuscript.

46. For Yang's suffering under Mao's rule, see E. Yang, *Yejian de ge*.

47. It was produced by Yuan Zhiming, who fled to the United States after the events in Tiananmen Square in June 1989 and later converted and became an active pastor.

48. Shen, "Huiyi wo de baba mama," 11–13.

49. Wen, "Xiamen shi Gulangyu Zhonghua Jidu jiaohui Sanyi tang."

50. Sanyi tang, *Sanyi tang bashi nian*, 8.

51. Orwell, *Nineteen Eighty-Four*.

52. Bays, *New History of Christianity in China*, 185–86.

Chapter 5

1. Borthwick, *Western Christians in Global Mission*.

2. The "glocalization" paradigm that attempts to produce a combined perspective on globalization and localization has been adopted in the study of Chinese Christianity. See, for example, P. T. M. Ng, *Chinese Christianity*.

3. Pieke, "Immigrant China."

4. Zhonggong zhongyang wenxian yanjiushi zonghe yanjiuzu and Guowuyuan zongjiao shiwuju zhengce faguisi, *Xin shiqi zongjiao gongzuo wenxian xuanbian*, 273–74.

5. Bays, "Chinese Protestant Christianity Today," 503; Dunch, "Protestant Christianity in China Today," 202.

6. A. Hunter and Chan, *Protestantism in Contemporary China*, 80–81.

7. Cao, *Constructing China's Jerusalem*, 60–61.

8. Baugus and Park, "Brief History," 93; Kang, *House Church Christianity in China*; McLeister, "Three-Self Protestant Church," 238.

9. Lyu, "Xiamen waiji Jidutu jiaoshi de zongjiao huodong."

10. Hirono, *Civilizing Missions*.

11. There are a few books edited by non-PRC churches or ministers that refer to the presence of international Christian agencies. These publications have seldom been mentioned in the pages of serious academic works. For example, Baugus and Park write that at least thirty-five hundred South Korean missionaries are serving in mainland China, and a number of Korean pastors have been able to preach to officially registered congregations without restrictions and have even provided continuing education to Lianghui pastors. See Baugus and Park, "Brief History," 91–93.

12. Dunch, "Protestant Christianity in China Today," 202.

13. The members of the mission organization all use English names. In this chapter, I follow the tradition and adopt English pseudonyms for people referred to.

14. The phrase "English corner" refers to informal instruction or casual chats in English held in schools and colleges in China. Sessions are often conducted by foreign teachers who are native English speakers. Their purpose is to improve participants' oral English skills.

15. Homans, *Human Group*.

16. For the reciprocal relationship between the degree of exclusivity and the degree of commitment, see Stark and Finke, *Acts of Faith*, chapter 6.

17. Van Gennep, *Rites of Passage*.

18. Iannaccone, "Why Strict Churches Are Strong."

19. It was officially approved as a "temporary venue for foreigners' Christian activity" (*waiguoren Jidujiao huodong linshi changsuo*) by the Xiamen RAB in 2005. It is referred to by the members as the XICF.

20. Lyu, "Xiamen waiji Jidutu jiaoshi de zongjiao huodong."

21. Snow, *English Teaching as Christian Mission*, 16.

22. See Lyu, "Xiamen waiji Jidutu jiaoshi de zongjiao huodong."

23. Baugus, "Introduction," 19.

24. I was well acquainted with the interior layout of the church building and the number of seats available for the congregation. Therefore, I could easily estimate the attendance at each gathering. According to my observations on several occasions, its Saturday gathering attracts 150 to 200 who attend regularly.

25. Bainbridge, "Sociology of Conversion," 180.

26. See, for example, Cao, *Constructing China's Jerusalem*; J. Huang, "Being Christians in Urbanizing China"; F. Yang, "Lost in the Market."

27. For a discussion, see F. Yang and Abel, "Sociology of Religious Conversion."

28. F. Yang, "Lost in the Market."

29. F. Yang and Abel, "Sociology of Religious Conversion," 150.

30. Since the 1980s, the Chinese universities have recruited a large number of full-time foreign personnel as "foreign experts," usually for short-term foreign language teaching rather than permanent academic research. At the present time, a very limited number of non-PRC citizens have been awarded full-time professorships. In the administrative system, the State Administration of Foreign Experts Affairs on the national level and the Bureau of Foreign Experts Affairs on the provincial and prefectural levels are in charge of issuing certificates and the management of these foreigners.

31. Cao, *Constructing China's Jerusalem*; F. Yang, "Lost in the Market."

32. *Renmin ribao*, "Fazhan Zhongguo tese shehuizhuyi zongjiao lilun, quanmian tigao xin xingshi xia zongjiao gongzuo shuiping."

33. X. Lian, *Redeemed by Fire*.

34. Translated from Z. Cai, "Xiamen Rongcun Zhonghua Jidu jiaotang jinian beiming."

35. M. Lin, "Cai Zhenxun xiansheng xiaozhuan."

36. In any probe into how Christianity has made significant inroads into Chinese society, social relationships (*guanxi*) should be taken into account. Western missionary enterprises and native Chinese churches have relied heavily on these *guanxi* for development. See, for example, J. T. H. Lee, "*Guanxi* and Gospel."

37. White and Liu, "Going Global and Back Again."

Conclusion

1. See, for example, F. Yang, "Cross of Chinese Christians."

2. Cao, "Spatial Modernity, Party Building."

3. Cao, *Constructing China's Jerusalem*.

4. Koesel, *Religion and Authoritarianism*.

5. Chau, *Miraculous Response*, 14.

6. Nora, "Between Memory and History."

7. Qiushi wang, "Qizhi xianming fandui lishi xuwuzhuyi."

8. The best-known example is that of Xu Chuncao, an elite Christian, who once publicly declared that "I am loyal to Christ Jesus, and have not compromised with those foreigners." See S. Zhang, "Xiamen Xinhai geming de linzhao," 22.

9. Pieke, *Good Communist*, 11.

10. Olick and Levy, "Collective Memory and Cultural Constraint," 922.

11. Misztal, *Theories of Social Remembering*, 73.

12. Lutz, "Women in Imperial China."

13. Murre-van den Berg, "Nineteenth-Century Protestant Missions."

14. For example, X. Cai, "Christianity and Gender"; Wong and Chiu, *Christian Women in Chinese Society*.

15. Cao, *Constructing China's Jerusalem*, 163.

16. Kuah-Pearce, *Rebuilding the Ancestral Village*.

17. White and Liu, "Going Global and Back Again."

18. Harrison, *Missionary's Curse and Other Tales*, 183.

19. Cited in Jenkins, *Next Christendom*, 87.

Bibliography

Adogame, Afe, and Shobana Shankar, eds. *Religion on the Move! New Dynamics of Religious Expansion in a Globalizing World*. Leiden: Brill, 2013.

Andrade, Tonio. *Lost Colony: The Untold Story of China's First Victory over the West*. Princeton: Princeton University Press, 2011.

Antony, Robert J. *Like Froth Floating on the Sea: The World of Pirates and Seafarers in Late Imperial South China*. Berkeley: Institute of East Asian Studies, University of California, 2003.

Arrington, Aminta. *Songs of the Lisu Hills: Practicing Christianity in Southwest China*. University Park: Pennsylvania State University Press, 2020.

Ashiwa, Yoshiko. "Positioning Religion in Modernity: State and Buddhism in China." In *Making Religion, Making the State: The Politics of Religion in Modern China*, edited by Yoshiko Ashiwa and David L. Wank, 43–73. Stanford: Stanford University Press, 2009.

Ashiwa, Yoshiko, and David L. Wank. "The Globalization of Chinese Buddhism: Clergy and Devotee Networks in the Twentieth Century." *International Journal of Asian Studies* 2, no. 2 (2005): 217–37.

———, eds. *Making Religion, Making the State: The Politics of Religion in Modern China*. Stanford: Stanford University Press, 2009.

———. "The Politics of a Reviving Buddhist Temple: State, Association, and Religion in Southeast China." *Journal of Asian Studies* 65, no. 2 (2006): 337–59.

Bainbridge, William Sims. "The Sociology of Conversion." In *Handbook of Religious Conversion*, edited by H. Newton Malony and Samuel Southard, 178–91.

Birmingham, AL: Religious Education Press, 1992.

Baugus, Bruce P. "Introduction: China, Church Development, and Presbyterianism." In *China's Reforming Churches: Mission, Polity, and Ministry in the Next Christendom*, edited by Bruce P. Baugus, 1–23. Grand Rapids, MI: Reformation Heritage Books, 2014.

Baugus, Bruce P., and Sung-il Steve Park. "A Brief History of the Korean Presbyterian Mission to China." In *China's Reforming Churches: Mission, Polity, and Ministry in the Next Christendom*, edited by Bruce P. Baugus, 73–95. Grand Rapids, MI: Reformation Heritage Books, 2014.

Bautista, Julius. "About Face: Asian Christianity in the Context of Southern Expansion." In *Christianity and the State in Asia: Complicity and Conflict*, edited by Julius Bautista and Francis Khek Gee Lim, 201–15. Abingdon, UK: Routledge, 2009.

Bautista, Julius, and Francis Khek Gee Lim, eds. *Christianity and the State in Asia: Complicity and Conflict*. Abingdon, UK: Routledge, 2009.

Bays, Daniel H. "Chinese Protestant Christianity Today." *China Quarterly* 174 (2003): 488–504.

———. "The Growth of Independent Christianity in China, 1900–1937." In *Christianity in China: From the Eighteenth Century to the Present*, edited by Daniel H. Bays, 307–16. Stanford: Stanford University Press, 1996.

———. *A New History of Christianity in China*. Chichester, UK: Wiley-Blackwell, 2012.

———. "A Tradition of State Dominance." In *God and Caesar in China: Policy Implications of Church-State Tensions,*

214

edited by Jason Kindopp and Carol Lee Hamrin, 25–39. Washington, DC: Brookings Institution Press, 2004.

BBC News. "Risky Road: China's Missionaries Follow Beijing West." Accessed June 3, 2020, https://www.bbc.com/news/world-asia-41116480.

Béja, Jean-Philippe. "Forbidden Memory, Unwritten History: The Difficulty of Structuring an Opposition Movement in the PRC." *China Perspective*, no. 4 (2007): 88–98.

Berger, Peter L. "The Desecularization of the World: A Global Overview." In *The Desecularization of the World: Resurgent Religion and World Politics*, edited by Peter L. Berger, 1–18. Washington, DC: Ethics and Public Policy Center; Grand Rapids, MI: William B. Eerdmans, 1999.

———. *The Sacred Canopy: Elements of a Sociological Theory of Religion*. Garden City, NY: Doubleday, 1967.

Berger, Peter, Grace Davie, and Effie Fokas. *Religious America, Secular Europe? A Theme and Variations*. Aldershot, UK: Ashgate, 2008.

Bol, Peter K. "The Rise of Local History: History, Geography, and Culture in Southern Song and Yuan Wuzhou." *Harvard Journal of Asiatic Studies* 61, no. 1 (2001): 37–76.

Borthwick, Paul. *Western Christians in Global Mission: What's the Role of the North American Church?* Downers Grove, IL: InterVarsity Press, 2012.

Bowra, Cecil A. V. "Amoy." In *Twentieth Century Impression of Hong Kong, Shanghai, and Other Treaty Ports of China*, edited by Arnold Wright, 813–28. London: Lloyd's Greater Britain, 1908.

Buswell, Robert E. Jr., and Timothy S. Lee. *Christianity in Korea*. Honolulu: University of Hawai'i Press, 2005.

Cai, Xiangyu. "Christianity and Gender in South-East China: The Chaozhou Missions (1849–1949)." PhD diss., Leiden University, 2012.

Cai, Zhenxun. "Xiamen Rongcun Zhonghua Jidu jiaotang jinian beiming" 厦门榕村中华基督教堂纪念碑铭 [The stele epigraph for the Xiamen Banyan Village Church]. *Daonan* 5, no. 7 (1931): 12.

Callahan, William A. *China: The Pessoptimist Nation*. New York: Oxford University Press, 2010.

Cao, Nanlai. *Constructing China's Jerusalem: Christians, Power, and Place in Contemporary Wenzhou*. Stanford: Stanford University Press, 2011.

———. "Spatial Modernity, Party Building, and Local Governance: Putting the Christian Cross-Removal Campaign in Context." *China Review* 17, no. 1 (2017): 29–52.

Chao, Jonathan, and Rosanna Chong. *Dangdai Zhongguo Jidujiao fazhan shi 1949–1997* 当代中国基督教发展史 1949–1997 [A history of Christianity in socialist China, 1949–1997]. Taipei: Zhongguo fuyinhui, 1997.

Chau, Adam Yuet. "Introduction: Revitalizing and Innovating Religious Traditions in Contemporary China." In *Religion in Contemporary China: Revitalization and Innovation*, edited by Adam Yuet Chau, 1–31. Abingdon, UK: Routledge, 2011.

———. *Miraculous Response: Doing Popular Religion in Contemporary China*. Stanford: Stanford University Press, 2006.

Chen, Bingling. "Gulangyu nanmin jigou he Guoji jiujihui" 鼓浪屿难民机构和国际救济会 [The Gulangyu refugee agency and the International Relief Committee]. *Xiamen wenshi ziliao* 12 (1987): 52–54.

Chen, Ronglan, and Li Xitai. *Xiamen fangyan* 厦门方言 [The Xiamen dialect]. 2nd ed. Xiamen: Lujiang chubanshe, 1999.

Chen, Yongming. *Qing dai qianqi de zhengzhi rentong yu lishi shuxie* 清代前期的政治认同与历史书写 [Political identity and history writing in the early Qing Dynasty]. Shanghai: Shanghai guji chubanshe, 2011.

Cheng, Yingheng. "Sing to the Lord a New Song: The Development and Influence of Minnan Hymns." In *Protestantism in Xiamen: Then and Now*, edited by

Chris White, 165–92. Cham, Switzerland: Palgrave Macmillan, 2019.

Cheung, David. *Christianity in Modern China: The Making of the First Native Protestant Church*. Leiden: Brill, 2004.

Ching, May Bo. "Guojia ruhe taoli: Zhongguo minjian shehui de beilun" 国家如何逃离：中国民间社会的悖论 [How to evade the arm of the state: The paradox of China's civil society]. *Zhongguo shehui kexue bao*, October 14, 2010, 11.

Chow, Alexander. "Calvinist Public Theology in Urban China Today." *International Journal of Public Theology* 8, no. 2 (2014): 158–75.

Chow, Christie Chui-shan. "Demolition and Defiance: The Stone Ground Church Dispute (2012) in East China." *Journal of World Christianity* 6, no. 2 (2016): 250–76.

Ci, Jiwei. *Dialectic of the Chinese Revolution: From Utopianism to Hedonism*. Stanford: Stanford University Press, 1994.

Cohen, Paul A. "Remembering and Forgetting: National Humiliation in Twentieth-Century China." *Twentieth-Century China* 27, no. 2 (2002): 1–39.

Colijn, Herman Abraham. "One House, Two Paths: Popular Religion and Protestant Christianity in Contemporary Chinese Households." PhD diss., Free University Amsterdam, 2018.

Confino, Alon. "Memory and Cultural History: Problems of Method." *American Historical Review* 102, no. 5 (1997): 1386–403.

Connerton, Paul. *How Modernity Forgets*. Cambridge: Cambridge University Press, 2009.

———. *How Societies Remember*. Cambridge: Cambridge University Press, 1989.

Cook, James A. "Bridges to Modernity: Xiamen, Overseas Chinese and Southeast Coastal Modernization, 1843–1937." PhD diss., University of California, San Diego, 1998.

———. "Reimaging China: Xiamen, Overseas Chinese, and a Transnational Modernity." In *Everyday Modernity in China*, edited by Madeleine Yue Dong and Joshua L. Goldstein, 156–94. Seattle: University of Washington Press, 2006.

Cubitt, Geoffrey. *History and Memory*. Manchester: Manchester University Press, 2007.

Dai, Yifeng. *Quyuxing jingji fazhan yu shehui bianqian: Yi jindai Fujian diqu wei zhongxin* 区域性经济发展与社会变迁：以近代福建地区为中心 [Regional economic development and social change: Focus on the modern Fujian region]. Changsha: Yuelu shushe, 2004.

Daily, Christopher A. *Robert Morrison and the Protestant Plan for China*. Hong Kong: Hong Kong University Press, 2013.

Davie, Grace. "Europe: The Exception That Proves the Rule?" In *The Desecularization of the World: Resurgent Religion and World Politics*, edited by Peter L. Berger, 65–83. Washington, DC: Ethics and Public Policy Center; Grand Rapids, MI: William B. Eerdmans, 1999.

Dean, Kenneth. *Lord of the Three in One: The Spread of a Cult in Southeast China*. Princeton: Princeton University Press, 1998.

———. *Taoist Ritual and Popular Cults of Southeast China*. Princeton: Princeton University Press, 1993.

Dean, Kenneth, and Zheng Zhenman. *Ritual Alliances of the Putian Plain*. 2 vols. Leiden: Brill, 2010.

De Groot, J. J. M. *The Religious System of China: Its Ancient Forms, Evolutions, History and Present Aspect, Manners, Customs and Social Institutions Connected Therewith*. Leiden: Brill, 1894.

De Jong, Gerald F. *The Reformed Church in China, 1842–1951*. Grand Rapids, MI: William B. Eerdmans, 1992.

Dikötter, Frank. *The Discourse of Race in Modern China*. New York: Oxford University Press, 2015.

Ding, Guangxun. *Ding Guangxun wenji* 丁光训文集 [Collected works of Ding Guangxun]. Nanjing: Yilin chubanshe, 1998.

Dirlik, Arif. *Revolution and History: The Origins of Marxist Historiography in China, 1919–1937*. Berkeley: University of California Press, 1978.

Dunch, Ryan. *Fuzhou Protestants and the Making of a Modern China, 1857–1927*. New Haven: Yale University Press, 2001.

———. "Protestant Christianity in China Today: Fragile, Fragmented, Flourishing." In *China and Christianity: Burdened Past, Hopeful Future*, edited by Stephen Uhalley Jr. and Xiaoxin Wu, 195–216. Armonk, NY: M. E. Sharpe, 2001.

Dunn, Emily. *Lightening from the East: Heterodoxy and Christianity in Contemporary China*. Leiden: Brill, 2015.

Evans, Grant. *The Politics of Ritual and Remembrance: Laos Since 1975*. Honolulu: University of Hawai'i Press, 1998.

Fagg, John Gerardus. *Forty Years in South China: A Biography of the Rev. John Van Nest Talmage, D.D.* New York: Board of Publication of the Reformed Church in America, 1894.

Fairbank, John K. "Introduction: The Many Faces of Protestant Missions in China and the United States." In *The Missionary Enterprise in China and America*, edited by John K. Fairbank, 1–19. Cambridge: Harvard University Press, 1974.

Fällman, Fredrik. "Calvin, Culture and Christ? Developments of Faith Among Chinese Intellectuals." In *Christianity in Contemporary China: Socio-Cultural Perspectives*, edited by Francis Khek Gee Lim, 153–68. Abingdon, UK: Routledge, 2013.

Fang, Youyi, et al., eds. *Xiamen cheng liubai nian* 厦门城六百年 [Six hundred years of Xiamen City]. Xiamen: Lujiang chubanshe, 1996.

Feuchtwang, Stephan, and Wang Mingming. *Grassroots Charisma: Four Local Leaders in China*. London: Routledge, 2001.

Fisher, Gareth. "In the Footsteps of the Tourists: Buddhist Revival at Museum/

Temple Sites in Beijing." *Social Compass* 58, no. 1 (2011): 511–24.

Flath, James. "'This Is How the Chinese People Began Their Struggle': Humen and the Opium War as a Site of Memory." In *Places of Memory in Modern China: History, Politics, and Identity*, edited by Marc Andre Matten, 167–92. Leiden: Brill, 2012.

Foucault, Michel. *Language, Counter-Memory, Practice: Selected Essays and Interviews*. Edited by Donald F. Bouchard. Translated by Donald F. Bouchard and Sherry Simon. Ithaca: Cornell University Press, 1977.

Freedman, Maurice. *Chinese Lineage and Society: Fukien and Kwangtung*. London: Athlone Press, 1966.

Gao, Bingzhong. "Yizuo bowuguan-miaoyu jianzhu de minzuzhi: Lun chengwei zhengzhi yishu de shuangmingzhi" 一座博物馆-庙宇建筑的民族志：论成为政治艺术的双名制 [Ethnography of a building both as museum and temple: The dual-naming method as political art]. *Shehuixue yanjiu*, no. 1 (2006): 154–68.

Giles, Herbert Allen. *A Short History of Koolangsu*. Xiamen: A. A. Marcal, 1878.

Goldman, Merle. *Literary Dissent in Communist China*. Cambridge: Harvard University Press, 1967.

Goldman, Merle, Timothy Cheek, and Carol Lee Hamrin, eds. *China's Intellectuals and the State: In Search of a New Relationship*. Cambridge: Council on East Asian Studies, Harvard University Press, 1987.

Gong, Jie. "Xiamen Tianzhu tang" 厦门天主堂 [The Xiamen Catholic Church]. *Siming wenshi ziliao* 5 (2009): 66–70.

Gu, Changsheng. *Awaken: Memoirs of a Chinese Historian*. Bloomington, IN: AuthorHouse, 2009.

———. *Chuanjiaoshi yu jindai Zhongguo* 传教士与近代中国 [Missionaries and modern China]. Shanghai: Shanghai renmin chubanshe, 1981.

Gu, Edward, and Merle Goldman, eds. *Chinese Intellectuals Between State and Market*. London: RoutledgeCurzon, 2004.

Guardian. "Chinese Cities Crack Down on Christmas Celebrations." Accessed August 2, 2020, https://www.theguardian.com/world/2018/dec/24/china-cracks-down-on-christmas.

Gulangyu guangongwei, ed. *Gulangyu qu aiguozhuyi jiaoyu cailiao xuanbian* 鼓浪屿区爱国主义教育材料选编 [Selected materials for patriotic education of Gulangyu District]. Xiamen, 1999.

Gulangyu guanweihui, ed. *Zhongguo shijie wenhua yichan yubei mingdan shenbao wenjian* 中国世界文化遗产预备名单申报文件 [Application documents for preliminary inclusion in China's World Cultural Heritage list]. Xiamen, 2012.

Guo, Yuhua, and Sun Liping. "Suku: Yizhong nongmin guojia guannian xingcheng de zhongjie jizhi" 诉苦：一种农民国家观念形成的中介机制 [Speaking bitterness: An intermediary mechanism for the formation of peasants' concept of state]. *Zhongguo xueshu* 4 (2002): 130–57.

Guojia zongjiaoju zhengce faguisi, ed. *Zhongguo zongjiao fagui zhengce duben* 中国宗教法规政策读本 [Chinese religious laws and policies reader]. Beijing: Zongjiao wenhua chubanshe, 2000.

Halbwachs, Maurice. *On Collective Memory*. Edited and translated by Lewis A. Coser. Chicago: University of Chicago Press, 1992.

Hao, Linren. "Yeying zhi si: Ji Xiamen zhuming nü gechangjia Yan Baoling" 夜莺之死：记厦门著名女歌唱家颜宝玲 [The death of nightingale: Story of Yan Baoling, distinguished singer in Xiamen]. *Jiayin*, no. 4 (2012): 23–26.

Hargett, James M. "Song Dynasty Local Gazetteers and Their Place in the History of *Difangzhi* Writing." *Harvard Journal of Asiatic Studies* 56, no. 2 (1996): 405–42.

Harrison, Henrietta. *The Missionary's Curse and Other Tales from a Chinese Catholic Village*. Berkeley: University of California Press, 2013.

Hattaway, Paul, Brother Yun, Peter Xu Yongze, and Enoch Wang. *Back to Jerusalem: Three Chinese House Church Leaders Share Their Vision to Complete the Great Commission*. Downers Grove, IL: InterVarsity Press, 2003.

He, Qiying. *Gonggong zujie Gulangyu yu jindai Xiamen de fazhan* 公共租界鼓浪屿与近代厦门的发展 [The Gulangyu International Settlement and the development of modern Xiamen]. Fuzhou: Fujian renmin chubanshe, 2007.

Hirono, Miwa. *Civilizing Missions: International Religious Agencies in China*. New York: Palgrave Macmillan, 2008.

Hobsbawm, Eric. "Introduction: Inventing Traditions." In *The Invention of Tradition*, edited by Eric Hobsbawm and Terence Ranger, 1–14. Cambridge: Cambridge University Press, 1983.

Homans, George C. *The Human Group*. London: Routledge and Kegan Paul, 1951.

Hong, Buren. "Houji" 后记 [Afterword], *Xiamen liushi nian jishi* 厦门六十年纪事 [Sixty years of Xiamen: A chronicle]. Xiamen: Xiamen daxue chubanshe, 2010.

Howell, Jude. "The Political Economy of Xiamen Special Economic Zone." In *Fujian: A Coastal Province in Transition and Transformation*, edited by Y. M. Yeung and David K. Y. Chu, 119–42. Hong Kong: Chinese University Press, 2000.

Huang, Jianbo. "Being Christians in Urbanizing China: The Epistemological Tensions of the Rural Churches in the City." *Current Anthropology* 55, no. s10 (2014): s238–47.

Huang, Ke-hsien. "Dyadic Nexus Fighting Two-Front Battles: A Study of the Microlevel Process of the Official-Religion-State Relations in China." *Journal for the Scientific Study of Religion* 53, no. 4 (2014): 706–21.

———. "Sect-to-Church Movement in Globalization: Transforming Pentecostalism and Coastal Intermediaries in Contemporary China." *Journal for the Scientific Study of Religion* 55, no. 2 (2016): 407–16.

Huang, Philip C. C. "'Public Sphere'/ 'Civil Society' in China? The Third Realm Between State and Society." *Modern China* 19, no. 2 (1993): 216–40.

Huang, Sen, and Liu Qi, eds. *Wenshi ziliao gongzuo gaishu* 文史资料工作概述 [Outline of historical materials work]. Beijing: Zhongguo wenshi chubanshe, 1992.

Huang, You, et al. "Xiaozhang yunji de Shao shi jiazu" 校长云集的邵氏家族 [The Shao family that produced ten principals]. In *Koushu lishi: Wode Gulangyu wangshi* 口述历史：我的鼓浪屿往事 [Oral history: My past in Gulangyu], edited by Zhonggong Xiamen shiwei xuanchuanbu and Xiamen shi shehui kexue lianhehui, 86–126. Xiamen: Xiamen yinxiang chuban youxian gongsi, 2011.

Hunter, Alan, and Kim-kwong Chan. *Protestantism in Contemporary China.* Cambridge: Cambridge University Press, 1993.

Hunter, Ian M. L. *Memory.* Rev. ed. Middlesex: Penguin, 1964.

Iannaccone, Laurence R. "Why Strict Churches Are Strong." *American Journal of Sociology* 99, no. 5 (1994): 1180–211.

Inouye, Melissa Wei-tsing. *China and the True Jesus: Charisma and Organization in a Chinese Christian Church.* New York: Oxford University Press, 2019.

Ireland, Daryl R. *John Song: Modern Chinese Christianity and the Making of a New Man.* Waco: Baylor University Press, 2020.

Jenkins, Philip. *The New Faces of Christianity: Believing the Bible in the Global South.* New York: Oxford University Press, 2006.

———. *The Next Christendom: The Coming of Global Christianity.* 3rd ed. New York: Oxford University Press, 2011.

Ji, Zhe. "Buddhism in the Reform Era: A Secularized Revival?" In *Religion in Contemporary China: Revitalization and Innovation,* edited by Adam Yuet Chau, 32–52. Abingdon, UK: Routledge, 2011.

Jiantang chouweihui. *Wei jianzhu Gulangyu Sanyi tang mujuan qi* 为建筑鼓浪屿三一堂募捐启 [Appeal for donations for the construction of the Gulangyu Trinity Church]. Xiamen, 1935.

Jing, Jun. *The Temple of Memories: History, Power, and Morality in a Chinese Village.* Stanford: Stanford University Press, 1996.

Johnson, Elizabeth. "Grieving for the Dead, Grieving for the Living: Funeral Laments of Hakka Women." In *Death Ritual in Late Imperial and Modern China,* edited by James L. Watson and Evelyn S. Rawski, 135–63. Berkeley: University of California Press, 1988.

Kang, Jie. *House Church Christianity in China: From Rural Preachers to City Pastors.* Cham, Switzerland: Palgrave Macmillan, 2016.

Kang, Wi Jo. *Christ and Caesar in Modern Korea: A History of Christianity and Politics.* New York: State University of New York Press, 1997.

Kao, Chen-yang. "The Cultural Revolution and the Emergence of Pentecostal-Style Protestantism in China." *Journal of Contemporary Religion* 24, no. 2 (2009): 171–88.

———. "Materiality in the Absence of the Church: Practising Protestantism During China's Cultural Revolution." *History and Anthropology* 31, no. 5 (2020): 563–82.

Kim, Rebecca Y. *The Spirit Moves West: Korean Missionaries in America.* New York: Oxford University Press, 2015.

Kindopp, Jason. "The Politics of Protestantism in Contemporary China: State Control, Civil Society, and Social Movement in a Single Party-State." PhD diss., George Washington University, 2004.

Kindopp, Jason, and Carol Lee Hamrin, eds. *God and Caesar in China: Policy*

Implications of Church-State Tensions.
Washington, DC: Brookings Institution Press, 2004.

Kipnis, Andrew. "*Suzhi*: A Keyword Approach." *China Quarterly* 186 (2006): 295–313.

Koesel, Karrie J. *Religion and Authoritarianism: Cooperation, Conflict, and the Consequences.* New York: Cambridge University Press, 2014.

Kuah-Pearce, Khun Eng. *Rebuilding the Ancestral Village: Singaporeans in China.* 2nd ed. Hong Kong: Hong Kong University Press, 2011.

Kuo, Cheng-tian. "Chinese Religious Reform: The Christian Patriotic Education Campaign." *Asian Survey* 51, no. 6 (2011): 1042–64.

Lai, Xinxia. *Zhongguo difangzhi* 中国地方志 [Local gazetteers of China]. Taipei: Taiwan shangwu yinshuguan, 1995.

Lane, Christel. *The Rites of Rulers: Ritual in Industrial Society—The Soviet Case.* Cambridge: Cambridge University Press, 1981.

Lee, Haiyan. "The Ruins of Yuanmingyuan: Or, How to Enjoy a National Wound." In *Places of Memory in Modern China: History, Politics, and Identity*, edited by Marc Andre Matten, 193–232. Leiden: Brill, 2012.

Lee, Joseph Tse-hei. "*Guanxi* and Gospel: Mapping Christian Networks in South China." In *Encountering Modernity: Christianity in East Asia and Asian America*, edited by Albert L. Park and David K. Yoo, 71–94. Honolulu: University of Hawai'i Press, 2014.

Le Goff, Jacques. *History and Memory.* Translated by Steven Rendall and Elizabeth Claman. New York: Columbia University Press, 1992.

Lehmann, Angela. *Transnational Lives in China: Expatriates in a Globalizing City.* Basingstoke, UK: Palgrave Macmillan, 2014.

Li, Si-ming, and Ling-xun Zhao. "Xiamen: Regional Center and Hometown of Overseas Chinese." In *China's Coastal Cities: Catalysts for Modernization*, edited by Yue-man Yeung and Xu-wei

Hu, 221–39. Honolulu: University of Hawai'i Press, 1992.

Li, Xiangping. "Zongjiao shengtai haishi quanli shengtai: Cong dangdai Zhongguo de zongjiao shengtai lun sichao tanqi" 宗教生态还是权力生态：从当代中国的宗教生态论思潮谈起 [Religious ecology or power ecology: Starting from the trend of religious ecology theory]. *Shanghai daxue xuebao* 18, no. 1 (2011): 124–40.

Li, Yongpu. "Qianyan" 前言 [Preface], *Quanguo geji Zhengxie wenshi ziliao pianmu suoyin 1960–1990* 全国各级政协文史资料篇目索引1960–1990 [Index to the table of contents of the CPPCC's historical materials, 1960–1990]. Vol. 1. Beijing: Zhongguo wenshi chubanshe, 1992.

Lian, Lichang. *Fujian mimi shehui* 福建秘密社会 [Secret societies in Fujian]. Fuzhou: Fujian renmin chubansge, 1989.

Lian, Xi. *Redeemed by Fire: The Rise of Popular Christianity in Modern China.* New Haven: Yale University Press, 2010.

Lin, May-li. "Zhonggong Zhengxie wenshi ziliao gongzuo de tuizhan 1959–1966: Yi Shanghai jingyan wei zhongxin" 中共政协文史资料工作的推展1959–1966：以上海经验为中心 [Promoting historical accounts at the Chinese People's Political Consultative Conference, 1959–1966: The Shanghai experience]. *Xinshixue* 26, no. 3 (2015): 145–203.

Lin, Muli. "Xiamen shi Jidujiao Rongcun tang shouren chuandao Cai Zhenxun xiansheng xiaozhuan" 厦门市基督教榕村堂首任传道蔡振勋先生小传 [A brief biography of Cai Zhenxun, the first preacher of Xiamen Banyan Village Church]. Unpublished manuscript, 2013. Microsoft Word file.

Lin, Renchuan. *Fujian duiwai maoyi yu haiguan shi* 福建对外贸易与海关史 [History of Fujian's overseas trade and customs]. Xiamen: Lujiang chubanshe, 1991.

———. *Ming mo Qing chu siren haishang maoyi* 明末清初私人海上贸

易 [China's private sea trade in the late Ming and early Qing periods]. Shanghai: Huadong shifan daxue chubanshe, 1987.

Lin, Xuezeng, et al., comp. *Tong'an xian zhi* 同安县志 [Tong'an County gazetteer]. Taipei: Chengwen chubanshe, 1967. First published 1929.

Lin, Yi. "Zhonghua diyi shengtang Xiamen Xinjie libaitang" 中华第一圣堂厦门新街礼拜堂 [The first holy church in China—Xiamen New Street Church]. *Xiamen wenshi ziliao* 7 (1984): 94–102.

Lin, Yueh-hwa. *The Golden Wing: A Sociological Study of Chinese Familism.* New York: Oxford University Press, 1947.

Liu, Jifeng. "From Vegetarian Hall to Revolutionary Relic: Overseas Chinese and the Reshaping of a Buddhist Temple in a Chinese *Qiaoxiang.*" *History and Anthropology* 31, no. 5 (2020): 583–99.

Liu, Jifeng, and Chris White. "Consuming Missionary Legacies in Contemporary China: Eric Liddell and Evolving Interpretations of Chinese Christian History." *China Information* 33, no. 1 (2019): 46–65.

———. "Old Pastor and Local Bureaucrats: Recasting Church-State Relations in Contemporary China." *Modern China* 45, no. 5 (2019): 564–90.

Liu, Xiaofeng. "Sino-Christian Theology in the Context of Modernity." In *Christianity*, edited by Xinping Zhuo, translated by Chi Zhen and Caroline Mason, 63–106. Leiden: Brill, 2013.

London Missionary Society. *The Chronicle of the London Missionary Society.* London: London Missionary Society, 1873.

Lozada, Eriberto P., Jr. *God Aboveground: Catholic Church, Postsocialist State, and Transnational Processes in a Chinese Village.* Stanford: Stanford University Press, 2001.

Lu, Zhuying. "Rikou yu zhong qiunan ji" 日寇狱中囚难记 [Record of life in a Japanese prison]. *Gulangyu wenshi ziliao* 4 (1999): 51–53.

Luo, Anping, ed. *Xiamen Jidujiao zhuanye zhi* 厦门基督教专业志 [Special gazetteer of Christianity in Xiamen]. Unpublished manuscript, 1993.

Luo, Guanzong, ed. *Qianshi bu wang houshi zhi shi: Diguozhuyi liyong Jidujiao qinlüe Zhongguo shishi shuping* 前事不忘 后世之师：帝国主义利用基督教侵略中国史实述评 [Review of the utilization of Christianity in the imperialist invasion of China]. Beijing: Zongjiao wenhua chubanshe, 2003.

Lutz, Jessie G. *China and the Christian Colleges, 1850–1950.* Ithaca: Cornell University Press, 1971.

———. "Women in Imperial China: Ideal, Stereotype, and Reality." In *Pioneer Chinese Christian Women: Gender, Christianity, and Social Mobility*, edited by Jessie G. Lutz, 29–47. Bethlehem: Lehigh University Press, 2010.

Lyu, Yunfang. "Xiamen waiji Jidutu jiaoshi de zongjiao huodong yanjiu" 厦门外籍基督徒教师的宗教活动研究 [Religious activities of foreign Christian teachers in Xiamen]. *Shijie minzu*, no. 5 (2010): 67–74.

Ma, Li, and Jin Li. *Surviving the State, Remaking the Church: A Sociological Portrait of Christians in Mainland China.* Eugene, OR: Wipf and Stock, 2017.

Macgowan, John. *Beside the Bamboo.* London: London Missionary Society, 1914.

Madsen, Richard. *China's Catholics: Tragedy and Hope in an Emerging Civil Society.* Berkeley: University of California Press, 1998.

———. "From Socialist Ideology to Cultural Heritage: The Changing Basis of Legitimacy in the People's Republic of China." *Anthropology and Medicine* 21, no. 1 (2014): 58–70.

Mao, Zedong. *Mao Zedong xuanji* 毛泽东选集 [Selected works of Mao Zedong]. Vols. 2 and 4. 2nd ed. Beijing: Renmin chubanshe, 1991.

Matten, Marc Andre, ed. *Places of Memory in Modern China: History, Politics, and Identity.* Leiden: Brill, 2012.

McCarthy, Susan. "Gods of Wealth, Temples of Prosperity: Party-State Participation in the Minority Cultural Revival."

China: An International Journal 2, no. 1 (2004): 28–52.

McLeister, Mark. "Chinese Protestant Reactions to the Zhejiang 'Three Rectifications, One Demolition' Campaign." *Review of Religion and Chinese Society* 5, no. 1 (2018): 76–100.

———. "A Three-Self Protestant Church, the Local State and Religious Policy Implementation in a Coastal Chinese City." In *Christianity in Contemporary China: Socio-Cultural Perspectives*, edited by Francis Khek Gee Lim, 234–46. Abingdon, UK: Routledge, 2013.

Mead, George H. "The Nature of the Past." In *Essays in Honor of John Dewey: On the Occasion of His Seventieth Birthday October 20, 1929*, 235–42. New York: Henry Holt, 1929.

Megill, Allan. "Foucault, Structuralism, and the Ends of History." *Journal of Modern History* 51, no. 3 (1979): 451–503.

Menegon, Eugenio. *Ancestors, Virgins, and Friars: Christianity as a Local Religion in Late Imperial China*. Cambridge: Harvard University Asia Center, 2009.

Misztal, Barbara A. *Theories of Social Remembering*. Maidenhead, UK: Open University Press, 2003.

Mok, Ka-ho. *Intellectuals and the State in Post-Mao China*. Basingstoke, UK: Macmillan; New York: St. Martin's, 1998.

Moon, Steve Sang-cheol. "Missions from Korea, 2019: Support Raising." *International Bulletin of Mission Research* 43, no. 2 (2019): 188–95.

Mullins, Mark R. *Christianity Made in Japan: A Study of Indigenous Movements*. Honolulu: University of Hawai'i Press, 1998.

Murre-van den Berg, Heleen. "Nineteenth-Century Protestant Missions and Middle Eastern Women: An Overview." In *Gender, Religion and Change in the Middle East: Two Hundred Years of History*, edited by Inger Marie Okkenhaug and Ingvild Flaskerud, 103–22. Oxford: Berg, 2005.

Ng, Chin-keong. *Trade and Society: The Amoy Network on the China Coast, 1683–1735*. 2nd ed. Singapore: National University of Singapore Press, 2015.

Ng, Peter Tze Ming. *Chinese Christianity: An Interplay Between Global and Local Perspectives*. Leiden: Brill, 2012.

Niu, Hezhi. "Gulangyu: Siqu haishi huozhe?" 鼓浪屿：死去还是活着? [Gulangyu: Dead or alive?]. Accessed May 10, 2020, https://www.douban.com/note /429133679.

Nora, Pierre. "Between Memory and History: *Les Lieux de Mémoire*." *Representations*, no. 26 (1989): 7–24.

Nosco, Peter. *Remembering Paradise: Nativism and Nostalgia in Eighteenth-Century Japan*. Cambridge: Council on East Asian Studies, Harvard University, 1990.

Oakes, Tim, and Donald S. Sutton, eds. *Faiths on Display: Religion, Tourism, and the Chinese State*. Lanham, MD: Rowman and Littlefield, 2010.

Olick, Jeffrey K., and Daniel Levy. "Collective Memory and Cultural Constraint: Holocaust Myth and Rationality in German Politics." *American Sociological Review* 62, no. 6 (1997): 921–36.

Ong, Aihwa. "Chinese Modernities: Narratives of Nation and of Capitalism." In *Ungrounded Empires: The Cultural Politics of Modern Chinese Transnationalism*, edited by Aihwa Ong and Donald Nonini, 171–202. London: Routledge, 1997.

Orwell, George. *Nineteen Eighty-Four*. London: Penguin, 1989.

Pan, Jennifer, and Yiqing Xu. "China's Ideological Spectrum." *Journal of Politics* 80, no. 1 (2017): 254–73.

Paramore, Kiri. *Ideology and Christianity in Japan*. Abingdon, UK: Routledge, 2009.

Park, Albert L., and David K. Yoo. "Introduction: Modernity and the Materiality of Religion." In *Encountering Modernity: Christianity in East Asia and Asian American*, edited by Albert L. Park and David K. Yoo, 1–15. Honolulu: University of Hawai'i Press, 2014.

222

Park, Chang-won. "Christian Reactions to Government-Led Cremation in South Korea." In *Christianity and the State in Asia: Complicity and Conflict*, edited by Julius Bautista and Francis Khek Gee Lim, 155–65. Abingdon, UK: Routledge, 2009.

Park, Chung-shin. *Protestantism and Politics in Korea*. Seattle: University of Washington Press, 2003.

Peng, Jingzhong. *Zhongguo fangzhi jianshi* 中国方志简史 [A brief history of China's local gazetteers]. Chengdu: Sichuan daxue chubanshe, 1990.

Peng, Yiwan. *Xiamen yinyue mingjia* 厦门音乐名家 [Noted musicians of Xiamen]. Xiamen: Xiamen daxue chubanshe, 2007.

Phan, Peter C., ed. *Christianities in Asia*. Chichester, UK: Wiley-Blackwell, 2010.

Pieke, Frank N. "The Communist Party and Social Management in China." *China Information* 26, no. 2 (2012): 149–65.

———. *The Good Communist: Elite Training and State Building in Today's China*. Cambridge: Cambridge University Press, 2009.

———. "Immigrant China." *Modern China* 38, no. 1 (2012): 40–77.

———. "Party Spirit: Producing a Communist Civil Religion in Contemporary China." *Journal of the Royal Anthropological Institute* 24, no. 4 (2018): 709–29.

Pitcher, Philip Wilson. *In and About Amoy: Some Historical and Other Facts Connected with One of the First Open Ports in China*. 2nd ed. Shanghai: Methodist Publishing House in China, 1912.

Popular Memory Group. "Popular Memory: Theory, Politics, Method." In *Making Histories: Studies in History-Writing and Politics*, edited by Richard Johnson, Gregor McLennan, Bill Schwarz, and David Sutton, 205–52. London: Hutchinson, 1982.

Potter, Pitman B. "Belief in Control: Regulation of Religion in China." *China Quarterly* 174 (2003): 317–37.

Qihuang Shanren. "Fanzai mu kou de bianqian" 番仔墓口的变迁 [The transformation of the barbarian cemetery]. *Gulangyu wenshi ziliao* 10 (2003): 151–54.

Qiu, Chengzhong. "Zhongguo pinyin wenzi yundong de xianqu: Lu Gangzhang" 中国拼音文字运动的先驱：卢戆章 [Pioneer of a romanized writing system for Chinese: Lu Gangzhang]. *Gulangyu wenshi ziliao* 3 (1998): 18–23.

Qiu, Yiling. "Xinhai geming qianhou de Xiamen baokan" 辛亥革命前后的厦门报刊 [Newspapers and periodicals in Xiamen around the 1911 Revolution]. *Xiamen wenshi ziliao* 18 (1991): 112–22.

Qiushi wang [Truth-Seeking Net]. "Qizhi xianming fandui lishi xuwuzhuyi" 旗帜鲜明反对历史虚无主义 [Taking a firm position against historical nihilism]. Accessed July 28, 2020, http://www.qstheory.cn/zt2015/lsxwzy823/index.htm.

Quanguo difangzhi ziliao gongzuo xiezuozu, ed. *Zhongguo xin fangzhi mulu 1949–1992* 中国新方志目录1949–1992 [A catalog of new gazetteers in China, 1949–1992]. Beijing: Shumu wenxian chubanshe, 1993.

Remmers, Phil. "The Emergence of Legal Christian Publishing in China: An Opportunity for Reformed Christians." In *China's Reforming Churches: Mission, Polity, and Ministry in the Next Christendom*, edited by Bruce P. Baugus, 245–67. Grand Rapids, MI: Reformation Heritage Books, 2014.

Renmin ribao [People's Daily]. "Fazhan Zhongguo tese shehuizhuyi zongjiao lilun, quanmian tigao xinxingshi xia zongjiao gongzuo shuiping" 发展中国特色社会主义宗教理论 全面提高新形势下宗教工作水平 [Develop a religious theory of socialism with Chinese characteristics; Comprehensively improve the level of religious work under the new conditions]. April 24, 2016, 1.

Renmin wang [People's Net]. "Zhejiang Yongjia yifa chaichu Sanjiang weifa zongjiao jianzhu" 浙江永嘉依法拆除三江违法宗教建筑 [Demolishing the illegal religious building of Three Rivers Church in Yongjia, Zhejiang Province, in accordance with the law]. Accessed May 25, 2020, http://zj.people.com.cn/n/2014/0429/c186938-21102950.html.

Reny, Marie-Eve. *Authoritarian Containment: Public Security Bureaus and Protestant House Churches in Urban China*. New York: Oxford University Press, 2018.

Sanneh, Lamin. *Disciples of All Nations: Pillars of World Christianity*. New York: Oxford University Press, 2008.

Sanneh, Lamin, and Joel A. Carpenter, eds. *The Changing Face of Christianity: Africa, the West, and the World*. New York: Oxford University Press, 2005.

Sanyi tang, ed. *Sanyi tang bashi nian 1934–2014* 三一堂八十年 1934–2014 [Trinity Church 1934–2014]. Xiamen, 2014.

Schudson, Michael. "Lives, Laws, and Language: Commemorative Versus Non-Commemorative Forms of Effective Public Memory." *Communication Review* 2, no. 1 (1997): 3–17.

———. *Watergate in American Memory: How We Remember, Forget, and Reconstruct the Past*. New York: Basic Books, 1992.

Schuman, Howard, and Jacqueline Scott. "Generations and Collective Memories." *American Sociological Review* 54, no. 3 (1989): 359–81.

Schwarcz, Vera. "Out of Historical Amnesia: An Eclectic and Nearly Forgotten Chinese Communist in Europe." *Modern China* 13, no. 2 (1987): 177–225.

Scott, James C. *The Art of Not Being Governed: An Anarchist History of Upland Southeast Asia*. New Haven: Yale University Press, 2009.

Shen, Daoxiang. "Huiyi wo de baba mama" 回忆我的爸爸妈妈 [Recalling my father and mother]. *Jiayin*, no. 2 (2012): 11–13.

Siming qu zhengfu. "2019 nian huji renkou ji qi biandong qingkuang" 2019年户籍人口及其变动情况 [Registered household residents and the change in 2019]. Accessed May 28, 2021, http://www.siming.gov.cn/zjsm/sjfb/rkmz/202101/t20210114_766531.htm.

Snow, Donald B. *English Teaching as Christian Mission: An Applied Theology*. Scottdale, PA: Herald Press, 2001.

Stanley, Brian. *Christianity in the Twentieth Century: A World History*. Princeton: Princeton University Press, 2018.

Stark, Rodney. *The Rise of Christianity: A Sociologist Reconsiders History*. Princeton: Princeton University Press, 1996.

Stark, Rodney, and Roger Finke. *Acts of Faith: Explaining the Human Side of Religion*. Berkeley: University of California Press, 2000.

Stockmann, Daniela. *Media Commercialization and Authoritarian Rule in China*. Cambridge: Cambridge University Press, 2013.

Sun, Anna. *Confucianism as a World Religion: Contested Histories and Contemporary Realities*. Princeton: Princeton University Press, 2013.

Sun, Yanfei. "The Rise of Protestantism in Post-Mao China: State and Religion in Historical Perspective." *American Journal of Sociology* 122, no. 6 (2017): 1664–725.

Szonyi, Michael. *Practicing Kinship: Lineage and Descent in Late Imperial China*. Stanford: Stanford University Press, 2002.

Takayama, K. Peter. "Revitalization Movement of Modern Japanese Civil Religion." *Sociological Analysis* 48, no. 4 (1988): 328–41.

Tan, Chee-beng, ed. *Southern Fujian: Reproduction of Traditions in Post-Mao China*. Hong Kong: Chinese University Press, 2006.

Tao, Feiya. "Wenhua qinlüe yuanliu kao" 文化侵略源流考 [A textual study of cultural aggression]. *Wenshizhe*, no. 5 (2003): 31–39.

Tao, Feiya, and Yang Weihua. "Gaige kaifang yilai de Zhongguo Jidujiao shi yanjiu" 改革开放以来的中国基督教史研究 [Study of the history of Christianity in

224

China since reform and opening up]. *Shixue yuekan*, no. 10 (2010): 5–21.

Unger, Jonathan. "Introduction" In *Using the Past to Serve the Present: Historiography and Politics in Contemporary China*, edited by Jonathan Unger, 1–8. Armonk, NY: M. E. Sharpe, 1993.

———, ed. *Using the Past to Serve the Present: Historiography and Politics in Contemporary China*. Armonk, NY: M. E. Sharpe, 1993.

Vala, Carsten T. "Pathways to the Pulpit: Leadership Training in 'Patriotic' and Unregistered Chinese Protestant Churches." In *Making Religion, Making the State: The Politics of Religion in Modern China*, edited by Yoshiko Ashiwa and David L. Wank, 96–125. Stanford: Stanford University Press, 2009.

———. *The Politics of Protestant Churches and the Party-State in China: God Above Party?* Abingdon, UK: Routledge, 2018.

Vanderbilt, Gregory. "Post-War Japanese Christian Historians, Democracy, and the Problem of the 'Emperor-System' State." In *Christianity and the State in Asia: Complicity and Conflict*, edited by Julius Bautista and Francis Khek Gee Lim, 59–78. Abingdon, UK: Routledge, 2009.

Van der Veer, Peter, ed. *Conversion to Modernities: The Globalization of Christianity*. New York: Routledge, 1996.

Van Gennep, Arnold. *The Rites of Passage*. Translated by Monika B. Vizedom and Gabrielle L. Caffee. Chicago: University of Chicago Press, 1960.

Walls, Andrew F. *The Missionary Movement in Christian History: Studies in the Transmission of Faith*. Maryknoll, NY: Orbis, 1996.

Walls, Andrew F., and Cathy Ross, eds. *Mission in the 21st Century: Exploring the Five Marks of Global Mission*. Maryknoll, NY: Orbis, 2008.

Wang, Ray. *Resistance Under Communist China: Religious Protestors, Advocates and Opportunists*. Cham, Switzerland: Palgrave Macmillan, 2019.

Wang, Xiaoxuan. *Maoism and Grassroots Religion: The Communist Revolution and the Reinvention of Religious Life in China*. New York: Oxford University Press, 2020.

Wang, Zheng. *Never Forget National Humiliation: Historical Memory in Chinese Politics and Foreign Relations*. New York: Columbia University Press, 2012.

Warnshuis, A. L. *A Brief Sketch of the Life and Work of Dr. John A. Otte*. New York: Board of Foreign Missions, RCA, 1911.

Watson, James L. "Standardizing the Gods: The Promotion of T'ien Hou ('Empress of Heaven') Along the South China Coast, 960–1960." In *Popular Culture in Late Imperial China*, edited by David Johnson, Andrew Nathan, and Evelyn Rawski, 292–324. Berkeley: University of California Press, 1985.

Watson, Rubie S. "An Introduction." In *Memory, History, and Opposition Under State Socialism*, edited by Rubie S. Watson, 1–20. Santa Fe, NM: School of American Research Press, 1994.

———. "Making Secret Histories: Memory and Mourning in Post-Mao China." In *Memory, History, and Opposition Under State Socialism*, edited by Rubie S. Watson, 65–86. Santa Fe, NM: School of American Research Press, 1994.

Wen, Yihan. "Xiamen shi Gulangyu Zhonghua Jidu jiaohui Sanyi tang" 厦门市鼓浪屿中华基督教会三一堂 [The Trinity Church in Gulangyu, Xiamen]. *Tianfeng*, no. 10 (1957): 32.

Wenger, Jacqueline E. "Official vs. Underground Protestant Churches in China: Challenges for Reconciliation and Social Influence." *Review of Religious Research* 46, no. 2 (2004): 169–82.

Wertsch, James V. *Voices of Collective Remembering*. Cambridge: Cambridge University Press, 2002.

White, Chris. "Appropriating Christian History in Fujian: Red Tourism Meets the Cross." *Studies in World Christianity* 23, no. 1 (2017): 35–50.

———. "History Lessons: Uncovering China's Protestant Past Today." *Review of Religion and Chinese Society* 6, no. 1 (2019): 126–45.

———, ed. *Protestantism in Xiamen: Then and Now.* Cham, Switzerland: Palgrave Macmillan, 2019.

———. "Sacred Dwellings: Protestant Ancestral Halls and Homes in Southern Fujian." In *Sinicizing Christianity*, edited by Yangwen Zheng, 233–60. Leiden: Brill, 2017.

———. *Sacred Webs: The Social Lives and Networks of Minnan Protestants, 1840s–1920s.* Leiden: Brill, 2017.

———. "To Rescue the Wretched Ones: Saving Chinese Slave Girls in Republic China." *Twentieth-Century China* 39, no. 1 (2014): 44–68.

———. "Waves of Influence Across the South Sea: Mutual Support Between Protestants in Minnan and Southeast Asia." *Ching Feng* 11, no. 1 (2012): 29–54.

———. "Xinjie Church and Christianity as Chinese Cultural Heritage." In *Protestantism in Xiamen: Then and Now*, edited by Chris White, 49–76. Cham, Switzerland: Palgrave Macmillan, 2019.

White, Chris, and Jifeng Liu. "Going Global and Back Again: The Transformation of Chinese Christian Networks Between Southeast Asia and China Since the 1980s." In *Annual Review of the Sociology of Religion 11: Chinese Religions Going Global*, edited by Nanlai Cao, Giuseppe Giordan, and Fenggang Yang, 115–37. Leiden: Brill, 2021.

Wielander, Gerda. *Christian Values in Communist China.* Abingdon, UK: Routledge, 2013.

Wong, Wai Ching Angela, and Patricia P. K. Chiu, eds. *Christian Women in Chinese Society: The Anglican Story.* Hong Kong: Hong Kong University Press, 2018.

World Heritage Centre. "Kulangsu: A Historical International Settlement." Accessed May 7, 2020, https://whc.unesco.org/en/list/1541.

———. "Properties Inscribed on the World Heritage List" and "Sites on the Tentative List." Accessed June 7, 2020, https://whc.unesco.org/en/statesparties/cn.

Wu, Bingyao. "Bainian lai de Minnan Jidu jiaohui" 百年来的闽南基督教会 [The Southern Fujian Church over the past century]. *Xiamen wenshi ziliao* 13 (1988): 76–102.

———. "Jidujiao Minnan dahui de yici shenghui" 基督教闽南大会的一次盛会 [A grand meeting of the Southern Fujian Synod of the Church of Christ in China]. *Xiamen wenshi ziliao* 14 (1988): 116–31.

Wu, Fei. *Maimang shang de shengyan: Yige xiangcun Tianzhujiao qunti zhong de xinyang he shenghuo* 麦芒上的圣言：一个乡村天主教群体中的信仰和生活 [Sacred word above the awn of wheat: Faith and life in a rural Catholic community]. Hong Kong: Daofeng shushe, 2001.

Xiamen Fojiao xiehui. "*Hong Yi Gulang xiejing* chongkan diancang yishi zai Gulangyu Riguangyan si longzhong juxing" "弘一鼓浪写经" 重刊典藏仪式在鼓浪屿日光岩寺隆重举行 [A grand ceremony held in the Gulangyu Sunlight Rock Temple on the occasion of the republication of the *Hong Yi Transcribing Sutra*]. Accessed May 7, 2020, http://xmfj.org/html/p/201311/2422.html.

Xiamen ribao [*Xiamen Daily*]. "Ben shi Junguanhui xuanbu guanzhi Jiushi yiyuan chanye" 本市军管会宣布管制救世医院产业 [The Municipal Military Management Committee takes over the Hope Hospital premises]. January 8, 1951, 1.

———. "Ben shi weishengju jieban Jiushi yiyuan ji fushe hushi xuexiao" 本市卫生局接办救世医院及附设护士学校 [The Municipal Health Bureau takes over Hope Hospital and its affiliated nursing school]. December 7, 1951, 1.

———. "Bu Xianli yi bei wo quzhu chujing" 卜显理已被我驱逐出境 [Henry A.

Poppen has been expelled]. March 5, 1951, 1.

———. "Shi Jidu jiaotu gonggu aiguo zhenxian, bodao Wen Yihan Du Zunneng fan Dang miulun" 市基督教徒巩固爱国阵线 驳倒温亦寒 杜尊能反党谬论 [Xiamen Christians are consolidating the patriotic front by refuting Wen Yihan and Du Zunneng's anti-Party fallacy]. May 11, 1958, 2.

———. "Zhou Qingze pizhe zongjiao waiyi fangdu fanghuo" 周清泽披着宗教外衣放毒放火 [Zhou Qingze plants poison and fire under the cloak of religion], September 12, 1957, 1–2.

———. "Zhou Qingze shi zongjiaojie de youpai fenzi" 周清泽是宗教界的右派分子 [Zhou Qingze is a rightist of the religious sector]. September 11, 1957, 7.

Xiamen shi difangzhi bianweihui, ed. *Xiamen shi zhi* 厦门市志 [Xiamen City gazetteer]. 5 vols. Beijing: Fangzhi chubanshe, 2004.

Xiamen shi tongjiju. "Xiamen shi 2020 nian guomin jingji he shehui fazhan tongji gongbao" 厦门市2020年国民经济和社会发展统计公报 [Statistical bulletin on national economy and social development of Xiamen]. Accessed May 28, 2021, http://tjj.xm.gov.cn/zfxxgk/zfxxgkml/tjsjzl/ndgb/202103/t20210319_2525636.htm.

Xiamen shi zhi bianweihui and Xiamen haiguan zhi bianweihui, eds. *Jindai Xiamen shehui jingji gaikuang* 近代厦门社会经济概况 [Social and economic profile of modern Xiamen]. Xiamen: Lujiang chubanshe, 1990.

Xiamen tongjiju and Guojia tongjiju Xiamen diaochadui, eds. *Xiamen jingji tequ nianjian 2019* 厦门经济特区年鉴 2019 [Yearbook of Xiamen special economic zone, 2019]. Beijing: Zhongguo tongji chubanshe, 2019.

Xiamen wanbao [*Xiamen Evening News*]. "Ya Bili jiqi houjizhe men" 雅俾理及其后继者们 [David Abeel and his successors]. November 17, 2013, 20.

Xiamen Zhengxie wenshi ziliao weiyuanhui. "Kantouyu" 刊头语 [Preface]. *Xiamen wenshi ziliao* 3 (1980): i.

Xiang, Biao. *Transcending Boundaries: Zhejiangcun: The Story of a Migrant Village in Beijing*. Translated by Jim Weldon. Leiden: Brill, 2005.

Xie, Zhibin. "Religion and State in China: A Theological Appraisal." *Journal of Church and State* 63, no. 1 (2020): 1–22.

Xinhua ribao [New China Daily]. "Mei le yanwu liaorao, duo le manmu xinlü 没了烟雾缭绕 多了满目新绿 [While smoke is gone, a new green is coming]. April 9, 2019, 3.

Xue, Qifeng, et al., comp. *Lujiang zhi* 鹭江志 [Xiamen gazetteer]. Vol. 1. Xiamen, 1769. Copy preserved in the Leiden University Asian Library.

Yang, C. K. *Religion in Chinese Society: A Study of Contemporary Functions of Religion and Some of Their Historical Factors*. Berkeley: University of California Press, 1961.

Yang, Enli. *Yejian de ge: Jingli yonghuo de zhen shen* 夜间的歌：经历永活的真神 [Songs in the night: Testament to the ever-living God]. Alhambra, CA: Zhongguo dalu shengtu jianzheng shigongbu, 2004.

Yang, Fenggang. "Chinese Conversion to Evangelical Christianity: The Importance of Social and Cultural Contexts." *Sociology of Religion* 59, no. 3 (1998): 237–57.

———, ed. "The Cross of Chinese Christians and Their Resistance to Suppression." Special Issue of *Review of Religion and Chinese Society* 5, no. 1 (2018): 1–130.

———. "The Failure of the Campaign to Demolish Church Crosses in Zhejiang Province, 2013–2016." *Review of Religion and Chinese Society* 5, no. 1 (2018): 5–25.

———. "Lost in the Market, Saved at McDonald's: Conversion to Christianity in Urban China." *Journal for the Scientific Study of Religion* 44, no. 4 (2005): 423–41.

226

———. "The Red, Black, and Gray Markets of Religion in China." *Sociological Quarterly* 47, no. 1 (2006): 93–122.

———. *Religion in China: Survival and Revival Under Communist Rule*. New York: Oxford University Press, 2012.

Yang, Fenggang, and Andrew Abel. "Sociology of Religious Conversion." In *The Oxford Handbook of Religious Conversion*, edited by Lewis R. Rambo and Charles E. Farhadian, 140–63. New York: Oxford University Press, 2014.

Yang, Fenggang, and Joseph B. Tamney, eds. *State, Market, and Religions in Chinese Societies*. Leiden: Brill, 2005.

Yang, Mayfair Mei-hui, ed. *Chinese Religiosities: Afflictions of Modernity and State Formation*. Berkeley: University of California Press, 2008.

Ying, Fuk-tsang. "Fandi aiguo yu zongjiao gexin: Lun Zhonggong jianguo chuqi de Jidujiao Gexin xuanyan" 反帝爱国与宗教革新：论中共建国初期的基督教革新宣言 [The Christian Manifesto and the making of a patriotic Protestant church in the People's Republic of China]. *Zhongyang yanjiuyuan jindaishi yanjiusuo jikan*, no. 56 (2007): 91–141.

———. "The Politics of Cross Demolition: A Religio-Political Analysis of the 'Three Rectifications and One Demolition' Campaign in Zhejiang Province." *Review of Religion and Chinese Society* 5, no. 1 (2018): 43–75.

Yip, Ka-che. *Religion, Nationalism and Chinese Students: The Anti-Christian Movement of 1922–1927*. Bellingham: Center for East Asian Studies, Western Washington University, 1980.

Yu, Anthony C. *State and Religion in China: Historical and Textual Perspectives*. Chicago: Open Court, 2005.

Yu, Feng, Zhang Zhenshi, and Zeng Shiqin. "Gulangyu lunwei gonggong zujie de jingguo" 鼓浪屿沦为公共租界的经过 [The process of Gulangyu's deterioration as an international settlement]. *Xiamen wenshi ziliao* 2 (1963): 76–107.

Yu, Yang. "Remaking Xiamen: Overseas Chinese and Regional Transformation

in Architecture and Urbanism in the Early 20th Century." PhD diss., University of Hong Kong, 2007.

Yue, Yongyi. "Chuantong minjian wenhua yu xin nongcun jianshe: Yi Huabei liqu miaohui weili" 传统民间文化与新农村建设：以华北梨区庙会为例 [Traditional folk culture and new countryside construction: The example of the temple festivals in northern China's pear-growing region.] *Shehui* 28, no. 6 (2008): 176–93.

Zhang, Qiang, and Robert Weatherley. "The Rise of 'Republican Fever' in the PRC and the Implications for CCP Legitimacy." *China Information* 27, no. 3 (2013): 277–300.

Zhang, Shengcai. "Xiamen Xinhai geming de linzhao" 厦门辛亥革命的鳞爪 [The 1911 Revolution in Xiamen]. *Xiamen wenshi ziliao* 18 (1991): 21–23.

Zhang, Xianqing. *Guanfu, zongzu yu Tianzhujiao: Shiqi zhi shijiu shiji Fuan xiangcun jiaohui de lishi xushi* 官府、宗族与天主教：十七至十九世纪福安乡村教会的历史叙事 [State, lineage and Catholicism: A history of the rural church in Fuan in the seventeenth to nineteenth centuries]. Beijing: Zhonghua shuju, 2009.

Zhang, Zhenshi, et al. "Gonggong zujie shiqi de Gulangyu" 公共租界时期的鼓浪屿 [Gulangyu during the international settlement era]. *Xiamen wenshi ziliao* 3 (1980): 1–84.

Zheng, Xijue, and Huang Heyuan. "Meiguo yisheng Yu Yuehan ruci ling ren" 美国医生郁约翰如此凌人 [The American Dr. John A. Otte was such a bully]. *Xiamen wenshi ziliao* 1 (1963): 64–66.

Zheng, Zhenman. *Family Lineage Organization and Social Change in Ming and Qing Fujian*. Translated by Michael Szonyi. Honolulu: University of Hawai'i Press, 2001.

Zhonggong zhongyang wenxian yanjiushi, ed. *Jianguo yilai zhongyao wenxian xuanbian* 建国以来重要文献选编 [Selected important documents since the foundation of the People's

Republic of China]. Vol. 1. Beijing: Zhongyang wenxian chubanshe, 1992.

Zhonggong zhongyang wenxian yanjiushi zonghe yanjiuzu and Guowuyuan zongjiao shiwuju zhengce faguisi, eds. *Xin shiqi zongjiao gongzuo wenxian xuanbian* 新时期宗教工作文献选编 [Selected works on religious work in the new era]. Beijing: Zongjiao wenhua chubanshe, 1995.

Zhongguo difangzhi zhidao xiaozu bangongshi. "1990 nian quanguo difangzhi gongzuo huiyi jiyao" 1990年全国地方志工作会议纪要 [Minutes of the 1990 national gazetteer work meeting]. *Xinjiang difangzhi*, no. 3 (1990): 4–7.

———, ed. *Difangzhi gongzuo wenxian xuanbian* 地方志工作文献选编 [Selected documents related to work on local gazetteers]. Beijing: Fangzhi chubanshe, 2009.

Zhongguo Jidujiao sanzi aiguo yundong weiyuanhui and Zhongguo Jidujiao xiehui, eds. *Jidujiao aiguozhuyi jiaocheng (shiyong ben)* 基督教爱国主义教程（试用本）[Christian patriotism textbook (trial edition)]. Beijing: Zongjiao wenhua chubanshe, 2006.

Zhongguo kexueyuan Beijing tianwentai, ed. *Zhongguo difangzhi lianhe mulu* 中国地方志联合目录 [The union catalog of Chinese local gazetteers]. Beijing: Zhonghua shuju, 1985.

Zhongguo shehui kexueyuan shijie zongjiao yanjiusuo ketizu. "Zhongguo Jidujiao ruhu wenjuan diaocha baogao" 中国基督教入户问卷调查报告 [An in-house questionnaire survey on Christianity in China]. In *Zhongguo zongjiao baogao 2010* 中国宗教报告 2010 [Annual report on China's religions, 2010], edited by Jin Ze and Qiu Yonghui, 190–212. Beijing: Shehui kexue wenxian chubanshe, 2010.

Zhou, Enlai. *Zhou Enlai xuanji* 周恩来选集 [Selected works of Zhou Enlai]. Vol. 2. Beijing: Renmin chubanshe, 1984.

Zhou, Haiyan. *Jiyi de zhengzhi* 记忆的政治 [The politics of memory]. Beijing: Zhongguo fazhan chubanshe, 2013.

Zhou, Kai, et al., comp. *Xiamen zhi* 厦门志 [Xiamen gazetteer]. Taipei: Datong shuju, 1984 [1839].

Zhu, Hongmo. "Ben hui zhi chengli yu jingguo" 本会之成立与经过 [The establishment and process of the church]. In *Gulangyu Sanyi tanghui niankan* 鼓浪屿三一堂会年刊 [Annual report of Gulangyu Trinity Church], edited by Trinity Church Committee, 5–10. Gulangyu, 1935.

———. "Gulangyu Sanyi tang jianzhu shimo" 鼓浪屿三一堂建筑始末 [The establishment of Gulangyu Trinity Church]. *Xiamen wenshi ziliao* 7 (1984): 108–25.

———. "Xiamen lunxian hou Gulangyu Yude nanmin shourongsuo" 厦门沦陷后鼓浪屿毓德难民收容所 [Lok Tek Girls' School refugee camp after the fall of Xiamen to the Japanese]. *Xiamen wenshi ziliao* 12 (1987): 55–59.

Zhu, Yujing. "Guojia tongzhi, difang zhengzhi yu Wenzhou de Jidujiao" 国家统治、地方政治与温州的基督教 [State rule, local politics and Christianity in Wenzhou]. PhD diss., Chinese University of Hong Kong, 2011.

Zhu, Zixian. *Gensui ai de jiaozong* 跟随爱的脚踪 [Following in the footprints of love]. Unpublished manuscript, 2010.

Index

Milton Keynes UK
Ingram Content Group UK Ltd.
UKHW020227030624
443570UK00004B/74